CRAIG J. GILL

Caddying on the Color Line

How Black Caddies Defined
and Redefined Golf in the South

Back Nine Press
Chicago, Illinois
www.back9press.com
Instagram and X: @backninepress

Copyright © 2025 by Craig J. Gill

All rights reserved. No part of this book may be reproduced in any form or by any means, electronic or mechanical, including photocopying, recording, or by any information storage and retrieval system, without permission in writing from the publisher. This book is in no way affiliated with Augusta National Golf Club.

9 8 7 6 5 4 3 2 1

First Edition

Library of Congress Control Number: 2024953130
Caddying on the Color Line /
Written by Craig J. Gill

Back Nine Press (USA)
Pages cm

ISBN 978-1-956237-26-9 (hardback)
ISBN 978-1-956237-28-3 (ebook)

For my partner, Stephanie,
and for my parents, John and Heather.

Contents

Note on Terminology vii

Introduction ix

Chapter 1. Getting to the Tee 1
    How White Golfers and Black Caddies Came to Meet

Chapter 2. "Caddying Would Be Their Lives" 25
    The Reality of Caddying in the South

Chapter 3. "Show Up, Keep Up, Shut Up" 45
    Navigating Racial Dynamics on the Golf Course

Chapter 4. Striking It Pure 73
    Labor Organizing Among Caddies

Chapter 5. From Caddies to Players 97
    Black Caddies Became Great Golfers and Changed the Game

Chapter 6. Cart Path Only 125
    Caddies, Mechanization, and the Search for Profit

Chapter 7. "Not a Man's Job" 143
    The Decline of Caddying Amid Societal Change

Chapter 8. Making Par 159
    Caddies and Civil Rights

Chapter 9. Green Jackets, White Overalls, Black Caddies 177
    A Complex End to a Southern Tradition

Epilogue 189

Acknowledgments 195

Bibliography 197

Notes 216

Index 252

Note on Terminology

Over the course of writing this book, I have encountered many approaches to writing about race and identity. The choices made here are not necessarily the only way or the "right" way to phrase these sensitive matters, but they are deliberate. As historians consistently reinterpret the past, the language they use to refer to people, places, and events change. Some readers may wonder why certain terms are used or words are capitalized. This note explains a few of my language choices.

In this book, the n-word is quoted in a few specific instances where it appears in the historical record. This word is a deeply offensive racial slur, and its historical inclusion here does not condone its use today. Its use here is not to perpetuate harm but to reflect the historical accuracy of the sources cited, offering an unfiltered view of the racial realities that Black Americans, especially Black caddies in the South, faced during the 20th century. To erase or censor this word in the quotations in which it appears would cover up the intense racial views of the time, which must be heard and seen by readers now, in order to more accurately understand this country's troubled past.

Throughout the book, I have chosen to capitalize Black and White when referring to racial identities. This decision reflects a recognition that these terms signify more than just skin color—they denote social, cultural, and historical identities. Capitalizing the word Black does not insinuate a universal Black experience, but rather it acknowledges the existence of a distinct community identity, shaped through centuries of collective struggles faced, triumphs celebrated, lives lived, and culture created by African Americans. I have also chosen to capitalize the word White. While some historians may argue that a collective White identity may not exist in the same way that Black identity does, choosing not to capitalize White while capitalizing all other races perpetuates the notion of whiteness as the default or the norm in society. Just as race is a social construct, so are the notions of what qualifies as "Black" and "White" in times and places where such identities determined whether you could be allowed access to a diner or to use a particular drinking fountain (with signs that read "Whites only"), where a human being fit into one of these labels meant the difference between opportunity and oppression.

Similarly, I capitalize South(ern) and North(ern) regions of the United States and the people from there when referring to the distinct identity and ideology of the place. In the time period that this book explores, the notions of "North" and "South" were strong markers—a diametric or binary opposition—that implied many social and cultural differences that date all the way back before the Civil War. While these distinctions may be lessened today (though they still exist), they were especially strong when these stories in the book take place. However, when used as descriptors for directionality or location, north(ern) and south(ern) are not capitalized. For example, a "Southern" approach to something (such as cooking or golf, or even personhood or legal justice), or a "Southernness," might refer to a common regional experience, a strong, cultural phenomenon that is shared and accepted widely, while a "southern" city or golf course refers simply to a geographical location that lies in the south of the country, or a place "north" of another location.

Introduction

The cover of the April 17, 1972 edition of *Sports Illustrated* magazine features Jack Nicklaus, arguably the greatest golfer of all time. The photographer's lens captured Nicklaus hoisting his putter high into the air after holing a putt on the 16th hole at Augusta National Golf Club. Nicklaus's trademark blonde locks, which earned him his nickname, Golden Bear, glimmer in the spring Georgia sun. His tanned arms extend from a hypnotizing red and white patterned shirt, and his white flared pants are as flawless as his scorecard that day. The expression on his face is one of concentration and poise; of a sportsperson unsurprised by their athletic excellence and focused on the work still to come.[1] Two holes later Nicklaus finished out his opening round with a score of 68, the lowest round anyone would shoot that week. Over the subsequent three rounds he held his nerve to win the tournament by three shots.

But Nicklaus is not the only subject of the image. Between Nicklaus and the camera is the striking figure of his caddie, Willie Peterson. The caddie is caught mid-stride, galloping toward the hole to retrieve Nicklaus' ball. Cigarette in mouth, single finger pointing to the sky, Peterson could be mistaken for the star of the show. But he was not; he was a caddie. Nameless on the cover of *Sports Illustrated*, nameless to all except the most knowledgeable of golf experts. His uniform—white tennis shoes, white coveralls, and a green baseball cap—contrast with his black skin; the one defining feature that all the caddies at the Masters shared until 1983. Willie Peterson was one of thousands of Black men in the South who chose to work as caddies over the course of the 20th century. And, like Peterson's anonymity on the cover of *Sports Illustrated*, African American caddies were at once central to golf in the South, and yet never fully acknowledged for their contributions to the game. Hidden in plain sight, they symbolized the racial structures of the South, where Black workers facilitated the activities of White leisure-seekers.

Three years later, in 1975, on that same 16th green at Augusta National Golf Club, Nicklaus and Peterson experienced the most memorable moment of their time together. Nicklaus was one shot behind the leader Tom Weiskopf, with only three holes to play. Chasing a record fifth Masters victory, Nicklaus's tee shot to the par-three 16th was not his best. "A disappointing one there, leaving him at least 40 feet short," remarked CBS announcer Ben Wright. A few minutes later—after assessing the long putt for birdie uphill through long shadows—Nicklaus addressed the ball. The putt was long enough that Nicklaus needed the flagstick to be held to ensure he could see his target. Peterson stood by the hole, tending to the flag, helping Nicklaus to home in on the cup. Back on the tee Weiskopf watched on, knowing that Nicklaus' opportunities to catch him were fading and that the chances of the storied champion holing the 40-footer were slim to none. Nicklaus drew the putter back and through the ball. The little white sphere began its journey up the hill toward the hole and the waiting caddie. As it passed into the section of the green covered by the shadows of tall pine trees in the late afternoon, Nicklaus and Peterson watched intensely. Halfway to the hole, Peterson removed the flagstick from the hole, with his right hand. A moment later, with the ball still 10 feet from the hole, he passed the stick to his left hand, freeing his right hand up to raise his fist to the sky in anticipation. Peterson had caddied for thousands of golfers on that green. He knew every slope and blade of grass on the course. He knew, 10 feet out, that the ball was only going to end up in one place. When the ball eventually dropped into the cup, he was airborne in celebration. Back on the tee, Weiskopf watched on in horror, now level with Nicklaus. Just 30 minutes later, Nicklaus would be confirmed champion.[2]

Nicklaus' fifth Masters victory in 1975 was his last with Willie Peterson on the bag and one of the last in the era of ubiquitous African American caddies at the Masters. Nicklaus won again in 1986, but by then the tournament committee at Augusta had dropped the requirements that professionals use local caddies during the Masters, all of whom were Black. Nicklaus—like most of the players on the professional tour—turned to their regular caddies to carry their bag at future Masters. For his victory in 1986, his son Jackie carried the bag. The last days of all-Black caddies at the Masters in the 1980s represented the symbolic end to a long history of Black caddying in the South. Owing to the popularity of the golf cart, more diverse job opportunities for Black workers, and an increasing White interest in caddying, Black caddies' monopoly faded.

But the history of Black caddies in Augusta stretched back to the late 19th century. The city's first course, the Bon Air Golf Club on the west side, employed local Black kids as young as seven years old to carry the bags of wealthy locals and tourists visiting the Bon Air

FIGURE 1: Nicklaus and Peterson celebrating a holed birdie putt on the 15th hole of the 1966 Masters (Getty Images).

hotel in the 1890s.³ In the years that followed—as the Bon Air Golf Club became the Augusta Country Club—African American workers tended to the course and caddied for the White golfers who played there. In 1933, when the famous Augusta National Golf Club opened its gates next door to Augusta Country Club, the *Atlanta Constitution* reported that "red-capped negro caddies waited" to tote the bags of arriving players.⁴ Peterson was part of a dynasty of Black caddies in Augusta that lasted for the best part of a century.

On tree-lined golf holes in Augusta, Black caddies labored tirelessly, carrying heavy golf bags for White golfers who used their increasing free time for outdoor pursuits. The Augusta Country Club was the scene of golf matches between the rich and famous, including President William Howard Taft and John D. Rockefeller. Taft made Augusta his winter golf capital, while Rockefeller spent six consecutive winters on Augusta CC's links between 1906 and 1912.⁵ These men of vast power and wealth, respectively, contrasted distinctly with the working-class Black men and boys who carried their bags. One of Taft's closest golfing companions, William Jarvis Boardman, who played with the president in both Washington, D.C. and Augusta, laid bare the considerable gap between White golfers and Black caddies in Augusta through a single act of philanthropy in 1910—he bought shoes for the caddies. On the morning of March 3rd, a group of 59 caddies descended upon a single shoe store on Augusta's Broad Street. One by one they turned over a token for one pair of shoes, fitted to their feet, gifted to them by W.J. Boardman—or "shoe man" as he became known among the caddies. Boardman's gift was an undoubted act of kindness, but it reveals a grim truth about the caddies: that many worked each day in bare feet or shoes ill-equipped to deal with the miles of walking that came with the job. This wealthy former attorney could afford to gift 59 pairs of shoes, while many of the caddies could not afford their own.⁶

As those caddies collected their shoes and returned to work, Hannah Peterson—the caddie Willie Peterson's grandmother—was pregnant and awaiting the birth of her sixth child. Located 20 miles south of Augusta Country Club, in Burke County, Georgia, she and her husband John lived and worked—like most Black southerners at the time—on a small farm, trying to build a family and financial independence.[7] That same year, 1910, Hannah gave birth to their son, Willie. Within a couple of years, the Petersons made the decision to move to Augusta, likely in search of better jobs and livelihoods than they could make in the exploitative world of tenant farming. This was the era of the Great Migration, when millions of African Americans left their rural lives and ventured toward the nation's growing and glowing cities in the North, in search of a brighter future. Not everyone wanted to leave the South, though. After all, this was their home, and all that they had ever known. Some, like the Petersons, ventured to nearer cities: Atlanta and Augusta, Durham and Charlotte. Cities offered jobs that paid a set wage, they promised a sense of financial security that tenant farming did not, and they were spaces where Black families could build community in numbers. So the Petersons moved to Augusta: a place familiar in its proximity to home, but alien in its urban pace.

By 1920, John and Hannah settled their family into a small house on Fitten Street in the west side of Augusta. John found work as a porter for a grocery store, while Hannah worked as a laundress for a private family.[8] Their neighborhood was entirely occupied by African Americans. As was the case in all Jim Crow cities at the time, local government and the housing industry strictly enforced racial segregation. The area was known as the Sand Hill, or Elizabeth Town. A map of the neighborhood, drawn by the Home Owner's Loan Corporation in 1937, noted that "most of the [neighborhood's] occupants are employed as servants ... and are chiefly butlers, chauffeurs, caddies, domestics."[9] The Peterson's work, then, was typical of African Americans in the city, and in their neighborhood.

While neither John nor his son, Willie Sr., ever worked as caddies, they were undoubtedly exposed to the job by those around them who did carry golf bags for a living. Sitting on their north-facing porch on Fitten Street, catching the first rays of the morning sun before it tracked to the south, the Petersons likely saw caddies making their way toward Augusta Country Club to start their day. If the breeze blew the right direction on a calm day, they could almost certainly hear metal golf clubs striking small white golf balls on the 17th fairway, less than 500 feet away. The proximity of Sand Hill to Augusta Country Club and Augusta National meant that in the decades that followed, many caddies made the neighborhood their home. The other area of town where caddies lived was known as Terry, another Black neighborhood just south of downtown. Terry was where John Peterson and his family moved in 1930.[10] By then his son, Willie, was 19 years old and had moved out. He had started working as a laborer at a local car garage and started his own life and family.[11] Soon they would welcome their first child, and then their second in 1932: Willie Jr, who would go on to caddie for Jack Nicklaus. Over the next 20 years, Willie Peterson's family would move a couple of times, but all within a small five-block radius.[12]

Living in the Terry, Willie Peterson Jr. was never far from someone who caddied at Augusta National or Augusta CC. For example, in 1940, when Willie lived on Gwinnett Street, walking a few minutes around the neighborhood he would have passed the house of a caddie named Joseph Edwards living a few blocks over on University Place, where the railroad lines passed through the neighborhood.[13] Another block west on Thomas Street were caddies Henry Bennett, Floyd Henderson, and Jack Aaron.[14] A couple of minutes farther south was Roulette Alley, where a number of caddies lived, including Arthur Home, Robert Roland, and Abraham Williams.[15] At eight years old in 1940, young Willie was probably not thinking much about his future career, but he would have been abundantly aware that caddying was an option for someone like him—a Black boy living in Augusta. In the two decades that followed, another caddie living on Roulette Alley, Willie Perteet, became a worker of nationwide fame, when the caddie master at Augusta National chose him to serve as President Dwight Eisenhower's regular caddie. The two Willies, Peterson and Perteet, lived within just a few blocks of each other for most of the 1940s and '50s. Little did either know that they would go on to become two of the most famous caddies in Augusta's history.

Willie Peterson Jr. first started caddying in 1949.[16] The job was one of several that he pieced together to make a living over the next decade. He first served in the Air Force, where he learned to cook and continued his cooking at the Augusta University Hospital, just steps from his home. Throughout his varied career, though, he continued to work as a caddie at Augusta National. His big break as a caddie came in 1960, when fortune and his eye for an excellent golfer combined to land him with the bag of young Jack Nicklaus. Still an amateur, Nicklaus was assigned another caddie that week: Leon McClady. But Nicklaus demanded a lot from his caddies; he was often the first golfer at the course and one of the last to leave on the practice days, and his caddie needed to be there to collect his golf balls on the driving range and attend to his needs around the course.[17] McClady found the demands too taxing and pulled out after the first practice day. That was when Willie Peterson got the call to take over. McClady's withdrawal was, in the end, a stroke of luck that set Willie on a path toward a successful caddying career with one of golf's greats. On their first day together Peterson told Nicklaus, "I'm going to stick with you if you'll stick with me, and you'll be the best there is." Nicklaus responded, "Okay, Willie, it's a deal."[18] In the years that followed the pair went on to win five of the next 16 Masters Tournaments: a run never seen before or matched since.

As a caddie for arguably the greatest golfer of all time, Willie Peterson's story is remarkable, but his is only the story of one individual, at one golf course, in one Southern city. In truth, thousands of African American golf caddies worked across the South, from coastal Virginia to central Texas, and they were central to the game. In the metropolises of Washington, D.C. and Atlanta, to the mountain towns of Knoxville, Tennessee, and Hot Springs, Virginia, to the coastal confines of Galveston, Texas and Biloxi, Mississippi, Black caddies were everywhere. For the first two-thirds of the 20th century, the vast majority of the South's country clubs, resorts, and public courses turned to Black men and boys as caddies. Elsewhere in the U.S., golf courses largely employed White schoolboys to carry golf bags.

The regional differences in caddying took hold while the game was in its relative infancy in the United States. As one account from 1899 summarized the state of caddying; "In the South the Ethiopian flourishes; in the North the Caucasian; in the West the son of the worthy pioneer; in the East the schoolboy."[19] Later, in 1927, one writer commented that he "never saw a caddie [in the North] darker than sun tan," while "all over the South, however, the Negro is part of the color."[20] Although exceptions existed—with occasional Black caddies among the caddie ranks of the North, especially after the Great Migration, and municipal courses in the South that employed White caddies—for the most part Black men and boys represented the vast majority in the caddy shacks of the South's burgeoning golf landscape throughout the 20th century.

Most African American caddies lived seemingly unremarkable lives, yet their stories reveal a rich portrait of life in the South for everyday Black people. This book is an account of their lives. It is not a chronicle of the greatest golfers and caddies of all time, nor is it a tale of extraordinary individuals who inspired a movement. It is a story of normal people: Black folks who—like millions of others around the South—worked tirelessly to improve their lives, support their families, and to shape their own path through an oppressive racial landscape. Their stories have been passed down through generations of Black families, but most have never been fully documented. It's time that these highly skilled workers get the recognition they deserve.

Peterson and Nicklaus' stories converged like the sand in the throat of an hourglass. Their lives began in such disparate worlds, defined by race, geography, and socioeconomics. For a brief few years together, they formed a formidable pair and shared success at Augusta National. In the decades after their victories, they once again grew apart. Nicklaus aged toward a busy life of business, family, leadership, and charity. In 2005, he retired from the game of golf as arguably the greatest player ever to play the game. His achievements included 18 major championships—five of which with Peterson by his side—and 73 wins on the PGA Tour. He also amassed a multi-million dollar empire built on golf course designs, golf equipment, and lifestyle products bearing his name and image. By the time Nicklaus retired, Peterson had been dead for six years. Taken by cancer in 1999, Willie Peterson died with little to his name but his stories and his connection to one of golf's greats.[21] For 20 years, his grave lay unmarked in a cemetery in Augusta, across the railroad tracks from the site of his caddying triumphs. No plaque listing his accomplishments, not even a headstone.[22]

With the passing of the last generation of Black caddies who worked the fairways of the South's golf courses, the need to tell their story has never been greater. The circumstances that produced the ubiquity of Black caddies for White golfers was undoubtedly rooted in the region's racial hierarchy. Yet, the generations of men and boys who worked the job for the best part of a century treated their role in the game with continuous professionalism and respect. Their stories are not to be forgotten, as if tossed onto the pile of relics from Jim Crow that some might prefer to forget than to address. These were not simply men who faced oppression and injustices on account of their race. The thousands of Southern Black men who called caddying their job over the course of the 20th century may not have lived extraordinary lives, but—like millions of other Black southerners—their daily struggles and triumphs abounded with resilience, pride, skill, and dignity. This is their story.

FIGURE 2: Golfers and their caddies at Pinehurst in the 1920s. Two other caddies provide entertainment on guitar (Tufts Archives).

CHAPTER 1

Getting to the Tee

How White Golfers and Black Caddies Came to Meet

In the heat of the summer in 1895, two men's paths converged in the North Carolina Sandhills region. There were once a million trees there—longleaf pines as old as time—that swayed to the stuttering rhythm of the wind. But in 1895, they were few and far between, chopped down for timber or tapped empty of their useful resin. Yet, James Walker Tufts—a Bostonian hundreds of miles from home—had a vision for this place. Out of desolate land, he devised a plentiful plan: to create the finest health resort in the country. A place where middle class and wealthy northerners—afflicted with the ailments created and/or exacerbated by urban life in New York, Boston, or Chicago—could cleanse their lungs with the reparative intake of pine air.

Looking out over the barren North Carolina Sandhills—a wasteland of shrubbery and pine-tree stumps—Tufts must have realized the immense task that stood before him. To convert this desolate rural area into an inviting and hospitable Southern playground required a vast operation and the planting of more than 200,000 trees and shrubs. For labor, he turned to the local workforce—poor Black and White North Carolinians, many of whom had done the work of clearing the land in the first place. Among them was Nicodemus Taylor, a man who had spent many decades laboring on North Carolina's unforgiving terrain. Tufts—Northern, White, and wealthy—and Taylor—Southern, Black, and comparatively poor—came together in the place that is now known as Pinehurst. Neither had any idea that they would have an early role in the creation of America's first golf mecca. Tufts was not a golfer and had no intention of building a golf resort. Taylor had almost certainly never seen a golf shot hit, let alone set foot on a golf course. Yet, just a few years later, Taylor would be one of the first caddies to work the Pinehurst golf courses, which would become world-renowned. Just as James Walker Tufts came to rely on the Black workers of Moore County to transform his 678 sandy acres of inhospitable land into a charming resort town, Pinehurst's golfers came to rely on Black men and boys to caddie for them on the course.

Tufts and Taylor's paths converged by chance—so too did those of the thousands of Black caddies and White golfers in the South. By 1902, when Pinehurst employed Donald Ross to design the now famed No. 2 course, golf courses across the South had already turned to Black workers as the almost universal source of caddies. It was a complex arrangement, and one that was loaded with social, racial, and economic meaning. While to some it may seem like an obscure footnote in the rich and storied history of the region, untold thousands of Black caddies carried clubs for untold thousands of White golfers. How did it happen that Black men like Demus Taylor—who had toiled for decades in the fields and lumber camps of the South—came to work on golf courses? Why were they drawn to the job, and why did the White golfers and golf course management in the region turn to Black labor as caddies in the first place? The circumstances which brought the two groups together was the culmination of decades of social and economic tumult and change in the South. It is not a straightforward story, but to understand how Willie Peterson and Jack Nicklaus found themselves winning five Masters tournaments together, you must first understand how thousands of Black caddies, like Demus Taylor, found themselves on the courses of the South in the early 20th century.

The Shackles of Sharecropping

Nicodemus Taylor was already well into his twilight years when he became one of the very first caddies at Pinehurst Country Club.[23] Demus, as he was known to all, was in his early 70s when James Walker Tufts drove a stake into the ground to signal the start of golf in the Sandhills. He did not know his age exactly, because—as with most born into slavery in the antebellum era—Taylor's enslaver did not keep detailed birth records. But Demus was certain that the year was either 1822 or 1823. In the seven decades that separated his birth and his first time caddying, he had lived a life that was similar to many millions of other Black Southerners, whose existence spanned the evils of slavery, the exploitation of sharecropping, and the backbreaking labor of industrial work. His trajectory from enslavement to carrying golf bags at Pinehurst was representative of the consistent labors of Black Southerners who strove for better jobs and better lives in the face of a society rigged against them.

Taylor's birthplace is unknown, but his birth into slavery is certain. He lived and worked, without compensation, for his first enslaver before being sold to another prior to the Civil War, a man named Guthrie in Chatham County, North Carolina. As the war brought financial difficulties to landowners in the region, Guthrie sought to cash-in and sold Taylor to a speculator for $1,300 in gold. Taylor's stature and strength made him an expensive purchase. Demus objected to the purchase as he did not want to be "taken off by any speculator." Soon after the transaction, he ran away from his new enslaver and made his way back to Guthrie's land. The sale most likely separated him from his family, and his desire to return to them fueled his decision to desert the speculator.[24]

Taylor stayed with Guthrie until the conclusion of the Civil War, when the promise of emancipation became a reality. The

Emancipation Proclamation signed by Abraham Lincoln in 1863 did not immediately impact Demus' status as enslaved property, just as it did not immediately free millions of others in the South. Southern enslavers chose simply to ignore the proclamation, hoping for a Confederate victory and a new country, with slavery once again as its bedrock. The slaveowners' dreams crumbled with the victory of the Union army and the surrender of Confederate forces at Appomattox in 1865. It was only then that Demus Taylor and most of the Republic's enslaved became free.

Demus Taylor's former enslaver, Guthrie, offered him 10 dollars per month to continue living and working on the same place that was previously his labor camp. With few alternatives, Demus accepted the offer and began life as a free citizen, working the same land he had for years.[25] The taste of freedom was sweet for those who had spent their entire lives shackled in bondage, yet their options were not plentiful after the war. General Sherman's promise of 40 acres and a mule did not materialize, and many Black southerners were left with nothing but the clothes on their back when their enslavement ended. Many turned to their former enslavers for potential employment and a new agreement that allowed them to work the land in return for compensation. Over the decades that followed, Taylor strove to make the most of his freedom—he worked in agriculture, the turpentine industry, lumbering, and finally as a caddie.

What Black Southerners like Demus Taylor most desired was to rise up the agricultural ladder to land ownership and control of their own time, land, crops, and profits. Financial independence was the antithesis to bondage, and it could render African Americans truly free. In theory, the steps toward land ownership were fairly straight-forward: Black farmers planned to earn and save money from working as paid field hands or from renting plots of land and making steady profits on the crop. In the end, they hoped their wages or profits would accumulate, and they could then buy their own land. When it came to facilitating Black financial independence, however, White Southerners steadfastly obstructed their progress. By the end of the 19th century—almost half a century after enslaved Southerners successfully fought to defeat the institution that had kept them in bondage for more than 200 years—around three quarters of Black farmers were stuck sharecropping or tenant farming.[26] In Demus Taylor's home state of North Carolina, fewer than one-third of Black farmers (32%) owned their land.[27] And that was a higher percentage than other southern states.

White landowners devised and honed the system of sharecropping as a means of maintaining their financial wealth, and their control over the South's large Black population. Left without an unpaid workforce who had farmed their land for decades or centuries, the White planter class created a new way to extract labor from newly freed citizens for as little cost as possible. At the start of the year, landowners rented out plots of land to tenants, along with the necessary tools for farming. Most Black farmers did not have the cash to rent the tools, so they rented them on credit. With little to no property upon which to leverage the credit, they mortgaged their future crop yield. At the end of the year, the Black farmers turned over the entirety of the crop to the landowner, who sold the output on the market. White landowners controlled the key transactions and rigged them in their favor. Many charged exorbitant rates for equipment rental and lied about the price they received for the crop. In the end, most landowners returned from the market and informed Black farmers that their debts outweighed the revenue from selling the crop, whether it was true or not. The only way for Black farmers to pay their debts was to stay on the same plot of land the next year and attempt to produce a greater yield.

Once a farmer was immersed in the system of sharecropping it proved almost impossible to escape, as debts to landlords and proprietors from one year spilled over to the next, creating a cycle of debt. Many Black Southerners in the late 19th and early 20th centuries remained perpetually stuck in the cycle.[28]

In their attempts to free themselves from the shackles of sharecropping, many Black people worked as paid field hands. Unlike in sharecropping, field hands had no stake in the crop output at the end of the year: they were paid by the day, week, or month, instead. Those who chose to work as field hands rather than sharecroppers hoped that doing so distanced them from cycles of indebtedness and gave them a wage that they could spend or save as they wished. However, paid labor was often as exploitative as sharecropping. For example, as previously stated, Demus Taylor's former enslaver, Guthrie, offered him 10 dollars per month to stay and work the land. But by the end of the month, the promised money often did not materialize, and "at the end of the year, the only pay Demas [sic] received was ten bushels of corn."[29] There were no viable ways to adjudicate the change in pay. Working as a field hand also made it difficult to purchase basic goods like food or clothing, because field hands had no future crop production to offer up as credit to local storeowners and proprietors. Left with no financial capital to show for their labors, field hands such as Taylor struggled to save any money toward land purchase or achieving their dreams of financial independence.

An Above Average Turpentine Worker

Like many Black workers, Demus consistently did whatever he could to find employment in any field other than agriculture. The changing southern economy in the late 19th century created the conditions for new jobs in industry. Investment from the North in naval stores brought a swell of industrial jobs to the region. As the industry expanded, camp owners required vast workforces to tap the trees. Many Black workers, such as Taylor—tired of sharecropping or wage labor on the farm, and attracted by the promise of good wages in turpentine work—joined the camps in search of a better life.[30]

At six feet four inches tall, Taylor was well built for turpentine work. Chippers—as these workers were called—spent long days moving from one tree to the next, carrying and swinging heavy axes. Being a chipper certainly brought in a steady stream of income for Black workers, but they ran into many of the same problems as tenant farmers. Because most turpentine work occurred in areas disconnected from any form of commerce, workers living in camps made all their purchases at the camp commissary. The commissaries—which were operated by the camp owner whose motivations were profit and maintaining a steady workforce—allowed workers to purchase on credit in the form of their future earnings. Just as for sharecroppers, the money they paid Black workers often came right back to them at a premium, and growing debts kept Black workers in turpentine camps.

Demus Taylor was an above average turpentine worker. He boasted that he was able to chip 31,000 trees per week—more than triple the average worker who could do only 10,000. Accordingly, the camp operator gave Taylor three times the regular daily rations of "four pounds of white meat, one bag of meal, and one quart of molasses." Taylor took the extra and exchanged it for better foods "like ham and chicken and such good things."[31] As an exceptional worker, Taylor eked out a livable compensation from the work, but average turpentine workers faced vast difficulties as they tried to use such work to build a living for themselves.[32]

Even with his salary of triple rations, Demus Taylor moved on from the turpentine industry into the lumber industry. Workers like Taylor did much of the work of clearing Moore County and other previously forested areas that became successful tourist resorts.[33] In 1930, more than a quarter of a century after leaving the lumber industry, Taylor still possessed his old axe, and posed for photographs with "the best hickory handle" (Figure 3), which cost him one dollar and 25 cents, and that he used to fell trees at wages of one dollar per day. Taylor later recalled, "That's the most wages I ever got."[34] The promise of such wages lured Black men into the booming lumber industry at the start of the 20th century. By 1910, in North Carolina, only 61 Black men remained employed in the turpentine industry, but almost 3,000 Black men felled trees for a living.[35] Over the next 50 years, sawmills employed more African American factory workers than any other industry.

Although the wages were more consistent in lumber work, most lumber firms operated with the same principle as landowners and turpentine firms—the most effective way to maintain a workforce of Black Southerners was to ensure their financial insecurity. They

FIGURE 3: Demus Taylor poses for a picture holding his old axe (Tufts Archives).

continued to exploit workers, by using cyclical debt or paying workers less than what they initially promised. In the end, wage labor in lumber camps, turpentine camps, and sawmills did not offer a clear path to financial independence for all workers who entered such industries. For the vast majority of Black workers in the South in the decades following the Civil War and well into the 20th century, financial independence was an elusive dream.[36]

The Settlements of Southern Pines and Pinehurst

Golf arrived in North Carolina just as workers like Demus Taylor turned away from the exploitative manual labor they had known for decades. The North Carolina Sandhills first experienced a tourism boom in the 1880s, which brought the sport to the South. John T. Patrick, a state immigration agent tasked with encouraging outsiders to settle in North Carolina, both permanently and temporarily, noticed the swell of northerners vacationing in the South for health reasons. The North Carolina Board of Agriculture searched around the state for areas that could appeal to potential immigrants from the North. Patrick settled on southern Moore County as the site for a new settlement after consultations with a state geologist and a local resident revealed that the area boasted a mild climate, excellent drainage, and long leaf pine forests; all attributes that medical professionals claimed were curative to many ailments.[37] He called the settlement Southern Pines, and within years it was a popular health resort for northerners seeking a reprieve from the damaging conditions of urban life. Patrick turned to his old profession—the printing press—to promote his resort and opened a printing house in nearby Pinebluff, which printed advertisements and pamphlets dedicated to spreading the gospel of the North Carolina Sandhills' health-restoring properties.[38]

Among those who read Patrick's pamphlets was James Walker Tufts. The bearded Bostonian arrived in the area to set up his own winter health resort in July 1895, with the semi-philanthropic aim of creating a tourist resort for middle-class northerners. He purchased the land at the sum of $1 per acre. A Massachusetts businessman, Tufts set about producing the finest winter retreat for northern tourists seeking to escape the polluted air of the increasingly urban and industrial North.

By any standard, Tufts was equipped with the business acumen and wealth to complete the monumental task at hand. In his hometown of Charlestown, Massachusetts, he entered the entrepreneurial world at the age of only 21, when he opened his own pharmacy after five years as an apprentice in the local apothecary store. Having expanded his operation to include three stores, Tufts soon became fascinated by the production of drug-store soda fountains, so much so that he sold his pharmacies and began manufacturing soda fountains himself. Over the course of the final third of the 19th century, Tufts' business grew substantially and eventually became part of the American Soda Fountain Company. By 1895, at 60 years old, Tufts began experiencing his own health problems and—having visited a number of southern health resorts on the advice of his doctor—dedicated himself to building his own resort. His vision was slightly different to other resort owners such as Henry Flagler on Florida's southern tip, or John Eugene du Bignon at Jekyll Island, Georgia, who both created luxury destinations for elite northerners. Tufts wanted to make the region's restorative qualities available to northerners of lesser means—middle-class professionals such as teachers, preachers, and small businessmen.[39] With his semi-philanthropic venture in mind, Tufts sold the remaining stake in the American Soda Fountain Company to focus on his massive new project.[40]

Tufts embarked on a scouting mission to find a site for his health resort in spring 1895. His trip down the Atlantic coast from Washington, D.C. to Miami gave him plenty of options, but none that matched his lofty expectations. On his return journey, he connected to the Seaboard Airline Railroad and scrutinized the Red Hills region of Florida and Georgia, where tourism had thrived for years. Again, Tufts left disappointed. By June, the grizzled old businessman seemed set to leave the South with nothing to show for it. On his way through North Carolina, however, he stopped in at Southern Pines for the evening. It was here at Southern Pines that Tufts saw Patrick's promotional pamphlets and received a guided tour of the region from Patrick himself. By the afternoon of June 16th—convinced by the health-giving properties of the region's climate and air—Tufts settled on a piece of land just five miles west of Southern Pines.[41]

The sandy, tree-cleared landscape provided a relatively blank canvas for Tufts' envoy, who began work at terrifying speed just one month after Tufts purchased the plot. Tufts drove a stake into the ground to mark the center of the village, and thus began the grueling construction of Pinehurst village.[42] He enlisted the skills of famed landscape architect Frederick Law Olmsted to design a New England village in the North Carolina Sandhills. Olmsted understood the scale of the task, especially the challenges of creating a village out of nothing. The land had no existing infrastructure, meaning that Tufts would need to install brand new basic utilities, including water, power, and sewage.[43] For labor, Tufts turned to the local population of poor Black and White Southerners, who spent the preceding years sucking every productive drop out of the region's landscape simply to survive.

In the heat of the summer, as he strolled the gravel of his fast-developing streets, he had the chance to observe the labors of local North Carolinians. What was clear to him then was that local Black Southerners suffered greatly from widespread poverty in the region, and they were desperate for work. Tufts commented in a letter to his wife that "It is strange and pitiful to see how anxious these men are to get to work." Three Black men, he noted, had walked eight miles to Pinehurst for one day of work: "If they got it, they would probably go back and forth until I get a shelter. Indeed, I am not expected to find shelter for them, and could employ hundreds." These workers toiled all day under the supervision of a well-paid overseer to clear the land for new buildings and roads, and they slept beneath bushes on pine straw. The overseer also ensured that the workers remained fed with meal and salt pork that he supplied "to the niggers and takes it from their pay."[44]

The Premier Golf Resort in the South

Pinehurst's growth into the premier golf resort in the South was never inevitable. Initially, James Walker Tufts had no interest in golf. He wanted to create a health resort for those of modest means to experience the healing benefits of the South in the same way that elites had done in the preceding decades. However, only a couple of years into the resort's existence, guests shaped the future of Pinehurst by creating their own ramshackle golf course on the local dairy farm. Quick to respond to the sporting needs of his guests, Tufts ordered the construction of a proper nine-hole golf course in 1898. Self-proclaimed golf enthusiast D. Leroy Culver designed and constructed the course with the help of local Black and White laborers, and it soon became a hive of tourist activity.[45] When James Walker Tufts died in 1902, leaving the stewardship of the village to his son Leonard, he still held out the hope that Pinehurst would become the modest health resort he set out to build seven years earlier.

Leonard Tufts had different ideas. Recognizing that the resort hemorrhaged money and was entirely propped up by his father's wealth, he set about restructuring the village as a modern capitalist enterprise. Alongside his decision to break with his father's policy of not selling any property, Leonard banked on the long-term viability of golf to the resort's success. One year before James Tufts died, Leonard convinced his father to hire a Scottish golf course architect and professional named Donald Ross—who had emigrated to America a few years prior and had carved out a name for himself in New England—to come to Pinehurst as head of golf operations. It was under Ross' stewardship, that Leonard Tufts' vision for a resort with golf at its center took hold. Leonard also enlisted and relied upon Frank Presbrey, a New York advertising executive, to create and promote the image of Pinehurst as a golfing mecca in the South. In turn, the sorts of tourists who would choose to visit Pinehurst soon did so primarily for the resort's golf courses and for the community of golfers who returned to these Sandhills every year. With time, the Pinehurst Country Club became the hub of the village, where vacation golf societies—the Tin

Whistles for men and the Silver Foils for women—took up residence. The new breed of guests who increasingly ventured to Pinehurst after 1902 created a recurring winter community around the two features they had in common: their wealth and their love of golf.[46]

Northern White folks were also attracted to the South for the region's distinctive racial demographics. In guidebooks and travel literature, writers consistently focused on the region's African American population and presented Black Southerners as a unique aspect of the culture and landscape. Overwhelmingly, such depictions reduced Black men and women in the South to demeaning caricatures.[47]

As northern tourists demanded vacations that offered interactions with nature and short-term sojourns to a more simplistic time, the South—with its apparent contented and primitive Black population—offered an appealing destination. According to the *Pinehurst Outlook*, guests desired souvenirs and post cards depicting Black locals: the best-selling post cards were "typical of the region," and cards depicting "negro subjects" topped the list.[48] Few images epitomized a visit to the South more than those of local African Americans. In fact, racial difference was part of the appeal of a southern vacation for White northerners, who ventured South to confirm for themselves what they found in promotional materials and travel guides.[49]

From the moment they left the North to the moment they arrived in Pinehurst, tourists were waited on by Black labor. The most common form of transport to the South was the railroad. In train cars and station platforms, Black waiters and porters facilitated the journey South of the Mason-Dixon line. Train line operators advertised the South's golf resorts and the ease with which they could be accessed by rail. Pamphlets for the Louisville and Nashville Railroad boasted of the "historical-romantic" courses along their tracks in the Gulf Coast, while the Atlantic Coast Line listed precise details about golf courses on their line.[50] Pinehurst advertising romanticized the journey south, with images of smiling bag-carriers along the way.[51] A 1930 cartoon depicted a Black Pullman Porter carrying a tourist's golf bag along a luxury cabin, telling a passenger that "de next stop sir, am Pinehurst."[52] Such depictions promoted the idea that a vacation to Pinehurst was one punctuated by charming—if dimwitted—Black service labor from start to finish.

Pinehurst guests were no different to tourists around the South who marked their vacations with interactions with Black locals. In the resort's early years, the local newspaper encouraged guests to venture just outside the village to the homes of local African Americans where they were promised they would find ramshackle "native cabins," offering them the chance to see "boys in every stage of raggedness."[53] Visits to the nearby African American church also proved popular among resort guests who sought to hear spiritual singing, another apparent unique and distinctive trait of "old-time" Black Southerners.[54] After the turn of the century, as a sense of community prospered among returning White guests, some took it upon themselves to create more formal ways to see Black Southerners and verify the images and stories they encountered in national media. Starting in 1899, committees of resort-goers collaborated with James and then Leonard Tufts to organize "cake walks" and "baby shows" at the Village Hall, in which local African Americans competed for significant prizes. During cake walks, White guests judged Black couples on the basis of their dancing, and in baby shows they judged Black babies on their beauty and charm. However, all judgments were rooted in a warped understanding of the ideal and unique Black Southerner that Northern White tourists had consumed in travel literature for years. Black locals understood that winning the lucrative prize—in 1899 the triumphant baby won five dollars, which was more than a week's earnings for an average agricultural worker—meant performing to White expectations of Black Southernness.[55]

While Golfers, Black Caddies

By the mid-1910s, golf became the central attraction of the Pinehurst resort, and guests took less interest in organized Black entertainment. These golfers needed an army of caddies to carry their clubs, and the resort recruited around 350 caddies, all of whom were Black.

According to a son of a White worker at Pinehurst in the 1930s, "A decision had been made in the early years that only Black men could work carrying golf clubs at Pinehurst."⁵⁶ Who made that decision is unknown, but the preferences of the resort guests were always top of mind. Pinehurst's White guests interacted with Black locals on the golf course for up to four hours for a single round, or eight if they chose—as many did—to play 36 holes in a single day. Interactions between White guests and Black North Carolinians increased dramatically due to golf's surge in popularity.⁵⁷

In the minds of Northern White tourists, employing Southern Black caddies became a convenient avenue to exercise their previous views and assumptions. Periodicals around the country published numerous stories about "native" wit of Southern Black caddies, especially those found at Pinehurst. On the pages of national golf magazines, readers found examples of uniquely African American workers who replied to their employers with charming quips. "Colored Caddies Unconsciously Funny" read the headline of a New York newspaper in 1928.⁵⁸ Other stories presented similar uniquely funny Southern Black caddies willing to poke fun at their employer, but rendered harmless by their perceived simplicity. In another Pinehurst account from 1915, a golfer asked his Black caddie, "What do you think of the war?" To which his caddie responded, "De wah … Done forgot all erbout it—dat wuz long while ergo."⁵⁹ The language and the deferential tone placed the caddies among other popular depictions of Southern African Americans as unique, charming, witty, and content.

Northern readers opened golf periodicals to reports on the South and expected to be transported to a place where caddies were "old-time" Southern African Americans.⁶⁰ In fact, the only magazine dedicated to golf in the south, *Southern Golfer and Tourist*, used a caricature of a Black caddie as their key marketing symbol (Figure 4).⁶¹ When readers travelled to Pinehurst and other southern resorts, they sought confirmation of the stories they read. By the time these stories reached the heights of their popularity, Pinehurst no longer held baby shows and cake walks in the Village Hall. Guests no longer needed to organize events that staged Black Southernness. Instead, they found

THE SOUTHERN GOLFER

Is a magazine full of unusual interest to those who winter in the Southland or who have friends who play in the South during the winter months.

Complete records of the Tournaments played and of unusual happenings on the links. Also numerous pictures, golf instruction articles, cartoons and comment well worth reading.

Our list of stars is greater than that of any golf magazine published, including such well known names as Walter Hagen, Jock Hutchison, Alex Smith, Francis Ouimet, Miss Glenna Collett, Bob Harlow, William E. Hicks, Ray McCarthy, John G. Anderson, Chick Evans and H. B. Martin

Send in your two dollar subscription and the magazine will follow you wherever you go.

Name_____

Address_____

_____

_____

FIGURE 4: Advertisement for *Southern Golfer Magazine,* January 15, 1924 (USGA Archives).

that their hours of daily interactions with Black caddies could fulfill their desire to see what they deemed unique and authentic Black Southerners. Even children were infatuated with the imagined reality created by popular depictions of the South, and they joined their parents in searching for a specific version of the region. In 1908, nine-year-old Charlie Taft, son of President William Howard Taft, for example, "rewarded his favorite caddies," in Hot Springs, Virginia, in what he understood to be "a characteristic way—by giving them a watermelon feast."[62] Caricatures and stereotypes of Black Southerners were so powerful that from as young as nine, many White Northerners developed a warped understanding of the South's Black population. For White tourists, caddies became another distinctive and attractive aspect of a southern vacation.

Pinehurst management understood early on that White guests sought interactions with Black locals, and by 1920s they used Black caddies in resort marketing. Frank Presbrey—who Leonard Tufts trusted to market Pinehurst around the nation—pioneered an aggressive print advertising campaign. Presbrey appealed to northern readers of magazines such as *Country Life in America*, *Town and Country*, and the various golf monthlies. Early ads from the start of the century foregrounded the benefits of Pinehurst's weather and outdoor activities as a pleasant winter reprise from the harsh winters in overcrowded and illness-inducing northern cities. Descriptions of Pinehurst set it apart from other winter resorts, particularly those in Florida based on the unique Pinehurst weather. One advertisement extolled that Pinehurst was "free from climatic extremes" and offered the "invigorating qualities of the wonderful climate found only in the dry, sandy, Long-leaf Pine regions of North Carolina," all only "one night out from New York, Boston, and Cincinnati."[63] Presbrey coupled these descriptions with illustrations of young and healthy-looking White people—strong men with their sleeves rolled up, as if taking a break from business on the golf course, and petite women in long dresses ready to strike a golf ball with finesse.[64]

As resorts in the South propagated, Pinehurst had to work harder to define its specific appeal to White Northerners, who could then

We are waiting for You at Pinehurst
North Carolina

THE three eighteen and one six hole practice courses at Pinehurst have become the center of golf and golfing interest during the late Autumn, Winter and Spring. They are acknowledged standards of quality and upkeep, and offer a variety unobtainable where play is limited to one course.

The Carolina now open. This house enjoys a reputation for hospitality and excellence of cuisine. The new addition, to be ready in January, adds a large number of rooms with bath, also sixteen sleeping porches and three private parlors.

Four excellent hotels, many cottages—all under one management.

HOLLY INN   BERKSHIRE   HARVARD

Open January 15th

All out-of-door sports. Tennis. Livery and saddle horses. Model dairy. Shooting preserve. Trap shooting. Good roads in a radius of 50 miles or more. No consumptives received.

Through Pullman Service from New York via Seaboard Air Line. Only one night from New York, Boston, Cleveland, Pittsburgh and Cincinnati.

Send for illustrated booklet giving full information

Pinehurst Gen. Office, Pinehurst, N.C.   Leonard Tufts, Owner, Boston, Mass.

FIGURE 5: Pinehurst advertisement depicting caddies, *Golf Illustrated & Outdoor America*, January 1915 (Public Domain).

choose from any number of southern destinations where the climate was fair and outdoor pursuits plentiful. In turn, Presbrey's advertising began to feature Black caddies alongside strapping White guests. The first ads to depict caddies placed them in scenes of White people relaxing on the clubhouse porch while golfers and caddies strolled the golf course in the background. Presbrey's illustrations of luxurious porches and vast fields in the background undoubtedly evoked images of antebellum plantation scenes.[65] Fewer than 10 years later, Presbrey moved caddies from the periphery to the center of Pinehurst's appeal. One advertisement in a nationwide golf magazine showed five young Black caddies sitting on a bench, all with wide smiles while the boy in the center holds a golf bag (Figure 5). Presbrey's caption read "We are waiting for You at Pinehurst, North Carolina."[66] The dual meaning of the word waiting was not lost on Presbrey. To a northern magazine reader, the caddies were "waiting" for their visit and "waiting" on their every need. In this description Presbrey presented caddies as both a permanent unchanging feature of Pinehurst resort and as servants to White guests. J.C. Bull, the vice-president of the Frank Presbrey Company, noted that Pinehurst ads "ought to be made to attract not so much by their novelty as by a definite individuality that means Pinehurst."[67] Clearly the image of Black servitude was one that Presbrey tied to the resort's brand, and also one that proved fruitful in attracting northern tourists, as it became a fixture in successful Pinehurst marketing.

At Pinehurst, and other golf resorts around the South in the early 20th century, employment of an African American golf caddie became part of the quintessential southern vacation for Northern Whites. Tourists from industrial cities ventured South in search of experiences uncommon in their hometowns. As soon as tourist hotspots marketed themselves as golf resorts, Black caddies became synonymous with the game in the South. The contrast between the two groups—wealthy White tourists, and working-class Black caddies—was undeniable. In 1922, Leonard Tufts undertook an investigation into the finances of the individuals who lived or owned property in Pinehurst and in the immediate vicinity. The results were a staggering portrayal of the vast gap between the two groups. Of course, Tufts categorized his investigation only by race: the region's key divide. Among the White population, the combination of personal wealth and real estate values came to $3,868,767. The total for the area's Black community was $28,245, less than 0.01% of the White total.[68] At separate ends of the racial and financial hierarchy, the two groups came together on the golf course—a stage upon which White tourists played out a warped fantasy of the South.

The "Mecca for Golf"

Elsewhere in the South, near the region's burgeoning cities, White southerners took up golf and began building their own country clubs at the turn of the century. No city caught the golf bug quite like Atlanta, Georgia. Founded in 1898 as a downtown organization for well-to-do White men who wished to experience the rigor and camaraderie of organized sports such as tennis and basketball, the Atlanta Athletic Club (AAC) grew into one of the city's key locales for Atlanta's "civic-commercial elite" to mix with those of their own ilk.[69] Early in the 20th century, the national golf craze reached the Gate City just as one writer in the *Atlanta Constitution* prognosticated that "golf in its many commendable qualities will become the great American game," and that "the time is nigh when they may become just as fascinated by the game as their northern brethren."[70] In 1900, businessmen took it upon themselves to create the Piedmont Park golf course, a nine-hole layout on the northside of the city. The truncated course proved inefficient for local enthusiastic AAC members who abandoned the Piedmont links in 1906 for a new 18-hole course designed by golf architect Tom Bendelow at East Lake, just a few miles east of the city. At East Lake, members could swim, sail, and play golf.

Although golf began in Atlanta in 1900, it was not until the construction of the first full course at East Lake that the game truly arrived. The *Atlanta Constitution* reported that the new course for the AAC was one of the best in the country.[71] Within five years, golf was the "king of local sports" in Atlanta; within six, boosters aligned golf with the city's booming industry and financial sectors when they noted that "Atlanta is now recognized as a Mecca for golf just as it is considered a leader in all other lines."[72] By 1920, Atlanta boasted five private golf courses—East Lake, Druid Hills Golf Club, Brookhaven (owned by the Capital City Club, another Atlanta social club), Ansley Park, and Ingleside Country Club—and one municipal course—Mozley Park.[73] Golf and Jim Crow arrived at similar times for Atlanta, and in the years that followed, both institutions became symbols for the city.

Elite Atlantans made themselves at home on the fairways and greens of East Lake, Brookhaven, and Druid Hills. The membership lists of Atlanta's private courses were a who's who of the city's White bankers, lawyers, real estate men, capitalists, businessmen, and civic leaders. It was these leaders of industry, law, and finance who also helped define a city that kept Black southerners at the bottom rung of society. There is no finer example than that of AAC member, golf fanatic, and judge Nash R. Broyles, who ruled the city's criminal court with an iron gavel for the first 14 years of the 20th century. One estimate suggests that he convicted around half of Atlanta's Black male population.[74] He even wore his discrimination on his sleeve when he boasted that "I have never sent young White boys or White girls to the stockade, as I have realized it would mean their complete ruin."[75] Of course, Broyles did not show the same concern for Black Atlantans who felt the heavy weight of his judgments.

Broyles also used the golf course as a place to implore Black men and boys to stick to their lane. One particular caddie, William "Tater" Cook, came before Broyles for theft twice in 1911. In the first instance, the *Atlanta Constitution* reported that on the golf course Broyles had "tried to instill into [Cook's] mind those precepts which tend to make one walk the straight and narrow path."[76] Of course, any African American living in Atlanta understood the double meaning behind such lessons from prominent Whites—they were intended to deter Black locals from transgressing racial norms or attempting to rise above one's status.[77] Broyles' lessons backfired somewhat: at the height of his judiciary powers, he struggled to obtain caddies to work for him. "Whenever he emerges from the clubhouse and yells for a caddie," the *Atlanta Georgian* reported in 1912, "there is a scurrying for cover."[78] According to the report, Broyles was left to carry his own bag on many occasions.

Other Atlanta golfers in real estate, finance, media, and government controlled the levers which kept Black locals in their place. One undeniable way that White Atlantans maintained the racial hierarchy was through strict labor segregation. Throughout the urban South, Whites occupied the best paid and most prestigious jobs, and restricted Black workers to jobs and pay that Whites felt were beneath them. In Atlanta by 1940, White men outnumbered Black men 20 to 1 in clerical and sales jobs, and White managers outnumbered Black managers 18 to 1. In the professional trades, the ratio of White-to-Black workers was slightly more equitable at 8 to 1, but still only 555 Black men worked in such jobs out of the 22,726 employed in the city.[79]

Despite the clearly discriminatory hiring practices, Black workers still preferred to earn a decent wage in a job serving Whites than a life of back-breaking indebtedness in agriculture or rural industry. Service jobs offered a less-intensive vocation. In towns and cities around the South, Black men entered into jobs as porters, attendants, janitors, waiters, and chauffeurs. The pay was better, and the working conditions were friendlier on their bodies; but above all, these positions allowed workers to leave the exploitation and cyclical debt in other industries. In a region in which the Black working-classes often had little choice other than to work for White people, it made most sense to choose the least exploitative of jobs.[80]

Alongside domestic workers, golf caddies were among the most prominent examples of exclusively Black workers serving exclusively White customers. At the city's five private courses, members employed only African American caddies to carry bags and find golf balls. The symbolic power of the job was striking. Up and down the fairways at East Lake, Brookhaven, and Druid Hills, Atlanta's most denigrated citizens facilitated the leisure time for the city's richest and most prominent men. Unlike the private relationship between Black domestic workers and White employers, caddies provided a public display of perceived racial difference. White Atlantans consistently promoted the notion that caddying required little skill other than the strength to carry the bag and the eyes to spot the golf ball. A traveling comedian even employed a donkey as a caddie in Atlanta after a round at East Lake, in which he reasoned, "If it is possible for all caddies to be asses, it should be possible for at least one intelligent ass to be a caddy."[81] Reports that belittled caddying skills contrasted greatly with the immense coverage of Atlanta's talented White golfers—including young Bobby Jones and Alexa Stirling—and further emphasized the perceived differences between Black and White Atlantans. The insinuation was clear for all those who played golf, worked as a caddie, or simply saw golf courses in person or in the newspaper: Black Atlantans were unskilled and existed solely to serve talented and productive White Atlantans.

The Story of America from the Eyes of One in the Melting Pot

While the circumstances which created Black caddies for White golfers were rooted in the South's deeply troubling racial structures, for individuals such as Demus Taylor—who had known nothing other than intensive labor—caddying was a relative reprieve. Taylor had spent his entire life in North Carolina's Chatham and Moore Counties—a rural region where service jobs were few and far between. Caddying was a brand-new vocation in the region early in the 20th century, and one that Black men and boys flocked to as a means of earning a living. Undoubtedly, caddies endured daily reminders of their place in the racial hierarchy in their interactions with White golfers and continued to have their incomes dictated by White management and customers. However, in the oppressive Jim Crow South, most caddies accepted the shortcomings of the job because it freed them from other more oppressive and soul-sucking occupations.

Demus Taylor's working life spanned from the evils of slave labor, through the exploitation of sharecropping and other industrial work, and culminated in his time serving White leisure-seekers at Pinehurst Resort. His final working years as a caddie placed him among a vast swath of Black workers who remained tied to White capital for employment throughout the South in the early 20th century. His job also offered some significant benefits over the back-breaking, and unprofitable occupations of his past.

Taylor also saw the promise of better times ahead for Black workers like his son Robert, and his daughters Bernice, Elnora, and Royia. Tragically, Demus and his wife Laura suffered the loss of 7 of their 11 children, and ensured that each of those who survived would have an education, and a chance for better careers than had been available in the 19th century.[82]

Demus' hope was realized, as his son Robert went on to become principal of the Black school just outside of Pinehurst, while also trading in real estate and managing the town that went on to take the Taylor family name: Taylortown.[83] In the decades that followed, Taylortown became home to thousands of Black caddies. For many of those men, it was a place that held promise of potential financial independence brought about through a new job, away from agriculture. The promise was unfulfilled for many, whose lives continued to be shaped by the heavy restrictions placed upon Black upward mobility in the Jim Crow South. But for some, caddying was a livelihood that offered new beginnings and exposure to a career which was impossible for their ancestors before them.

Demus Taylor died in 1934, having lived a long and full life. A tribute in the local newspaper read, "Monday Uncle Demus passed to the great beyond. His story will probably never be written, the story of America from the eyes of one in the melting pot."[84] Taylor's cadre of caddies, the first men and boys who picked up golf bags in the South, paved the way for the generations that followed.

CHAPTER 2

"Caddying Would Be Their Lives"

The Reality of Caddying in the South

Black youngsters across the South rarely had their hearts set on a life carrying clubs on the golf course. Most had relatively few interactions with the game at all in their early years—every course other than the few Black country clubs banned Black golfers. Like an explorer who sets out with little intention but stumbles upon something spectacular, many caddies encountered the game and became forever a part of it. For Charlie Sifford, who went on to be one of the great Black golfers of all time, finding golf at the age of 10 was a revelatory "discovery." In that moment when he first found the game and began caddying, he knew he would make a career of it.[85]

Similar stories proliferate around the South. At 10 years old Carl Jackson, who has caddied in more Masters Tournaments than anyone else, spent many hours standing at the fence which separated Sand Hill, a predominantly Black neighborhood of Augusta, and the prestigious Augusta Country Club. Less than a year later he was shagging balls on the range and by age 11 he was skipping school on

Thursdays and Fridays to caddie. Two years later, Jackson graduated from Augusta Country Club to Augusta National, dropped out of school, and was on the path toward a lifetime of carrying golf bags.[86] Not all Black caddies shared such a linear path. But so many of them discovered golf and made a career out of it—not because the pay was spectacular, nor was the work a walk in the park. It was an honest way to make a living, and one which created a distinct camaraderie within the South's caddy shacks. Every day they showed up, spent time honing their craft, shooting the breeze and playing cards with their buddies while waiting for their next bag, or even working on their short game with castoff clubs and balls. Rarely glamorous, yet more appealing than field work or industrial labor, caddying became normality for many thousands of Black men and boys across the South.

Mastering the Basics

What was the job like for those Black men and boys who discovered golf and made a career of it? Caddies showed up early in the morning and awaited their bag for the day. Once they were matched with a player, they carried their golfer's bag to the 1st tee. Caddies carried the golf bag, attended to some basic tasks, and offered their advice to players. The golf bags of the first half of the 20th century differ greatly from modern, lightweight golf bags: back then, the bags were significantly heavier and often filled with an unnecessary amount of gear. Until regulations regarding the number of golf clubs allowed by a single player changed, there was no limit to how many clubs a player could use, and caddies often had to carry bags stuffed with heavy clubs. When the rule changed to limit players to just 14 clubs in 1938, Pinehurst caddies rejoiced.[87]

Alongside carrying the bag, caddies needed to keep a close eye on their player's ball to ensure it did not get lost in deep rough or in the woods. Caddies also tended the flagstick when players were on the green, removing the flag when golfers putted. Some golfers also expected their caddie to provide guidance and advice. Such expectations differed from player to player but often included tasks such as suggesting what club to hit, estimating a distance, or judging the slope of a putting green. While these were the commonalities of most workdays for a caddie, the job offered a significant amount of novelty compared to many occupations available to Black Southerners during Jim Crow. No two rounds of golf have ever been played the same way, meaning that the subtleties of the job changed every day. Because the standard of golfer also varied wildly from one player to the next, caddies learned to be adaptive to different skill levels and had to offer different advice based on the player. Furthermore, the fact that golf courses had 18 different holes meant that over the course of a single round, the job offered some novelty. The hours of caddying were comparably short. An average round of golf took around four hours and thus a caddie could expect to work eight-hour days if he carried two bags in a day. Caddies worked at a comparatively engaging occupation, making it popular for those who sought a break from the monotony of repetitive agricultural labor or grueling turpentine work.

The exact system of employment for caddies varied from club to club and resort to resort, but most followed a general pattern. Almost universally, caddies were not employees, nor did they have contracts. The golfers themselves—rather than country clubs—employed caddies on a day-to-day basis. Caddies received their pay and potential tip directly from the golfer at the conclusion of the round. Country clubs and resort management facilitated the hiring of individual caddies to individual players and set pay scales but did not pay caddies themselves. This arrangement provided a level of uncertainty for both caddies and management that came with positives and negatives for both parties. For caddies, the temporary nature of the work gave them the relative freedom to choose their working hours and days without employers dictating their time. It also allowed workers in other industries to caddie as a means of extra income without being tied into the job. Thaddeus McRae, a Pinehurst caddie in the 1930s and '40s, worked full-time at the local pharmacy but carried a bag whenever he could, especially on Saturdays.[88] But the uncertainty also meant that caddies did not receive any protection from their employers, and they could be banned from caddying at a particular course without any legal claim. One mistake or overstep in a single round could leave a black mark against their name in management's books, and they could find themselves out of work at that golf course indefinitely. For management, the lack of contracts freed them of any pressure to provide workers with benefits supplemental to their income, not to mention fundamental worker's rights. A lack of labor rights also gave management the power to dictate acceptable and unacceptable conduct on the golf course amid the looming threat of firing.

Master Caddies

Because caddies could choose to stay home and choose when to show up, country club and resort management sometimes struggled to secure a consistent workforce. When other industries offered caddies comparable benefits, especially during World War I and World War II, golf course managers struggled to find enough caddies to carry bags.[89] The problem became particularly stark for Atlanta's golf clubs during World War II, as caddie masters went door-to-door in search of available men and boys.[90] Country clubs and resorts understood that their access to willing Black caddies depended on a lack of Black labor opportunities elsewhere in the economy. When other opportunities become more plentiful, courses needed to provide at least some level of basic amenities for their caddies to maintain their workforce.

Caddies who worked at seasonal locations such as Pinehurst were especially attuned to the positive aspects of caddying. For much of the first half of the 20th century, most golf resorts aimed at White tourists operated only in the colder months of the year. Marketed as winter resorts for vacationing northerners, these locales opened their gates between October and December, and usually closed for the summer by the middle of May. This schedule meant that caddies who carried bags all winter at resorts turned to alternative forms of income in the summer. More often than not, the available jobs were in farming.[91]

Long summers back on the farm undoubtedly reinforced the benefits of caddying and ensured that men would return to caddying when the golfing season arrived late in the year. Back-breaking and monotonous farm work in the southern summer heat made carrying a golf bag on mild winter days all the more appealing. However, not all caddies lived locally. In fact, many caddies travelled to Pinehurst only for the winter golf season, returning to their homes for summer. While most came from elsewhere in Moore County or neighboring counties, some travelled from South Carolina.[92] Black workers who made tourist hotspots their seasonal home often lived in Black-owned guest houses, such as the one operated by Demus Taylor after he finished caddying early in the 20th century. During peak weeks, when the most important golf tournaments took place, Pinehurst occasionally struggled to supply enough caddies due to of a lack of adequate housing in the area.[93]

Once caddies arrived at golf courses, the system of allocating them to a player varied widely. At many clubs such as Pinehurst, the caddie master assigned caddies to players on a first-come, first-serve basis. Caddies lined up in the order they arrived and once they had completed their round they took "their place, still numerically, at the other end of the lane and begin over again."[94] The logic behind such a system was to discourage players from requesting their personal favorite caddies—which may have brought with it delays to tee times and disagreements between different golfers who requested the same bag-carrier.[95] After many years of standardized pay for all caddies employed at that course, management around the country began devising new and innovative ways of categorizing caddies based on their skills and experience. Most country clubs and resorts created caddie classes, usually ranging from "A" to "C." Class A, according to one caddie manual of the time, was "composed of the most efficient caddies," and were "given the largest fees and preference when a caddie is needed." On the other hand, Class C caddies were often the youngest among the ranks, had little experience, and were a cheap hire. The separation of caddies into different classes meant that initial pay could be quite measly for first-time caddies. However, for those who stuck with the job and caddied for many years, the pay and consistent employment made the job a steady source of income. Caddies who made their way into Class A status could expect to be hired on a more consistent basis than those of lower classes.[96]

The management of caddies usually fell to a full-time caddie master employed by the country club or resort. These individuals were directly responsible for maintaining a respectable and hard-working force of caddies available to golfers at all times. While a select few clubs and resorts employed Black caddie masters, most courses employed White men for the role. At Pinehurst, the first caddie master, A.A. Ruffner, was employed at a rate of $8 dollars per week, plus the use of a room at one of the hotels and full-reimbursement of his railway ticket from New York to Pinehurst. Needless to say, Ruffner's weekly guaranteed wage was much greater than the caddies over whom he was given charge. The cost of full board at the same hotel was $3 per week, or he could upgrade to a more expensive room for $5 per week. Regardless, Ruffner was left with roughly half of his wage as disposable income.[97] Ten years later, in 1911, Pinehurst caddie fees were at a level at which caddies might be lucky to earn half the wage of the caddie master in a week.[98]

Management tasked caddie masters with a few key duties. First and foremost, they had to be able to provide golfers with a caddie for their round at all times. Caddie masters needed to maintain a steady supply of caddies at the caddy shack who were ready and waiting to work. During peak season, the demand could be hard to satisfy, and caddie masters devised methods of ensuring consistent supply, such as facilitating transport to the golf course, or actively going out into the Black neighborhoods and bringing caddies to work. The latter occurred occasionally in Pinehurst, and it often impinged on efforts to keep local Black children in school for full days of learning. In the mid 1920s the principal of the Black school in Taylortown had to institute a system in which school aged caddies could only be employed at Pinehurst on weekdays if they showed credentials proving they had attended a full day of school that morning.[99] Caddie masters also needed to ensure that the standard of individuals who caddied at the course was up to scratch. Doing so at some clubs meant keeping detailed records of caddie competence. Donald Currie, Pinehurst's caddie master during the 1920s, revamped the caddie system and boasted that he kept such thorough records on caddies and former caddies that he knew what had happened to the men on the "list of undesirables." According to Currie, the majority of the men whom he had banned from caddying had been killed as outlaws or jailed.[100] Alongside maintaining a plentiful supply of respectable caddies, the caddie master also ensured that caddies remained in their designated space on the course and trained new caddies on the basics of the game.

For Black caddies, the existence of a White caddie master was a signal of White authority over their working arrangements. The job title—master—also evoked the long-standing master-slave relationship between White and Black Southerners. Although caddie management in the North, where caddies were White school children, were also given the title of master, it carried extra weight in the South with its long history of racial slavery. News articles as late as the middle of the 20th century continued to refer to caddie masters in the South simply as "masters."[101]

Caddies also operated in a peculiar working dynamic in which they had two bosses: the customer and the caddie master. The golfers were their bosses in many ways, because it was they who caddies spent most of their time working for and who they reported to. And yet, the caddie master held final say over caddies and their livelihoods. The player acted as a de facto supervisor—the caddie master's deputy on the course—with a responsibility to report any missteps to the caddie master. Caddies, therefore, worked under consistent supervision and understood that they must be on their best behavior at all times.

Diving for Golf Balls

The pay that caddies received brought many Black workers into the job. Although caddie fees varied from course to course, many clubs and resorts shared similar practices and communicated with each other about hiring tactics.[102] At the start of the century, caddies could expect to earn about 20 cents for the first hour of a round, and 5 cents for every subsequent 20 minutes.[103] The caddie fee for a four-hour round, therefore, totaled roughly 30 cents. Over the course of a six- or seven-day workweek, and once tips were added to the equation, caddies earned between 5 and 10 dollars per week. Compared to agricultural wage labor—where wages ranged from 30 to 75 cents per day in the regular season and from 60 cents to one dollar per day in the high season—caddying was certainly competitive and often more lucrative than agricultural wage work.[104] By the 1930s, caddies earned over 1 dollar per round. At Pinehurst in 1924, Donald Ross increased caddie fees from a flat rate of 75 cents per round to 1 dollar in response to caddie shortages, indicating that wages were a driving factor in the appeal of the job to Black Southerners.[105] Even in cities around the South, caddying offered a competitive wage. Charlie Sifford—the first Black golfer to join the PGA Tour—began caddying in Charlotte in 1933 when he was just 10, and 3 years later, at the age of 13, earned as much from his time working on the golf course as his father did as a laborer at the local fertilizer plant.[106]

While earning decent wages through caddie fees and tips, caddies also sought other supplemental income on the golf course. Specifically, they could make a little extra selling the golf balls they found on the job. "Members are buying and paying good prices for golf balls found by the boys," wrote one golfer at Atlanta Athletic Club's East Lake course, "and in that way encouraging them to make small efforts to find lost balls."[107] The average golfer had an uncanny ability to hit their golf balls into the many lakes, ponds, and rivers that dotted the South's golf courses. Between rounds, or when the course was quiet, caddies took to the water to recover such treasures. In one tragic turn of events in 1922, two Black caddies drowned in the lake at Atlanta's Brookhaven golf course when diving for golf balls.[108] Selling balls was clearly profitable enough to encourage caddies to search tirelessly—even dangerously—for them.

Many White golfers disliked the system that allowed caddies to sell lost balls back to those who played the course. They argued that the practice encouraged caddies to steal from their golfer's bag and negligently search for their player's balls during the round, to allow them to return to the spot afterward to recover the ball for sale. "Before long," one disgruntled Atlantan wrote, "at the present rate of going, even the balls in the members' lockers will not be safe from the raids of the caddies."[109] By 1923, the apparent problem had reached such a stage that Atlanta clubs enlisted law enforcement to help. "County Officers Declare War on Caddies" read one *Atlanta Constitution* headline detailing the story of one caddie who was charged with petty larceny after officials found 19 golf balls in his possession. Neither the club nor the newspaper, it seemed, considered the possibility that the caddie found the balls innocently in his own time.[110] Seven years later, in Savannah, Georgia, a local policeman fatally shot a Black caddie on the golf course. In his defense, the officer claimed the caddie "put his hand to his pocket as though to draw a weapon," and that the "negro caddy had been stealing golf balls."[111] Around the same time, Pinehurst officials introduced a rule that caddies could not sell golf balls because the practice encouraged caddies to "steal balls from bags or pick up balls lost by players." Exceptions were made for caddies who the caddie master knew to be "honest and reliable."[112]

A Profound Sense of Ownership

Caddies travelled to the course in many ways, but their journey was not always straightforward. At Pinehurst, in the early years, caddies lived in a number of surrounding towns and villages including Jackson Hamlet, Smoke, West End, and even as far as Carthage, 12 miles away. Those who lived along the railway line had the option of commuting by train. Pinehurst even offered discounted rates to caddies and to laundry workers who used the railroad in the first decade of the century—a rate of 5 cents each way, as long as their ticket was signed by the caddie master or manager of the Pinehurst laundry.[113] The discount was beneficial to Pinehurst management, as it maintained a steady supply of workers while keeping their wages relatively low. Other caddies who did not live along the rail line had more arduous journeys into the golf course. Traveling by foot was the most common means of commuting in the first decades of the century, as groups of caddies rose before dawn and walked many miles to the golf course to take their place in line.

Later, as motor vehicles became more common, caddies packed into old cars and made their way to work. Pinehurst caddie master Donald Currie noted that it was not uncommon for "eight, ten, twelve" caddies to "start out in an old Model T Ford, run out of gas two or three miles from town, and walk the rest of the way in."[114] As the decades passed, Pinehurst Resort created formalized modes of transportation for caddies to the course. They instituted a bus, which picked up teenagers from the local Black schools in the early afternoon and transported them to the golf course for work.[115] It was important for Pinehurst to ensure a consistent supply of workers, and such infrastructure made that possible. Though convenient for caddies, these forms of transport added to their employer's control over their working life. Caddies who relied on the provided transport became reliant on their employer, and consequently lost some of their freedom to define their own working hours.

In cities like Atlanta, public transportation offered the most straightforward form of commuting. Early in the 20th century, when Atlanta's Black population was scattered around the city, many caddies likely lived close enough to walk to the golf course. As the population of the city increased between 1890 and 1930, and as housing discrimination entrenched racially distinct areas of the city, Black Atlantans migrated westward in the city, while Whites moved north. The biggest employers of caddies were the Druid Hills and the East Lake clubs—both located in the east of the city—meaning that most caddies lived too far from the courses to walk. The streetcar that stretched from downtown to East Lake gave caddies an efficient mode of transport. Caddies represented a significant proportion of the streetcar's ridership in some areas of the city. According to a manager at the Georgia Railway and Power Company in 1922, the section between Springdale Road and Druid Hills Golf Club "was used chiefly by caddies and servants."[116] Riding the streetcar came at a financial cost, though—one that caddies wished they could do without. In the 1930s, the railway company experienced "a lot of trouble with caddies from the golf club stealing rides." One caddie, A.J. Hammond, received a sentence of a $12 fine or 20 days in prison when he was caught climbing into a streetcar through the window. Other caddies devised clever schemes to avoid paying the fare. Sometimes one caddie would pay the fare, walk to the back of the car, and step onto the back door treadle, allowing his colleagues to enter at the back.[117] In the Jim Crow economy rigged against Black workers, saving a 10-cent fare felt like a trivial crime to Black caddies.

Riding the streetcar to work also subjected Black Atlantan caddies to the realities of Jim Crow accommodations. Following the 1906 riot in the city, White authorities segregated the streetcar to entrench strict racial divides in public spaces. Such segregation was a consistent reinforcement of Black Atlantans' place at the bottom of a societal hierarchy. For caddies and other Black workers throughout the city, the journey to work reflected the racial dynamics they would face on the job.[118]

Though commuting added time to the workday, it also made caddying a more desirable vocation than many jobs that required African American workers to live in close proximity to their White employers. Being able to return home every day to their own neighborhood—away from White oversight and control—was a benefit of wage work. After decades of impeded Black mobility, the simple act of commuting gave Black workers a sense of freedom that had been relatively impossible in sharecropping or turpentine farming. It meant that, should they not want to turn up for work one day, then they would not find their employer at their door within minutes. Commuting gave them a more profound sense of ownership over their time than existed in fieldwork or other industries in which they lived close to their employment. Domestic workers who lived in-house for White families and farmers who lived on the land they rented from White landlords learned that proximity to bosses often gave employers the power to blur the lines between work and leisure, creating an overall increase in demands on their labor.[119] The act of commuting provided a buffer between them and their work that often did not exist in the previous decades.

Waiting for Work

Upon arrival at the golf course, Black workers discovered immediate differences between caddying and other intensive jobs performed by Black Southerners. At the start of each day, caddies made their way to their designated waiting area: the caddy shack. Every country club or resort that employed caddies had a caddy shack of some sort. Usually, the space fulfilled only the basic needs of workers who awaited their round. Four walls, a roof, somewhere to sit, and the simplest of bathroom facilities gave the men shelter from the elements and a place to await their next bag. The caddy shack—as a separate space for Black workers and out of sight of White leisure-seekers—reinforced the worker's position in the race- and class-based hierarchy of southern society. White country club and resort management ensured that Black caddies stayed in their designated areas as a means of finely managing the separation of Black workers and White leisure-seekers. Donald Ross, the head of golf operations at Pinehurst, was steadfast in his belief that caddies be discouraged "in every way, from hanging around the clubhouse."[120] The four walls of the caddy shack provided a simple solution to any potential intermingling of caddies and golfers when the game was not in progress. While waiting for their next bags, Black caddies were to remain out of sight.

Time spent in the caddy shack, however, was not always engrossing and enjoyable. Long days often passed without work, and caddies certainly experienced the boredom that came with waiting for a customer who wanted to play. In the age before accurate weather reporting, caddies did not know if a rainstorm that kept golfers off the course in the morning would last an hour or the whole day.[121] A caddie might clock in at work first thing in the morning and not set foot outside the caddy shack until late in the afternoon, once it became clear that he would not be employed that day. The dark and enclosed caddy shack across the South must have seen many days of boredom. Being trapped in the caddy shack for entire days when inclement weather ruled out the possibility of employment also brought financial stress to these workers. In a job that paid cash in hand on a day-to-day basis, returning home without a single cent may have proved traumatic to families who relied on daily earnings.[122]

Idle time in the caddy shack ranged from boredom to excitement. When the golf course was not busy, caddies could spend days sitting and waiting for golfers to request a caddie. The workers, therefore, needed to come up with ways to pass the time. Among the more common means of entertainment was gambling. According to DeWayne Wickham, a former caddie who worked at Woodholme Country Club in Maryland, when caddies "were in high abundance, the caddy shack resembled a casino."[123] In one corner of the caddy shack, a craps game might occupy some of the men, as older caddies controlled the dice and orchestrated the betting from those gathered around them. In another corner some caddies might be engaged in a game of tonk—a popular game among the younger men, each of them trying to gather enough winnings to enter the craps game in the other corner. Outside and out of view of the White golfers, the youngest caddies might have "pitched pennies" against the caddy house wall, hoping to land theirs closest to the wall and win the pot. Occasionally, law enforcement descended upon caddy shacks to arrest those who partook in games of chance.[124] In the dark and dingy caddy shacks of the South, where uneven floors brought added excitement and nerves to every roll of the dice, gambling created a consistent hum of excitement as the waiting workers cheered and groaned as their fortunes ebbed and flowed.[125]

Every game came with the possibility to multiply or lose a day's pay, yet caddies engaged in gambling as more than an avenue for increased earnings: it was a form of entertainment, a stay against boredom. For those caddies who took the most interest in gambling, "winning wasn't nearly as important … as the rush he got from just being part of the action," as DeWayne Wickham put it. As with many gamblers, the exhilaration brought caddies back into a game as much as the hope of taking home a few extra dollars. It was, as Wickham noted, "the heart-thumping excitement that came with every roll of the dice, every turn of the cards or toss of the penny." Images of caddies playing various games of chance show men enjoying each other's company and sharing in a moment of excitement (Figure 6).[126] Many younger caddies also saw their initiation into the games of craps and cards as part of their transition into adulthood. Just as they began their professional lives as caddies on the golf course, they placed meaning on their first experiences of gambling in the clubhouse. According to Wickham, "it was their Bar Mitzvah—a coming of age that announced their arrival into manhood."[127]

Black caddies' propensity for gambling certainly received the attention of White golfers and country club management. In fact, gambling became such a common sight in and around the caddy shacks of the South that White golfers began describing craps as "African Golf" and "Nigger Golf." The disparaging terms reinforced White beliefs that caddies could not possibly be skilled at the actual game of golf, and they criticized caddies for their potentially wasteful use of their money.[128]

However, for caddies and all Black wage workers of the South, gambling was another avenue which demonstrated their financial independence from employers. In other dominant industries such as sharecropping, the payment was often made in non-cash forms such as crops or tools—or a reduction in debt. Cash gave workers a freedom to choose how to spend their earnings, and gambling was a signal that their lives and livelihoods would not be defined by White employers. In the face of disparaging White comments about the futility and risk involved in gambling, placing bets may actually have represented a means of defying White prescriptions regarding appropriate behavior. It is important to note though that gambling, of course, was not conducive to financial security or long-term wealth. For caddies, the problem was likely exacerbated by the length of time spent idle in the caddy shack. Hour after hour of boredom made the thrill of gambling all the more appealing to the men who awaited their shift.

FIGURE 6: Four caddies involved in a dice game, 1913 (Getty Images).

As a means of passing time, caddies sometimes turned to liquor to make the hours pass quicker. However, it must be emphasized that drinking among caddies was relatively rare, and drinking to the point of intoxication was even rarer. At the start of the century, the Pinehurst caddie master kept a book that listed every caddie by name and an accompanying picture. Under many pictures, the caddie master wrote a one-word comment—most often the phrases were "good" or "sorry." For some of the men, the comment read "drunk"—a sign that the drinking culture among caddies occasionally spilled over and certain men developed addictions that inhibited their work.[129]

The Comforts of the Caddy Shack

Despite the potential for excessive drinking and gambling among caddies, the caddy shack offered a space of relative freedom to Black men to enjoy each other's company while at work. According to one former caddie, it was a "single space controlled by Black folks in this enclave of White wealth and power."[130] Unlike on the course where Whites placed explicit expectations on Black caddies both as employees and as members of a prescribed underclass, the caddy shack was a distinct area where caddies had the freedom to relax. In the caddy shack they shared occupational expertise, told stories about their round the previous day, and spread knowledge about the golfers who played there. Out of sight and earshot of their employers, caddies could easily bluntly discuss the golfers whom they caddied for. At Sedgefield Country Club in Greensboro, North Carolina, for example, every player who regularly played the course was "classified and listed by the caddies according to his vanity, language, and graciousness."[131] Sharing such knowledge in the caddy shack helped caddies prepare for their next golfer. At courses with a large caddie corps, the caddy shack may even have had a small kitchen where caddies could prepare meals. At Pinehurst, there was a distinct kitchen dedicated to selling lunches to the caddies. The kitchen not only kept caddies fed, but, in the words of Donald Ross, "The fact that the boys get good food at reasonable prices is a very important factor in bringing the boys there."[132] Those who chose to caddie for many years took comfort in the confines of the caddy shack.

On the golf course, caddies presented themselves how they wished to be seen. At certain courses, caddies chose to dress in their finest attire while on the job. In 1911, the caddie master at Pinehurst decided to take pictures of all caddies who worked there, for purposes of identifying the workers. The images show men and boys dressed in clothing that seem more fit for a church service or wedding than a golf course. The men wore dark suits, shirts, ties, and smart shoes. Their outfits indicate that the caddies thought the work both required it and bestowed status upon them. Unlike in other occupations of the time, where clothing was largely functional and likely to become dirty over the course of a day's work, caddies had the freedom to use clothing as a tool for self-definition. Wearing a fine suit and smart shoes served to imbue caddying with a sense of importance and prestige that did not exist in other occupations around the South. Even if the pay for caddies did not make them affluent, the ways they chose to dress themselves gave them a cultural and social wage that elevated the status of the occupation among Black Southerners.[133]

"Now We Dance"

Golf's high barriers to entry—in the form of exclusionary gatekeeping by facilities and exorbitant cost of equipment—meant that almost no African American Southerners could play the game even if they wanted to. Caddying offered Black men the opportunity to learn a new sport that they had almost no exposure to by any other means. Once caddies became workers at golf courses, they engaged with the game on a daily basis. In turn, they learned the ins and outs of golf and observed what constituted good and bad play. Caddies built their own golf clubs, or accepted hand-me-downs from players and began playing the game in their own communities or by sneaking onto White golf courses at night.[134]

Eventually, country clubs and resorts allowed caddies to play the courses where they worked on days when the course was otherwise closed for maintenance. Once they began, many caddies became engrossed in playing the sport and took every opportunity to play more golf. At Pinehurst, a caddie by the name of "Swamp" built a short course for caddies not far from the caddy shack where the men could spend their time between rounds brushing up on their own skills.[135] For most of the first half of the 20th century, caddying was the avenue by which most African Americans who came to play golf were exposed to the game.

Working at a site of White leisure offered the double-edged sword for Black caddies: making money by entertaining White golfers. White management organized shows that often took the form of demeaning and infantilizing entertainment. At Pinehurst, the cake walks and baby shows from the beginning of the century encouraged those on stage to act in ways that reinforced White expectations and stereotypes about Black Southerners. Financial imbalance and the promise of potential cash prizes for the best dancers or most handsome babies made it hard for Black locals to resist taking part. In historian Louis Moore's *I Fight for a Living*, a former Augusta National worker and future national boxing star, Beau Jack, remembered Black men and boys being pitted against each other in blindfolded fights, which became bloodbaths for the entertainment of club guests. In these instances, entertaining White golfers in ways that reinforced harmful stereotypes was part of what it took to make a living.[136]

Yet in other ways, Black caddies sought out opportunities for impromptu entertainment and shows that displayed their talents. In images from Pinehurst, there are caddies playing guitars, dancing, and singing. Reports of caddies performing at clubhouse events reached newspapers and promotional material in cities and resorts. At Pinehurst, events featured "the pick of caddie entertainers and other colored talent," while in Atlanta the opening of a new clubhouse at West End included a "dancing contest among the West End caddies."[137] In the early 1940s, when Pinehurst caddie Willie McRae completed his first round alongside veteran caddie Robert "Hardrock" Robinson, the latter turned to the former and said, "now we dance." Hardrock made his way to the practice putting green by the clubhouse and collected his fellow caddie Robert Stafford, who brought a washboard. Stafford kept a beat with the washboard, and Hardrock danced to the delight of the growing crowd of White golfers. McRae remembered that "Hardrock didn't just *dance*, he drew the crowd right *into* his tapping." His talents "sent a charge like electricity right through the crowd," and "his feet moved so fast ... with such rhythm ... only a man born to dance coulda done it."[138] Prior to becoming a caddie, Robinson had spent time as a professional dancer and entertainer—how he turned to caddying is uncertain. However, caddying offered an opportunity for these men to demonstrate their skills and cultural talents in ways that were not possible in many other jobs.

When caddies engaged in entertaining on their own terms, they reaped some financial and cultural benefits. The soul-sucking, regimented, and repetitive occupations that most Black Southerners occupied offered almost no avenues for creative freedom, and certainly no financial compensation for such self-expression and creativity. When Hardrock danced, "the money poured into [his] tub." Caddies could supplement their income with these performances and also reinforce their sense of self-worth. When the dancing was over and Robert Stafford asked Hardrock for some of the takings, the latter replied, "When they come to see *you, then* the money's yours." It was not just the payment that mattered to Robinson; it was also that those tourists came to see him. His talents as a dancer and the crowds he drew reinforced his personhood in a region in which Black men were made to feel as insignificant as possible. Caddying offered small avenues for self-fulfillment that were lacking in the monotonous jobs elsewhere in the southern economy.[139]

While Black workers may have preferred caddying to many other opportunities available to Black workers seeking an honest wage and some degree of financial independence, it also reinforced the racial hierarchy. The symbolic importance of Black servitude was not lost on Black caddies, as caddies understood their position as facilitators for White leisure time and often detested the subservient role they were required to play. For some, it was simply too much to ask. Famed Black writer Richard Wright caddied for a single round in Mississippi before realizing how much he hated working a job in which the main role was serving White folks' every need. Wright returned home, "disgusted, tired, hungry, hating the sight of a golf course," and never caddied again.[140] Charlie Sifford caddied at the Carolina Country Club in Charlotte because the job gave him the possibility to play golf; but it pained him to continue to exist in the racial hierarchy that underpinned the game.[141] Sifford, Wright, and many others took their earliest chances to leave the occupation in search of something better, and many ventured North in the hopes of finding a life where their incomes were not tied to White employers.

Those who continued to caddie in the South were not more accepting of their position in the South's racial hierarchy. They stayed because the job offered them a life that was better than what they had before. It offered them some degree of financial independence. Caddying allowed them to foster community, to become skilled in a profession, and to learn a new sport themselves. When Black Southerners decided whether to uproot their lives and follow the Great Migration to the North, they weighed the potential for a better life with the upheaval of breaking ties with the communities they and their families had called home for many generations. For most who continued to walk the course every day, it gave them a livelihood that was far better than the ones their parents—and their grandparents—had experienced before them.

While caddies' working lives were by no means ideal, the list of reasons to quit or move were slightly shorter for Black caddies than for many millions of other Black Southerners. The job offered them something different. It offered them an escape from the drudgery of exploitative farm labor. It offered them a chance at a somewhat consistent wage. It offered them a community of similar men and boys who enjoyed each other's companionship. It offered them the opportunity to learn a new game and hobby. It was little wonder that thousands of Black men would choose to enter the caddy shacks of the South over the course of the 20th century.

CHAPTER 3

"Show Up, Keep Up, Shut Up"

Navigating Racial Dynamics on the Golf Course

Willie McRae was 10 years old when he first picked up a golf bag at Pinehurst in 1943. He approached the group of golfers on the first tee at the famous No. 2 course with trepidation, and with a deep sense of anger toward his father who had forced him into caddying. "Right then I hated my dad for getting me into this mess," McRae later remembered. World War II had taken its toll on the family, and Willie's father, Thaddeus Herman McRae, decided that Willie needed to start earning a wage to help put food on the table for him and his 10 siblings at home in Taylortown. They grew much of their own food on the farm they shared with Willie's grandparents on his mother's side of the family, but it was not enough to keep him out of the workplace. Earlier that year, he began working with his grandfather at the Pinehurst Saw Mill. Before long though, his father pulled him aside and told him, "It's time you learned. Caddying is a way of life for most of us in Taylortown. Besides, I know everything you need to know. I'll teach you." Thaddeus McRae worked weekdays at the local pharmacy but caddied as a side job whenever he could to earn a little extra for his large family.

As they stood under an old tree on their property, a tree they called "The Tree of Knowledge," Thaddeus imparted the key lessons for any young Black caddie to learn before he picked up his first golf bag. He grabbed a branch and an old bag to show him how best to carry it. "Pretend this here's a golf bag and this branch a club. When the player approaches you, stand the bag up, hold it still but back up a step," he said, holding the bag at arm's length. This advice was simple enough for Willie to follow, but the subsequent explanation of different golf clubs might as well have been a foreign language to the 10-year-old. "You watch a player hit a few shots with different clubs, and you see how far he hits each one. He might hit a 1-wood 200 yards or just 150. He might hit a 5-iron a 100 … or 125." Willie stared back blankly. "Give it time," his dad reassured him, "in the meantime, the important thing is to *show up, keep up, and shut up.*"[142]

Willie McRae soon picked up the basics on the job, with help from his colleagues in the caddy shack. A few months of experience did not stop him from being on the receiving end of his father's lectures after word got back to Thaddeus that his son had spoken out of turn on the golf course. "You got a tongue on you that needs controlling. Just because you *thought* that golfer yesterday was too proud, don't mean you *say* it. You keep your mouth shut. Hear me? No sass!" Thaddeus wanted the best for his son and the best for his family. "Look, Son, the idea out there is to make money right—money to help your mom. All of us, right? You wanna do that, right? … Good. But to do that you have to be *professional*. … And you're professional when you make the man happy," Thaddeus lectured.[143]

A few days later, Willie had his father's words ringing in his ears as he carried the bag of Richard Tufts, the third generation of Tufts men to own and operate Pinehurst Resort after his father, Leonard Tufts, and his grandfather, James Walker Tufts. Willie's feet ached in his old shoes, worn to threads on the sole, with cardboard inserts stuffed inside to provide meager padding. He desperately wanted to ask Tufts if he would be willing to spare some money toward a new pair, but he had to bite his tongue and heed his father's advice. Over the first three holes, he opted to say nothing at all rather than risk opening his mouth and potentially airing his true feelings. When Tufts asked for club recommendations, Willie simply picked the one he felt was best suited for the shot and handed it to him. On the 14th hole, Tufts—unsure of his caddie's silence—asked Willie if something was wrong. McRae kept his silence, his father's voice in his head kept telling him "Don't do it Willie Lee, ya hear? Don't you do it!" The voice competed with the ache of his feet, each step making it harder to resist asking Tufts for help. Soon it became too much. "It's like we can ask you for anything. You're that nice," Willie blurted out, to which Tufts simply nodded his head and said, "Ah huh, I'd like to think that people who work for me can come to me if they need to." The voice inside Willie's head grew louder, telling him, "Shut up, Willie, just shut up. Just *stop*, now!" But the pain became too much to bear, and he finally gave into his needs, "I need a new pair of shoes. These hurt so bad." At this point there was no turning back for Willie. He immediately regretted his honesty. Tufts gave a brief acknowledgement, "I see," and the pair did not exchange words for the rest of the round. McRae's need for new shoes gave way to a desire to be as far from the golf course as possible. He later remembered, "I never shoulda opened my mouth. Keep up and shut up, that's what I shoulda done. Why couldn't I just do that?"[144]

In the days that followed, Tufts gave McRae a new pair of shoes, yet their interaction that day encapsulated the complexities of etiquette on the golf course between a Black worker and a White leisure-seeker. From his father's lectures to his own internal monologue, Willie McRae understood his precarious position as a Black person in a White space. Although McRae's recollections did not implicitly reference the color line that separated him from Pinehurst golfers, like every Black southerner, he would have been continuously aware that the politics of race permeated every interracial interaction. His father's instructions—on how to hold the bag out while taking a step back, on staying quiet unless spoken to, and on repressing his true feelings about employers—were all cloaked in racial etiquette and decorum. The small step back demonstrated the Black caddie's deference to the White golfer, and the unspoken truths spoke to a difference in standards of acceptable speech for White and Black individuals on the course. Of course, race intersected with other variables, such as the power relations between employee and employer, as well as the age, class, and gender dynamics at play. However, race dominated every interaction, just as it did for other African Americans and Whites in the South whenever they met.

McRae's early career confusion about how to act and speak while on the job also points to the unique lens that encounters between caddie and golfer offer into the workings of racial behavior in the South. The overlapping layers of golf etiquette and racial etiquette made those who walked the fairways especially aware of their actions. In Pinehurst, Atlanta, and throughout the South, many White golfers hoped their interactions with their Black caddies would reflect their assumptions about race—in particular their belief in a natural racial hierarchy—and that their adherence to golf etiquette would help uphold their middle- and upper-class sensibilities. Black caddies, on the other hand, approached each interaction with the knowledge that any infractions of racial etiquette might lead to violent retribution or firing amid a rigged and racially segregated labor market. Nonetheless, these workers insisted on demonstrating their humanity and their skill, and at times outrightly challenged White prescriptions for their conduct.

Consideration, Courtesy, and Gentlemanly Feeling

While the Rules of Golf were decided upon by the game's major governing bodies, the codes of etiquette were the result of community creation. New golfers who sought to understand the basic rules of the game could purchase rulebooks that detailed the basics of scoring and penalties, and explained how players should navigate obscure scenarios—such as what to do if your ball strikes another player. Rules and etiquette differed both in spirit and in practice. While the rules were in place to provide the basic structures of the game, the etiquette existed to inform the character and nature of golf. Knowing *the rules* taught a player that they legally had five minutes to find a lost ball; understanding *etiquette* meant a player knew not to spend five minutes searching for a ball that was lost beyond doubt. As one golf writer noted in 1909, "consideration for others, courtesy, gentlemanly feeling; this is the basis of all golfing etiquette."[145] The game's reputation hinged on etiquette, as writers and commentators consistently took to the pages of golf periodicals bemoaning the moral declension of the game when etiquette was not properly upheld. As a game that defined its players, golf required an image of respectability and class befitting of those who could afford to play it. While most sports in the United States had a defined rulebook, few came close to the expectations regarding a player's conduct like golf. Upholding the game's etiquette was linked to upholding the image of the class of people who played the game. Elitist beliefs posited that golf promoted the same values that made someone an upstanding member of society, and most often those values were prescribed by the elite individuals who played the game.

Golf's strict codes of conduct served elites as purposefully exclusionary of other social classes. New players, who were not outrightly excluded on the basis of country club membership or playing costs, were often deterred by the game's elitist mores. High costs of entry and membership requirements to play most courses gave the game an exclusive air and allowed players to differentiate themselves from the general mass of the population who played more accessible sports. Furthermore, golf's stringent codes of conduct made the game unique compared to others, and golfers celebrated in the way that golf etiquette added a collective identity to the sport. In one poem that made the pages of *American Golfer*, the author wrote,

> "Now baseball has its many rules,
> Lawn tennis has its laws,
> There's statutes, too, for pingpong,
> Although they may have flaws;
> But, Golfing is the only sport,
> That has restrictions set

> On how to walk and how to talk—
> 'Tis called golf etiquette."[146]

Elites did not deem etiquette a relic of bygone days or a pretentious part of the game recently imported from Great Britain. Rather, they seized upon golf's rigorous etiquette as another tool for identity-making. In turn, as golf grew more popular and municipal courses opened the game up to working- and middle-class White Americans, elites consistently bemoaned the lack of gentlemanly conduct among the new golfing masses. One editorial argued that "the direct cause for this carelessness in regard for golf rules and its attendant etiquette can be traced back in a large measure to the fact that in the last few years the ranks of golfers have grown so rapidly."[147] A parody set of "rules of etiquette for public courses" listed in *American Golfer* sneered at municipal courses and listed the many flaws of those who played them. Those who frequented public golf courses, the author argued, talked loudly, did not repair their damage to the course, and played dangerously.[148] Elites consistently used expected codes of conduct in golf to emphasize their status in the upper echelons of society.

Although some rule books dedicated space in the closing pages to codes of conduct, golf etiquette was largely enforced by golfers themselves on the course. Any new golfer who came to the game experienced any number of potential golfing faux pas. However, new players quickly learned about etiquette simply by watching their more experienced peers. In one northern city, for example, local clubs "universally agreed that their players ... shall maintain this etiquette themselves and by example teach the others." If example was not enough and an individual transgressed a fundamental rule, other players would take it upon themselves to reprimand the offender and explain how best to avoid making the same mistake in the future, "so that with an accumulation of the results of that endeavor, players new to the game will gather a golfing education."[149] Golfers also believed that the game's tradition and legacy relied on the passing of proper etiquette from one generation of players to the next, and that upholding unwritten codes lay at the bedrock of golf's future. Writing in 1931, one contributor to *Golf Illustrated* claimed, "The only way to maintain golf as it is today, and to build its standards even higher is to practice, and in so practicing, preach the etiquette of the game of golf as it has been handed down from those grand old players of times gone by."[150] While the rules of the game changed, players hoped that the general character of the game would be defined by its long-standing etiquette.

Caddies needed to learn the etiquette of golf in particular ways that applied to their role on the course. Perceptions of the caddie's role were not always consistent from one player to the next. One golfer may have seen the caddie as a companion on the course, someone to talk to or confide in. Others saw caddies as simple bag-carriers, who were there only to allow the player to play without having to lug their heavy bag of clubs over the hilly terrain. Players also differed in their expectations of caddie involvement in their game as some valued the caddie's insight and local knowledge, while others preferred the caddie to keep quiet and let the golfers fend for themselves. Caddies learned when to speak and when to keep quiet. A witty comment to one mild-mannered player after a poor shot might result in a shared laugh, while the same words to a short-tempered golfer risked angry retribution.

Learning what a player wanted was a delicate balance and something that caddies needed to learn, either over the course of a round or over the course of many years caddying. Caddie etiquette was learned in much the same way that regular golf etiquette was, through experience. When caddies transgressed the strict lines of etiquette, players might reprimand them verbally or reduce the tip at the end of the round. Each transgression contributed to an accumulated understanding of golfer expectations. Older and more experienced caddies also taught younger caddies the tricks of the trade, how to read the slope of the green and interpret the effect of wind or the direction of the grain on the ball. Such golf knowledge often came alongside more general tips of how far to stand from the player, when to offer advice, and how to hold the flag. They shared knowledge between them about individual players in a collective endeavor to help each caddie become better prepared for the bag they were about to carry.[151]

Jim Crow on the Course

Just as golf etiquette existed to bolster the elite's collective identity, racial etiquette existed as a tool for White Southerners to orchestrate and extract an expected behavior from Black Southerners. Jim Crow laws and control over financial capital did much of the work of creating racial hierarchy, but racial etiquette buttressed it daily. In many spaces where Black and White people interacted, there were no clear boundaries or structures in place to indicate that White individuals held authority over Black individuals. In stores or on streets, Whites did not often have a visible representation of their higher rank in the racial hierarchy and therefore developed codes of behavior that made clear what may have been unclear.[152]

Although Jim Crow is understood as a system of laws, politics, and violence that sought to enshrine White supremacy, it was also a cultural phenomenon that manifested itself in the everyday interactions between southerners in shared spaces. When Black and White southerners came into contact, each party understood that the color of their skin impacted the way they were expected to act. Take, for example, the expectation that Black Southerners step aside and remove their hats when White people approached them. Or the belief that handshakes between the races was unacceptable. Black and White people could not use the same doors to houses. Black shoppers were expected to let White shoppers in front of them at check-out lines. The list of unwritten rules was expansive. In such instances, Black individuals understood the power imbalance that encouraged them to show deference and yield to their White counterparts. At the same time, White Southerners also acted according to their race in choosing not to step aside. Each interaction often also had a third participant: the audience. Those who watched interactions between White and Black individuals were involved in three major ways—firstly, their presence reminded the two central actors that they were in pubic and needed to adhere to societal standards. Secondly, the audience themselves learned proper conduct by watching the encounter. Each interaction informed the audience how they should act in such situations. Third, those who observed the interaction could hold the actors accountable.[153]

Black and White Southerners learned racial etiquette in the same ways that golfers and caddies learned sporting etiquette, at first with a basic education of conduct and then through experience. As children, Black and White Southerners learned from authority figures in their lives, such as parents and teachers, how to navigate the world according to their race to avoid publicly transgressing norms. In schools and at home, White adults taught their children to avoid intimate interactions and familiar behavior with African Americans, thereby enshrining an understanding of racial difference from an early age. Black parents taught children the skills of navigating interactions with White individuals—how to act with deference and restraint to avoid potential physical retribution for their actions. Willie McRae's father was sure to teach his son the importance of showing deference before his first time caddying. In turn, the lived experiences of public interactions fine-tuned both parties' ability to perform according to their respective racial expectations. Of course, White Southerners also used violence to enforce etiquette when Black individuals transgressed expectations.[154] Just as wealthy golfers passed down golf etiquette to differentiate themselves from working- and middle-classes who played other sports, White Americans maintained racial etiquette across generations to ensure a continuation of racial norms in the South.

Because racial etiquette was never written down or enshrined in law, it was malleable and subject to daily change. Every single interaction between White and Black people in the South offered the possibility to move expectations in one direction or the other. Black individuals could use their accumulated knowledge of hundreds of previous interactions to find small holes in the system that might allow them to assert their personhood. When they challenged prescribed behaviors, they also questioned the authority of Whites in society in small but not insignificant ways. The buildup of these acts alone did not independently represent a significant challenge to the foundational structures of racial hierarchy. However, over time the continued practice of small challenges contributed to a Black political consciousness that manifested itself in the widespread resistance that became the Civil Rights Movement.[155]

In certain spaces, Whites actively avoided segregation and practiced purposeful inclusion of Black southerners but only when doing so reinforced the racial stratification. Some trains, for example, allowed Black domestic servants to ride on White carriages with their employer because doing so highlighted the unequal relationships between White and Black passengers. Under no circumstances, however, would other (especially wealthy) Black individuals be able to ride on White carriages, because doing so broke down the artificial distinctions between the races.[156]

On the golf course, the same phenomenon existed. Every course in the South strictly banned Black golfers from playing on the course, yet purposefully included Black workers as caddies. Doing so reinforced the master-servant relationship that White Southerners tried to enshrine between themselves and Black Southerners. In spaces like golf courses and private homes, Black presence was not only tolerated, it was actually encouraged when it upheld the racial hierarchy of the South.

Racial etiquette took hold on golf courses where White players expected Black caddies to perform according to their place. Indications of status could range from the language both parties used to the many basic and subservient acts involved in caddying, such as carrying the bag, holding the flagstick, or picking up the player's ball. In every interaction each actor was expected to uphold their end of the bargain. An author in *American Golfer* from 1920 demonstrated that White golfers expected caddies to act in certain ways when writing that one of John D. Rockefeller's caddies "conformed" to the "proverbial type of lazy, listless, but rather keen-witted southern negro boy."[157] Conforming was the name of the game. White golfers expected that

Black caddies not only perform to societal standards of servitude, but also to do so with a smile on their faces. White descriptions of Black caddies—as well as promotional material—claimed that Black caddies were contented and happy. One tourism advertisement for New Orleans and the Gulf Coast boasted golf "under huge oaks draped with Spanish moss—three sporty courses, rolling fairways, velvety greens—grinning, willing, colored caddies—in short, golfing under ideal conditions."[158] Another description of Black caddies around the South claimed that golfers found "obliging and cheerful" helpers. The same newspaper report also commented on the tendency for Black caddies to approach the game as if they were partners with their players. When White players asked, "Whose ball is that near the pin?" caddies replied, "That's ours, sir."[159] Reports of contented Black caddies who viewed themselves as part of a team also reinforced wider White beliefs about the harmonious Jim Crow society in which African Americans were happy with their role as servants to Whites.[160] It helped Whites feel like everything was fine.

Golf courses implemented rules and etiquette for caddie behavior that further emphasized the distance between White golfers and Black caddies in the South's racial hierarchy. At Pinehurst, management carefully managed caddie mobility around the property. The use of a distinct caddy shack —initially adjoined to the club house and then separated entirely—made clear that the corridors of the clubhouse were not for African Americans. However, the closeness of the caddy shack to the clubhouse contributed to the idea that Jim Crow society was one of purposeful separated inclusion, in which Black workers who served White leisure-seekers existed in relative proximity to their employers.

Although the proximity of the clubhouse and the caddy shack served as a symbol for Jim Crow's racial harmony for Whites, it was an obvious demonstration of hierarchy. The segregation made clear the racial difference between White leisure-seekers and Black workers. At Pinehurst Donald Ross ensured that caddies were always kept under tight control. Of particular import to Ross was his belief that "we must discourage, in every way, caddies from hanging around the clubhouse."[161] Likewise, the caddies were not allowed into the main streets of the village except for a few hours on Saturday afternoon, or when they were purposefully included as workers and entertainers.[162] Pinehurst functioned largely as a sundown town.[163] Country club and resort management understood the double-sided problem of Black existence in what was a predominantly White space. While it made sense to keep caddies nearby for practical reasons, it also became a problem when caddies crossed the border into so-called White spaces. Clubhouses did not have the outright signage to mark "White" and "Colored" areas as existed on train platforms or water fountains, in part because southern golf courses were not integrated spaces (in terms of players) until the middle of the century. The lack of clear signage caused issues for Ross and others who subsequently policed caddie movements and discouraged any indication that African Americans belonged in the verandas or hallways of the clubhouse. When Atlanta Athletic Club built their first caddy house in 1912, its stated purpose was as a space where caddies "will be required to stay while not on the links."[164] Black existence at the golf course was a carefully procured image that Whites cultivated and managed.

The same policing of mobility existed on the golf course where caddies walked alongside their White employer on the same grass and at the same pace. To maintain the critical racial distinction, early in the century caddies could not enter certain parts of the course. At Pinehurst caddies were "not permitted to walk through the bunkers or into the traps or pits or upon the green." Regulating caddies in these ways allowed Whites to demarcate an apparently colorblind landscape as one that had racially designated spaces. It also reinforced to caddies that although they walked the course with their employer, it was the golfer who was supposed to inhabit the spaces of skill and talent. The greens and bunkers were a place for talented White golfers and not for servile, unskilled, Black caddies. Exceptions to caddie mobility only emphasized their servitude to White golfers. For example, at Pinehurst the only caddie who could enter onto the green was "the boy pulling out the pin."[165] Black caddies would keep a distance from other players, when players were confined to the small, defined space of the green. The inclusion of only one caddie into the space of White talent, and with the explicit direction to remove the flagstick for White golfers, made clear the difference between White golfers and Black caddies.

White golfers also expected Black caddies to function as entertainers. Every morning caddies lined up outside the caddy shack and awaited their bag for the day. At most courses the line functioned on a first-come, first-serve basis. On occasion though, White golfers devised new methods to decide the order of caddies. At Pinehurst, when the competition was fierce between caddies to secure a job, White golfers sometimes encouraged the competing caddies to perform their best Charleston dance to decide which caddie to use.[166] The first caddie master at Pinehurst, A.A. Ruffner, had a stipulation in his contract that dictated that he should assist "at entertainments that may be projected for the amusement of Pinehurst or Hotel Guests."[167] Black workers shouldered the assumption that they should consistently acquiesce to White demands on their behavior, regardless of whether if it was part of the job description. It was the color line that made such expectations possible on southern golf courses.

Expectations of racial and caddie etiquette did not always translate into the lived experience. The prolonged time spent together during a round of golf and the long-term relationships that developed between caddies and players offered advantages and disadvantages to Black caddies who wished to challenge their prescribed place in society. The longevity provided the opportunity for them to prove themselves as intelligent humans who were fit for more than just serving others. However, the same intimacy meant that overstepping the mark could forever damage their livelihood if players reported individual caddies and had them punished. Caddies in these circumstances were not nameless and faceless like they might be in everyday interactions on the street; the players knew who they were and therefore held greater control over the caddies' financial well-being.

Once a caddie had a firm grasp of the basics of their expected behaviors, any purposeful challenge to these codes of conduct came with the potential for retribution or for redrawing the lines of expected behaviors. Small challenges, such as holding their own on club selection or encouraging a player to rethink their strategy, might provide freedom to do so again later should the player respect the caddie's advice and benefit from it. A player who made a better score on a hole because of their caddie may have been more inclined to listen to or respect caddie input in the future. On the day that Willie McRae caddied for Richard Tufts, Tufts asked him to read a putt on the 3rd hole. After he carefully judged the slope and the grain, McRae gave his best advice which proved correct, as Tufts rolled in the putt and smiled. McRae later remembered that he "smiled back" and found himself "opening up more and more on just about every hole."[168] In that moment, his professional competence gave McRae the confidence to become more assertive in his role.

On the other hand, caddies who challenged players in too forceful a manner risked appearing above their racial station. A reprimand from a White golfer made caddies think twice about overstepping in the future, while a concession encouraged caddies to step outside their previously prescribed lane. In his very first round as a caddie, McRae experienced the difficulty of correctly judging how much advice to give his player, when he finally bucked up his courage and offered advice on the line of a putt on the 14th hole. McRae was mistaken as the ball rolled the opposite way and the player left the green "disgruntled" with him.[169] A fictionalized 1930 cartoon imagining an interaction between a player and a caddie at Pinehurst revealed the propensity for White players to distrust their Black caddie's knowledge. The scene depicted a caddie who told the golfer that his shot was not as good as he thought, to which the player replied, "That's a hot one! I split the flag with a mashie-niblick ... That caddie is either a humorist or a dumbskull." Upon arriving to the green with no ball in sight, the golfer inquired as to the ball's location, given that it landed on the green. "Dat's jest it," the caddie responded, "when dey land on dese hard sand greens dey bounces 20 yards into de rough."[170] While the scene was a fictionalized imagining, and framed the caddie as inarticulate, it suggested that Black caddies had the knowledge and the confidence to challenge their employer. What made the task for caddies even harder was that even if they gave correct advice, their golfer may not have had the ability to carry it out and could easily place the blame for their lack of talent on the advice given by their caddie. Golfers everywhere often like to blame their caddie for bad advice or outcomes, and those golfers are far from being right in their judgment, well before race comes into play. In the Jim Crow South, the line between appropriate behavior and overstepping was razor thin, and often fraught with danger.

An Army of "Boys"

Among the most basic ritualized behaviors in interracial interactions was the names White and Black individuals used to address one another. The titles both parties used encapsulated racial power structures of the South. Caddies almost always addressed their player as "Sir," "Mister," or "Ma'am," and, depending on the player's preference they might add the golfer's surname after the formal prefix. White golfers did not reserve the same level of respect when referring to their caddies. The most common name given to a caddie during conversation was "Boy." Since slavery, Whites used "Boy" and "Girl" to address African Americans. White Southerners used such phrasing in part because assigning a single, demeaning term for all Black people diminished their individuality and humanity. Referring to someone by their name reinforced that they had importance as an individual and not just as another member of a subordinate race of nameless "boys." An article from the *Pinehurst Outlook* in 1931 noted that, "During March, an average five hundred boys a day, drawn from all the colored families within a radius of 10 square miles, supply the army of Pinehurst golfers." Although some of the Pinehurst caddies at this time were children, the vast majority were grown men. The article even acknowledges that fact; "'Boys' they are called, although most of them are grown men, and many of them are old."[171] The phrase infantilized Black caddies of all ages. Belittling Black men in such a way further contributed to common beliefs at the time that the entire

African American race was in need of both protection and direction from mature, adult, White masters.[172]

Racial etiquette and golf etiquette were made and unmade every round, as both caddies and players navigated a world of comfort and discomfort in each other's company. Being a Black caddie on a White golf course was a nuanced dance—knowing when to challenge a White golfer, when to hold their ground, how to phrase advice, how to flatter a player who might offer a larger tip, how to tease certain players who enjoyed the fun of it, and how to offer as little as possible to the most racist players without appearing shiftless. Like dancing, it had a flow—a give and take—each step was delicately balanced, and caddies learned and relearned when to step forward, back, or to the side.

For White players, racial etiquette loomed over every interaction they had with caddies. When faced with transgressions by Black caddies, whether accidental or on purpose, White golfers needed to decide upon an appropriate response. Country clubs and resorts instituted systems of discipline and accountability for caddies who did not perform to expectations—whether as a worker or as a member of the so-called subservient race. All clubs employed caddie masters to administer and discipline caddies, but they also deputized golfers and encouraged them to report caddies whose behaviors were out of line. Pinehurst management reassured guests that if they "ever had any criticisms of [the caddies] we are always anxious to correct it."[173] During the 1920s, Pinehurst even paid local law enforcement to coerce caddies into acceptable behavior. Head of golf operations, Donald Ross, noted that Sheriff Knight was "absolutely indispensable to us at the country club." The sheriff, he continued, "keeps the boys under complete control, as far as their behavior is concerned and has a strong influence over them."[174]

At Pinehurst in the 1930s, the caddie master Donald Currie held detailed records of every caddie, including report cards. Currie noted that caddies "realize they must co-operate because if they ever get a black mark on this course, they are blacklisted from ever caddying on any Pinehurst course."[175] Accepting transgressions may have encouraged such behavior in the future, yet at times White golfers may actually have appreciated moments of Black humor, or Black skill when it benefitted their golf game. According to Pinehurst advertising, at their best Black workers "perfected [caddying] to an art thru [sic] their efficiency and their droll darky character."[176] It was a fine balance to decide whether a caddie should be reminded of their place or given some degree of freedom to act how they wished. Certain acts demanded obvious correction, such as moments when caddies did not properly address players as "Sir." Other acts, such as witty retorts, filled a gray zone as Whites often promoted the notion of the happy and witty Black caddie, but likely did not appreciate jokes made at their expense. As one *Golf Illustrated* writer wrote, "The negro caddies, found on most of our southern courses, are delightfully original in their observations and wholly without contempt."[177] On the occasions where caddie contempt spilled over, golfers may have been less charmed.

One example of a Black caddie transgressing both racial and golf etiquette reveals much about the nature of expected behaviors in interracial interactions. In 1913, at the Atlanta Athletic Club's East Lake course, a White golfer—Mr. W.P. Hill—employed a young Black caddie just as he would every other round. Despite reminding the caddie of his basic duties prior to the round, Hill became frustrated as the caddie performed incompetently. The caddie consistently walked to the wrong ball on the fairway and proclaimed it as belonging to his player. Each time Hill reminded the caddie to pay close attention to the ball in flight and to walk to the correct one. The White golfer interpreted his caddie's incompetence as a symptom of his stupidity. Hill's exacerbation soon turned to anger on the 11th hole when, just as he was at the top of the backswing, his caddie loudly commented "Mister, your britches is split." The caddie committed the cardinal sin of golf etiquette by talking during a golfer's swing; doing so during his own employer's swing rendered the transgression all the more affronting.

The caddie's noise alone would have angered the player, but the content of his outburst compounded Hill's humiliation and rage as the caddie also broke the rules of racial etiquette. The unwritten codes of racial conduct certainly forbade Black Southerners from making comments that might embarrass Whites. The caddie's outburst highlighted a wardrobe malfunction that alone might be cause for distress, but coming from the mouth of a Black service worker took on an extra layer of embarrassment. In a rage, Hill immediately turned on the caddie after the comment, and a report of the incident in *American Golfer* highlighted the racial overtones behind Hill's response when it noted that "You can also imagine—for it would not look well in print—what Mr. Hill said to that little imp of darkness." Both the golfer and the newspaper highlighted the caddie's race as a major reason for retribution. After lambasting and then chasing the caddie over 50 yards until it became clear that the caddie had the pace to outrun him, Hill returned to the tee to the welcome of his playing partners who took great amusement in the incident. He carried his own bag for the rest of the round.[178]

Hill's actions demonstrated that Whites sought to police Black behavior on the golf course through instruction and, when deemed necessary, verbal, physical, and financial retribution. In his lectures on the role of the caddie, Hill sought to instill clear rules of etiquette for the caddie to follow, and in his angry outburst and chase he tried to punish a Black worker who overstepped acceptable racial conduct. The racialized description of the caddie as an "imp of darkness" highlighted the golfer's belief that his Black caddie's greatest sin was the public embarrassment of a White person. The moment at which the caddie stopped simply breaking caddie etiquette and transgressed racial etiquette was the one at which Hill attempted to punish him. While the caddie managed to avoid physical injury, Hill may have felt that the caddie learned somewhat of a lesson through his loss of wages for that round. The caddie likely worked at least two hours to complete the first 10 holes and received no financial compensation for his labor. White golfers likely felt that the overlapping threat of verbal, physical, and financial punishment kept caddie behavior largely in check.

Purposeful Sabotage

Approaching the confrontation between Hill and his caddie from the perspective of the Black worker offers a slightly different interpretation of events. Prior to the round, Hill asked the caddie if he was familiar with his duties, to which the worker replied that he had caddied many times in the past. However, the report of the incident noted that "Hill proceeded to explain to him what he was expected to do, and that his special duty was to watch his ball." While Hill interpreted the caddie's inability to walk to the correct ball on repeated occasions as a symptom of "his stupidity," an alternative explanation might be that the caddie purposefully walked to "the first ball he came to" to frustrate his employer who patronizingly lectured him on his basic duties despite his past experience. During Jim Crow, Black service workers throughout the South practiced numerous forms of purposeful sabotage or disruption that hindered White leisure time.[179] Such an explanation seems even more plausible given that later in the round, the caddie pointed out Hill's ripped trousers at the exact moment of his swing, which caused grave embarrassment. Reports of the incident in *American Golfer* gave no credence to the potential that the caddie was purposeful in his actions and his attempts to annoy and embarrass a White golfer who had belittled and patronized him. Caddies did, on occasion, retaliate to players who questioned their professional competence. One caddie in Asheville even attacked a golfer who continuously reprimanded him for not watching the ball.[180] The incident at East Lake may have been a more subtle means of payback.

In the end the golfer, W.P. Hill, was the butt of the joke and a victim of embarrassment, which are not legal transgressions. Perhaps the caddie's actions were a purposeful demonstration of resistance to demeaning White employers. Perhaps the caddie knew that the public embarrassment may have encouraged Hill, or even his peers, to reconsider future interactions with Black caddies. Because the historical archive is silent on the caddie's motivations, we do not know what he was thinking, but we do know that he—just as any Black Southerner living at the time—would have understood the societal expectations on his behavior that strictly discouraged making such comments to White people. That he so publicly broke with prescribed behavior encourages historians to analyze and interpret his motivations. In this case, he seemed motivated to challenge the prescribed roles of talented White masters and unskilled Black servants.[181]

Caddies at times transgressed racial etiquette in collective ways as well. Examples, such as incidents when caddies chose not to work in the rain or not to work at all and instead attend other events, offer a unique insight into the everyday politics of the South. At Pinehurst, when caddies decided not to work in the rain, the dominant White narrative of the event dictated that the collective action was representative of the shiftlessness of African Americans and demonstrated the lack of ambition and work ethic among Black locals.[182] Of course, that narrative also further fueled White beliefs that Black workers would be entirely unproductive on their own terms and required White overseers in a master-servant relationship. However, when approached from the perspectives of Black caddies, the action seemed less about their shiftlessness and more as a direct challenge to the racial etiquette that demanded Black service at the drop of the hat. Caddies who collectively refused to work in unpleasant conditions reminded Whites of the importance of Black labor to White leisure and challenged White demands for ever-present Black service.

One of the great ironies of White beliefs about the unskilled nature of Black workers in the South was that they were so reliant on Black labor in every way.[183] In fact, the choice to avoid caddying in the rain seems all the more subversive, as it would have forced White golfers to carry their bags at their heaviest, sodden with water and with a damp golf bag strap against their shoulder. Black caddies perhaps withdrew their services not as a symptom of their shiftlessness, but as a direct challenge to White expectations of Black servitude and behavior. While such challenges did not shake the sandy ground of the golf course, they certainly reaffirmed Black workers' humanity and self-worth in an environment that did as much as possible to reduce them to servants. Every challenge was not always obvious to White golfers, but to Black golfers every challenge had meaning and importance.

Black transgressions of racial etiquette that sought to undermine White perceptions of Black inferiority faced a remarkably stubborn Jim Crow mindset. For White golfers, the evidence of skilled caddies challenged their belief that African Americans were idle and shiftless, and replaced it with the notion that African Americans were well-suited to subservient roles. Initial discussions of caddying in golf magazines and newspapers noted that the job was one that required no learned skills. A 1907 article in the *New York Tribune* described the widespread belief that the caddie was "a human express wagon, invented to save the player from fatiguing himself by carrying a half dozen sticks uphill and downhill," who was also able to "indicate where the ball rolled."[184] Accordingly, as racial hierarchy took hold in the South, caddying became a job reserved for African Americans, as was the case with all unskilled jobs.

Over time the White perception of Black caddies changed. Caddies demonstrated their talents and golfing prowess on the job, and articles that mentioned the "shiftlessness of the darky character," gave way to mentions of contented and skilled Black caddies.[185] World famous golf professional Walter Hagen wrote, in 1929, "If one gets the idea that the colored caddie doesn't know the game he is soon disabused. These boys know golf from A to Z, and they quickly learn all there is to learn about each player's game."[186] In 1926, a member of management at Pinehurst boasted that "I have played golf through the south and north considerably and as a general rule have found the caddies here to be superior to those at any other places."[187] Years later, three-time major winner Tommy Armour claimed that Black caddies at Pinehurst "know every inch of every green like you know your face for shaving."[188]

By the 1920s and '30s, some White golfers began reporting that Black men were better suited to the role than the White children used on courses in the North. Donald Currie, Pinehurst's caddie master for much of the middle of the 20th century, argued that Black men were particularly adept for the role because they "have no higher ambition than to be good caddies. They aren't like northern caddies, because you will find that northern caddies are often too ambitious and are most unreliable." A local White golfer in High Point, North Carolina, praised the abilities of Black caddies, noting that "colored caddies make much better caddies: they need the money more; they are bigger and older, and most of them are able to improve the game of the average duffer."[189] Once Black caddies around the South proved that they were as skilled as—if not better than—their White counterparts in the North, Donald Currie and others trumpeted false narratives about innate Black characteristics that made them perfect for the job, such as how "eternally happy they are," and their "excellent eyesight."[190] Whites initially racialized caddying as a Black job, because it required no skills other than carrying a bag and watching the ball—traits that they felt suited apparently inferior and unskilled African Americans. In turn, as Black caddies demonstrated their talents and turned the job into a skilled profession, White golfers once again racialized the role with their claims that African Americans were suited to the job because of their innate characteristics, not their ability to learn, or their work ethic. These golfers joined a long list of Jim Crow advocates who adjusted their logic when the evidence before them contradicted their previous reasoning.[191]

Small Acts of Black Self-Worth

White golfers changed the way they discussed Black caddies in the 1930s—around the same time that they noticed a changing demographic among the caddie ranks. Over the first third of the 20th century, Whites consistently promoted the notion that the perfect caddie on a southern course took the form of a grizzled old African American, born during slavery. Pinehurst promotional materials highlighted "befo-de-wah" caddies as a benefit of golfing at the resort.[192] In the 1930s, as the number of caddies who were born in slavery dwindled, White onlookers reflected with nostalgia on the passing generation. The *Pinehurst Outlook* bemoaned that "The old days in the caddy house were more picturesque than the present. Numbers of the old type of darky, unfortunately fast dying out, were among the caddies then."[193] The younger generation, with their professional competence and confidence to challenge White authority on the course, undermined White assumptions about Black inferiority. In the end, White observers who had known Jim Crow for decades were never likely to accept African American competence as a sign of Black humanity and equal ability. The path for Black Southerners out of the lowest paid and most subservient of jobs was never going to be through White acceptance, whether in the form of Black demonstrations of skill or conformity to White expectations.[194]

Yet, Black caddies who challenged White stereotypes were a consistent reminder to White golfers that the project of racial hierarchy was entirely manufactured. Moments when Black caddies held their ground on advice to players, and were proven correct, demonstrated both their professional capabilities and their bravery in standing up to White golfers. A caddie at Pinehurst in the 1940s, for example, "put down the bag and started to walk off the course," when his player ignored his advice. When the player relented and accepted the caddie's advice he went on to make a birdie on the hole.[195] Likewise, in 1938, a report about Pinehurst's caddies noted that among them were such skilled and talented caddies who not only knew "exactly what club you should use for each shot but will refuse to give you a club you ask for if he knows it is wrong."[196] Black challenges on the golf course did not redefine the stranglehold Jim Crow had over the South, but they perhaps reminded White Southerners that racial hierarchy was built on an unsubstantiated set of beliefs. A system built on such unsteady foundations needed consistent restructuring in the form of the ever-changing and often contradictory mindset. Over the course of a few decades, Pinehurst's caddies went from being described as a group who "rarely suggest advice," to a collection of workers who at times insisted that their employers follow their instruction.[197] Small acts that asserted Black self-worth and humanity each represented small dents in the gradual destruction of the Jim Crow system.[198]

* * *

Even if caddies undermined White assumptions about Black inferiority on the course, they inadvertently ran the risk of increasing expectations upon their working standards. Initially, when White golfers expected Black caddies to simply keep up, carry the bag, and find the golf ball; any service above and beyond the minimum—such as correctly estimating a distance, or reading the slope of the green—may have resulted in an increased tip at the end of the round. However, after years of continuous demonstrations of their talents, Black caddies raised the expectations on their work to a standard that, for some observers, was the highest in the country. Walter Hagen, in his discussion of differing golf customs in the nation, noted that Black caddies "hand out the right clubs, and their judgement is just as good, if not better, than the average boy in the North."[199] At Pinehurst, once the standard of caddying had been raised by a select few caddies—most notably Ed Gaines, "the model caddie from the 1920s"—all other caddies needed to raise their professional competence. This included acts like "making sure they always showed ear-to-ear smiles."[200] In turn, caddies carried the weight of increased expectations without a corresponding increase in pay. Early in the century, the average Black caddie could make an honest wage, one reporter commented, even if they strolled the fairways as "inscrutable and expressionless" workers. As the 20th century progressed, White golfers demanded greater effort from Black caddies, with little reward.

Importantly, caddies in the South could often not aspire to better jobs than caddying, given that better jobs were reserved for White workers. Willie McRae acknowledged that Black Southern caddies differed from White caddies in the North, who only caddied in the summer and until they were no longer in school. Black caddies took the job more seriously because "for many of them, caddying would be their lives—how they got by—what they had to look forward to."[201] In the racially segregated labor market where caddying was a lifetime job, increased expectations coupled with a lack of commensurate pay increase may have actually been detrimental to caddies' livelihoods. Increasing expectations may have made tips more difficult to earn.

Finances and the rigged system that restricted Black Americans to subservient or menial jobs were also foundational to the outward image of a harmonious paternalistic society. Without the strict racial boundaries for acceptable Black labor in the South there was little necessity for caddies to act as happy and subservient in jobs where they served White golfers. Looming over every interaction was the complete financial imbalance that allowed the coercion in the first place. The threat of firing—and the knowledge that caddying was perhaps as lucrative and comfortable a job as many African Americans could hope to fill—created the expectation that caddies should act contented with their position. Had Black Southerners been allowed to progress up the employment ladder into higher paying jobs and into financial security, had they been allowed to build up capital and property, then they would no longer be entirely beholden to White expectations regarding their workplace behavior. Meanwhile, reports about happy and content Black caddies created the false impression that Black Southerners had always been willing servants.[202] White golfers perpetuated an enduring cycle when they encouraged Black caddies to act joyously on the job using financial incentives, and then saw that forced happiness as evidence of Black suitability and contentedness with their place in society.[203]

Whites often proactively enforced racial etiquette in the South, rather than reactively.[204] The power of financial imbalance over expected behavior was immense. In the places where White and Black individuals had their most prolonged and intimate contact—such as on the golf course between player and caddie or in the home between a family and their domestic servant—the power of financial control was the single biggest tool for enforcing expected behavior.[205] Thaddeus McRae knew so when he told Willie that the way to make money was to "make the man happy," by keeping his mouth shut. Pinehurst even advertised that "the men and boys earn their living by caddying, and are therefore well-behaved and efficient."[206]

Country clubs and resorts understood that the rigged system of labor in the South strengthened their hand in enforcing strict behavioral norms onto their Black employees. As Pinehurst admitted, the smiles on the faces of Black caddies, and their contented behavior, were not evidence of their natural joy at serving wealthy White golfers. Rather, caddies conformed to racial and golfing etiquette, because they understood the financial inequity in Jim Crow society and made sacrifices to put money in their pockets and food on their family's table. In the end, racial etiquette serves as another example of just how manufactured the racial difference was between White and Black Americans. If racial difference held any basis in reality or nature, it would not have required such powerful tools—like financial control and violent retribution—to maintain, and it certainly would not have required consistent upkeep.

Close attention to behavioral expectations on golf courses also reveals that racial etiquette was not a distinct tool of Jim Crow, separate from violence, financial control, disenfranchisement, and segregation. Rather it was a binding force that both upheld and underpinned these other, more visible tactics.[207] As noted, violence provided a reactive means of enforcing expected behaviors as golfers reprimanded their caddies who stepped above their racial station. But racial etiquette also informed violence throughout the South because clearly defined, yet unwritten, codes of conduct gave White Southerners their reasoning for committing atrocities against Black Southerners. An employee at Jackson Country Club, Mississippi, reportedly assaulted a number of Black caddies, because "he was tired of these negroes talking back to him."[208] Without the twisted justification that Black individuals transgressed acceptable behavioral norms, violence would have seemed even less justifiable than it already was. Racial etiquette gave violence some rationale in White minds. Likewise, White Southerners used racial etiquette, specifically Black refusal to act deferent in every situation, as justification for racial segregation—separation removed much of the unease and uncertainty.[209] When it came to disenfranchisement, the same logic applied. Whites justified banning Black Southerners from voting because equality in the ballot box may have encouraged African Americans to demand social equality in everyday interactions—a situation that would have seemed frightening to many White Southerners.[210] These tools of oppression were all arms of the same beast, and racial etiquette played a significant role in growing the most damaging of them.

The intimacy of the golf course provided the stage upon which many White individuals, with their malleable racial worldview and their support from the rigged labor market, both reinforced and found evidence to support racial hierarchy through racial etiquette. Yet, for Black caddies, their lives as caddies were not defined by the things they had done unto them by their employers. Rather, they chose to use their employment as a space to consistently demonstrate their humanity and their self-worth. They turned a job that was once seen as menial into a skilled profession, and the money they earned gave them some freedom to enjoy their time off and enabled their families to eat.

FIGURE 7: A caddie follows behind their golfer on at Pinehurst in the 1920s. (Tufts Archives).

CHAPTER 4

Striking It Pure

Labor Organizing Among Caddies

"Caddie boys are all right; caddie boys on a strike," sang the 50 Black caddies employed at Richmond, Virginia's Hermitage Golf Club on June 12, 1901. The caddies sang their song for an hour while they marched around the golf course waving their hats and coats. Earlier that day, 50 of the caddies employed at the club—who all hailed from the city's Jackson Ward—held a conference to discuss their working conditions. Unsatisfied with their wages of 10 cents per hour, they decided to strike as a body, demanding 15 cents per hour. Newspaper reports on the strike took great care to highlight the Blackness of the caddies, and the disbelief that Black workers would demand better working conditions. "Nothing but negro caddies are employed according to the rules of the club," stated the report in the *Washington Evening Star*, "and all of the 50 caddies are very black." The *Norfolk Landmark* referred to the disgruntled workers as "ebon-faced strikers." A report in the *Nashville American* noted that "The whole of Richmond's upper crust is shocked almost into silence at the audacity of the pickaninnies in daring to demand anything." Any disruption to society life was an inconvenience, but when the disruption stemmed from Black workers, it was an affront.[211]

If the caddies who carried the golf bags at the club were "very black," the golfers were very White, and very rich. The Hermitage Golf Club in Richmond, Virginia, conformed to the stereotype of the lavish southern country club at the turn of the century. Formed in 1900, the founding members hoped the club would promote the "revival of athletics in Richmond." But it was athletics for only the White elites. According to one report, to join the club a prospective member needed nothing "less than a four-hundred-year-old pedigree," or a "bank account of six figures." The clubhouse—completed three months prior to the strike—was appointed with expensive furniture and broad verandas. It was a Saturday home to Richmond's well-to-do who sought outdoor pursuits and social events with others of their like.[212]

On the golf course, the Black caddies were expected to act as willing and contented helpers. The strike that occurred in June 1901 represented quite the opposite. Not only did the caddies reject the prescriptions placed upon their behavior, but they also demonstrated their distinct understanding of the value of their labor. In turn, the 50 strikers brought the course to a complete standstill. While their actions were ultimately unsuccessful, it revealed a great deal about the power dynamics at play between White golfers and Black caddies. It was the first recorded strike of its kind—Black caddies withholding their labor—but it was followed by a number of others in the years and decades that followed.

Analyzing caddie strikes, from the first grumblings of discontent in the caddy shack to the moment the strikes were won and lost, is a laborious but worthwhile task. These fleeting strikes reveal both the daily struggle of Black workers to define their own place in the Jim Crow economy, and the ways that White employers used the economic, legal, social, and political tools at their disposal to uphold racial hierarchy.

Before poring over the details of individual strikes and what they reveal about race, labor, and golf in the Jim Crow South, it is important to analyze the wider trends of caddie strikes across the United States. The first caddie strikes in the country started not long after the game began growing in popularity. Chicago, Illinois was the site of the first recorded incident in which caddies withheld their labor, in July 1895.[213] Very few strikes occurred over the subsequent five years, but at the turn of the century several caddie corps around the country withheld their labor with at least five strikes taking place every year between 1899 and 1902. Between then and the early 1910s, the number of strikes per year remained consistently fewer than five before a spike in strikes in the mid-1910s followed by an even greater spike in the early 1920s, with 16 recorded strikes in 1922 alone. The rest of the 1920s was a fallow period for caddie strikes before a wave of consistent strikes in the 1930s. Evidence exists for more than 90 caddie strikes throughout the 1930s—a period of unmatched caddie labor unrest before or after. In the years that followed caddies rarely withheld their labor and recorded strikes appeared once every year or two by the 1950s (Figure 8).[214] Of course, these statistics only capture the strikes that made it into newspapers. Many likely went unrecorded but the evidence of those that did reveals the general trends of caddie unrest.

The Strike Microbe

The rising and falling trend line of caddie strikes over time prompts the simple question: Why did caddie strikes happen often at some times and not at others? The answer is not so simple. Newspaper reports about striking caddies occasionally framed them within a "fever" or "epidemic" of strikes that was sweeping the country.[215] "Strikes are contagious," one newspaper declared in reference to a caddie unrest.[216] The strike of 50 Black caddies at the Hermitage Golf Club in Richmond prompted one newspaper writer to ask, "Wouldn't it be a good idea for our scientists to begin investigating the strike microbe? Its existence in the atmosphere is strikingly in evidence."[217] Of course, strikes were not contagious, but caddies may have taken inspiration from other successful strikes to gain better wages or conditions by withholding labor. Broader societal and cultural conditions likely played some role in the changing trends. For example, the low

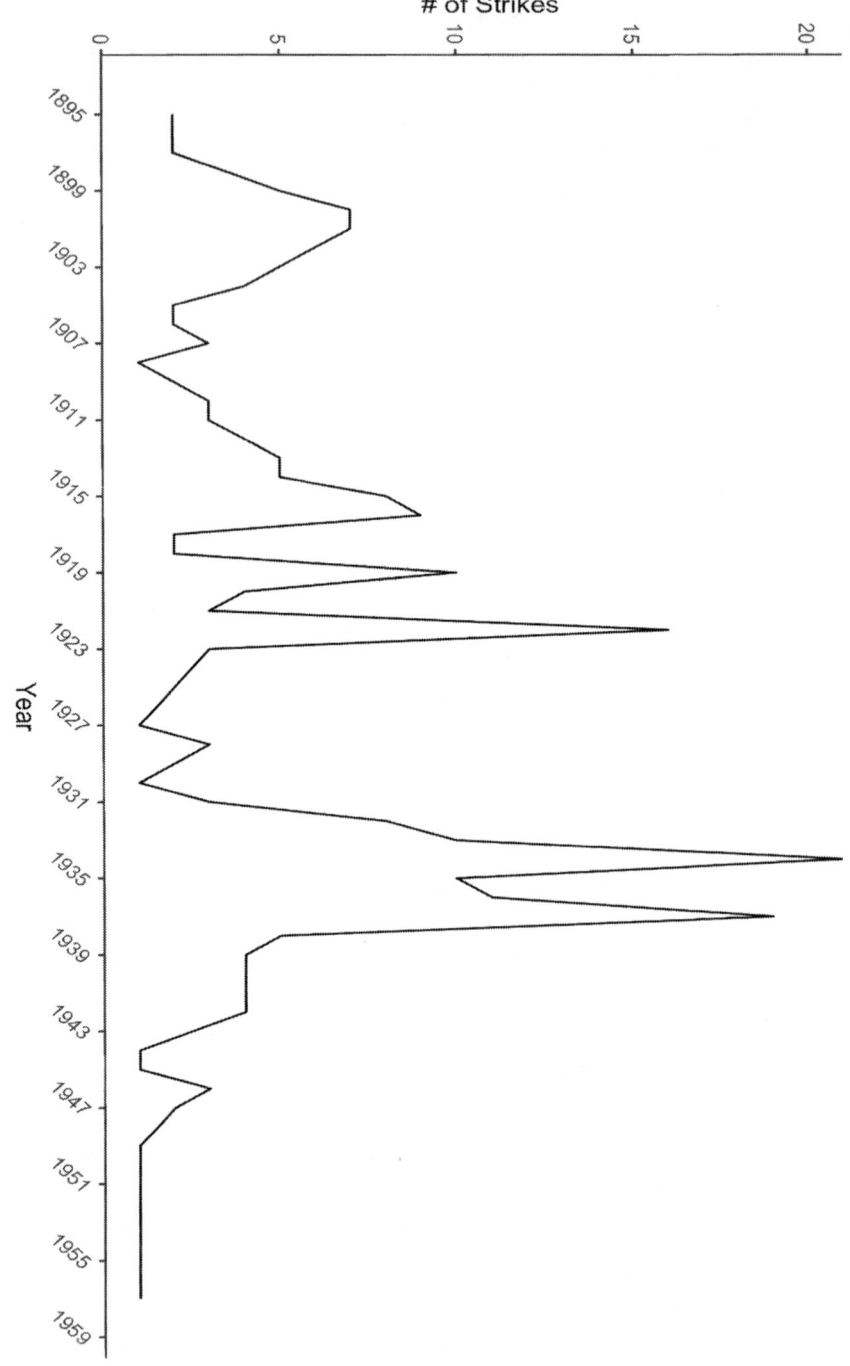

Figure 8: Strikes by caddies in the United States per year, 1895-1957.

number of strikes in the 1920s correlates with a booming national economy and the rapid expansion of country clubs around the nation.[218] Caddies may have fared well from the thriving golf industry and may have been well compensated at the time. Likewise, the Great Depression tore through the country in the '30s, causing financial hardship to millions while workers organized for better rights. In the '40s, less caddie unrest might be attributed to the impact of the war, as less golf was played and many caddies found work in the war industries.[219] These hypotheses might hold some truths, but the numbers alone cannot reveal the true character of the strikes. Each strike had its own context and its own logic.

Data also reveals that the clustering of caddie strikes varied by time and region (Figure 9). Early in the century, as golf was still largely concentrated in the northeast, caddie strikes occurred mainly in the North. Over the subsequent decades, though, strikes could be found throughout the country, and by the 1930s, the number of caddie strikes in the South rivaled the North. In that decade, strikes occurred in every state in the South from Texas to Virginia. North Carolina and Tennessee both experienced more than 10 documented strikes in the 1930s, as many as any state in the rest of the country. These regional trends show that caddie strikes were not confined to White child caddies in the North. The growing number of strikes in the South from 1900 to 1939 also indicates that caddies in the South became more likely to make demands for adequate compensation and decent working conditions over time.

In attempting to understand why caddies chose to strike, it is important to place their work within the context of golf at the time. As golf grew into the South in the late 1890s and early 1900s, White golfers saw Black caddies as "beasts of burden," and as individuals who were there to only carry bags and spot balls.[220] They might ask, "Why should such workers receive more than basic compensation for such work?" But caddies likely saw it differently: they knew that the work at times was hard. Long hours in the sun carrying two heavy bags and keeping track of multiple golf balls in the long grass or fescue was not easy. But they also understood that their labor was vital to the

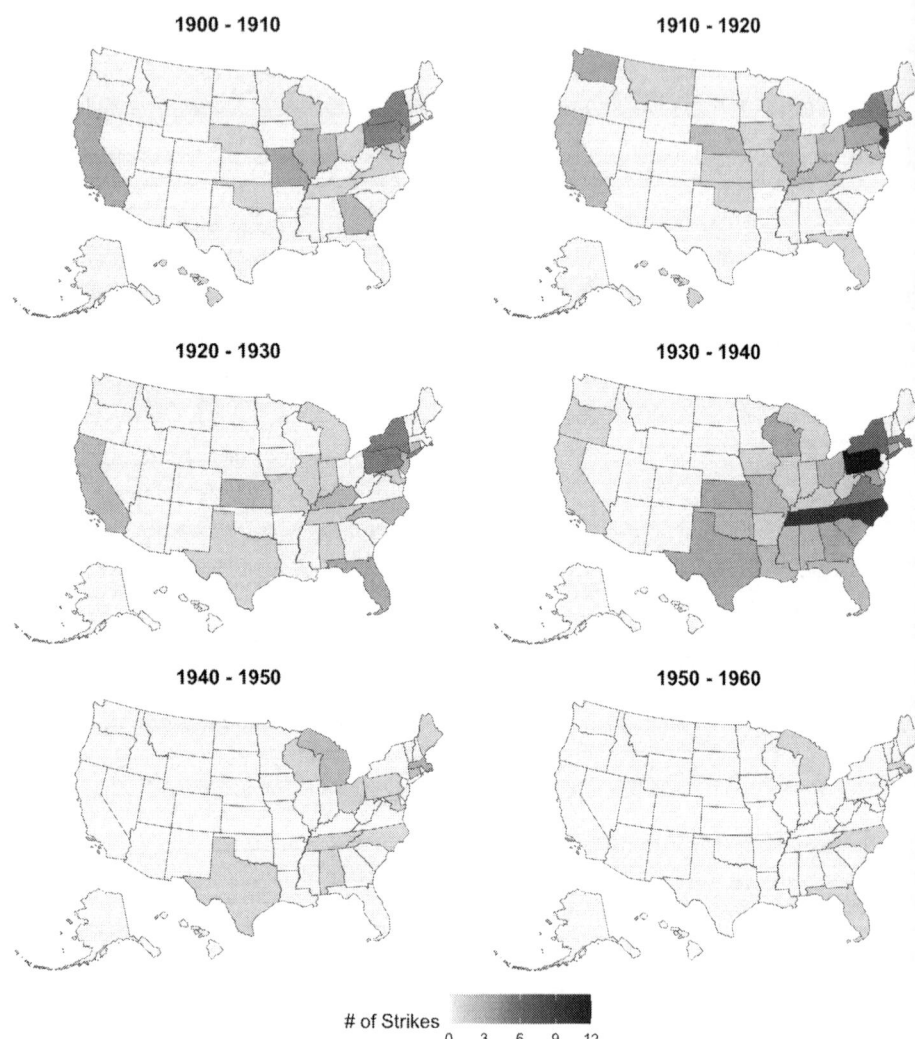

FIGURE 9: Number of U.S. caddy strikes by state and decade.

facilitation of White leisure. It was not as if White golfers employed caddies as a luxury. For the first third of the century, at least, caddies were used almost every time a golfer played, because the bags were heavy and carrying them while trying to have an enjoyable experience was difficult. Understanding that caddies were foundational to a golfer's ability to play 18 holes and get the accompanying enjoyment out of their leisure time, it becomes clear that the labor was essential.

For Black caddies in the South, the decision to withhold their labor was carefully managed and calculated. On a simplistic level, the calculation that caddies needed to make was to evaluate whether the value they provided the golfer matched their pay. If their contributions did not reflect their income, they might strike. Things were never that simple, though. An array of complex factors made the decision much more difficult.

Black caddies were most likely aware of the fraught history of Black labor in the South, and the potential costs of going on strike. From slavery and well into the Jim Crow era, Black workers who rejected the conditions of their work faced violent retribution from their White enslavers and bosses.[221] White management rarely accepted—and certainly did not appreciate—acts of collective resistance to the labor status quo in the region. It was not out of the question that a strike of caddies might be met with violence, either from the management or from local law enforcement. The looming threat of violence was, of course, not just a form of reactive retribution toward unruly workers: it was an active deterrent that served as an example to Black workers across the region, that should they choose to reject their place in the Jim Crow system they did so at the risk of violence.[222]

Black caddies considering a strike also needed to consider how replaceable they were. As with the threat of violence, the availability of replacement caddies varied both by location and by time. Black caddies laboring in places like Pinehurst, where the supply of local labor was sparse, likely understood that the management would struggle to replace them if they withheld their labor.[223] On the other hand, in cities with large Black populations, such as Atlanta, caddies knew that there may have been a larger pool of workers who might break the strike. During an extreme economic downturn, such as the Great Depression, mass unemployment meant that management could quickly find replacements. Caddies also had to consider whether management would consider abandoning their commitment to hiring caddies along racial lines. In cities in the upper South—not far from where White child caddies were the norm—it was possible that a club might use White children as strikebreakers, and in turn close caddying off as a viable profession for the Black workers who had performed it and relied on it for years.[224] The calculation also probably changed as the century progressed and caddies became more skilled than they were at the turn of the century. It was far easier to replace caddies when their working brief was to watch the ball and carry a bag than it was once they had become expert strategists on the course. Certainly, the decision to strike was one that could not be taken lightly, and it required a great deal of both consideration and risk on the part of the workers.

The Feature Event of the Season

Strikes were also not always about money. At times they reflected caddies' desire for proper working conditions and respect for their time and labor. Some strikes, like one at Asheville Country Club in 1921, underscored the close links between caddies' labor and their own leisure time. The Black caddies employed there staged a walk-out that lasted an entire week, yet they were not concerned about their pay. On May 23, the caddie corps were set to play their annual tournament at Asheville CC. Golf clubs often allowed these tournaments—they offered something of intrigue for White onlookers, but also provided caddies with a distinct day that they were allowed to play, which might discourage them from sneaking onto the course to play at other times.[225] In 1921, the event was set up as an all-day affair, with a qualifying round in the morning and a final round in the afternoon. Members donated their clubs for the caddies to use and offered cash prizes. In the weeks leading up to the tournament, the

Asheville Citizen described the day as "the feature event of the season for the caddies."[226] It was expected that more than 50 caddies would play, and that a large audience would be in attendance. Yet on May 23, the tournament was brought to a crashing halt as the 100 caddies employed by the club walked out *en masse* and began a strike.

What caused the strike at Asheville Country Club in 1921? The caddie tournament was not usually a day for a labor dispute. Quite the opposite, in fact. As the local newspaper reported, the tournament "always caused a great deal of fun for the golfers." The strike materialized because the management at Asheville Country Club refused to "allow spectators to follow the players in the Caddie tourney." The caddies who chose to play expected that their colleagues who were not competing would be allowed to watch. The *Asheville Citizen* reported that "only 50 players were in the tourney, but the other 'bearers of the clubs' went out in sympathy with their 'brothers.'"[227] When the management chose to ban the crowd, the caddies not only abandoned their tournament but also decided to withhold their labor in protest. In the days that followed, it appeared that neither the caddies nor the club would budge. Club manager George A. Miller made no statement on the first day of the strike and mistakenly believed that the caddies "would be on hand" the following morning, Tuesday, May 24.[228] The caddies did not return until Monday May 30, one week after they had first walked off. The club's board of governors met on Saturday May 28 and unanimously decided that the striking caddies would be given until Monday to "return to their work without conditions or concessions of any kind, either expressed or implied, and that in the event they did not return, the board might take such action as it might see fit."[229] The board's decision appeared to have the desired effect when some caddies returned to work the following day and the rest returned another day later. In the meantime, Asheville's golfers, including Edith and Cornelia Vanderbilt who played a round on Wednesday May 25, had to go without the services of the club's Black caddies.[230]

Asheville Country Club's unique caddie strike in 1921 reveals the importance that Black caddies placed on demonstrating their skill.

While most caddie strikes around the nation revolved around salary, the Asheville caddies were concerned over their right to have spectators at their annual tournament. No reports on the incident included any interviews with the striking caddies, so it is impossible to know their exact thought process when they decided to walk out, but their action illuminates the value that the caddies placed on their freedom to enjoy the game.

The men and boys who caddied at Asheville CC chose to give up a full week of pay to protect their ability to play a tournament, but the strike was about much more than simply being allowed to play. Most caddies found ways of playing in their own time outside of the caddie tournaments—sneaking onto courses and building their own.[231] Caddie tournaments were different: they offered one solitary day in the golf calendar when Black golfers could demonstrate their capabilities—on the White members course where they worked—to those who may have subscribed to flawed beliefs about Black inferiority and lack of sporting talent. In the weeks before the tournament, the *Asheville Citizen* noted that "a number of the young players have become quite proficient and will probably make enviable records," and that the tournament was set to "draw a large gallery" that included club members.[232] Other caddie tournaments around the South commanded significant viewing audiences.[233]

One can only speculate why the Asheville CC management chose to ban spectators. One potential explanation is that they did not want to give the caddies a platform upon which to show their capabilities. All segregated sport was, at least in part, predicated on the belief of Black inferiority—and the only way to maintain that belief was to restrict African American opportunities to dispel that myth. Displays of Black sporting excellence undermined the idea that Black individuals were less capable than White folks and—in the minds of many White southerners—potentially encouraged other African Americans to reject their subordinate position.[234] Of course, White golfers were sold on the image of willing and contented Black caddies, not the notion that Black golfers might be better than them.[235] In fact, the very first caddie tournament in Asheville revealed the ways that Black sporting excellence could subvert White notions of Black inferiority. The announcement of the 1898 tournament in the White-authored *Asheville Gazette* read, "'White Supremacy is going to have to take a back seat at the golf links,' as "the grounds are to be turned over to the little negro 'caddies.'"[236] Black caddies spent the entire year caddying for White golfers who likely had no idea that the caddies were talented golfers in their own right. Just a few years after the Asheville caddie strike, a young Black man named John Brooks Dendy discovered the game on the Asheville CC links. Dendy went on to win three National Negro Opens.[237] The caddie tournament was the only opportunity for caddies to demonstrate their talents to their peers and White onlookers, and they were unwilling to let that opportunity slip by.

Striking to preserve a viewing audience, the Asheville caddies saw their labor as a way to define their leisure time. The strike was not a straightforward labor dispute—over wages, or working hours, or workplace safety. The caddies purposefully withheld their labor to protect their right to spend their time off work exactly how they wished. While the caddie tournament may have been a workplace benefit, the caddies were not working on the day of the tournament—it was a day off work, and an important one. They knew that their employers—the golfers and the club—would suffer as a result of their walk-out, and they also believed that such action was an effective way to retake control of their leisure. For them, caddying for a living and playing the game in their free time were closely connected, and they hoped that they could withhold the former to achieve the latter.

Golf Clubs, Bricks, and Other Weapons

Occasionally, caddie labor struggles turned violent. Perhaps the most prominent example occurred in Atlanta, at the Atlanta Athletic Club's East Lake golf course. The details of the unrest appeared in print years after the incident occurred, when famous White golfer Chick Evans wrote an article about southern Black caddies in 1914. In his telling of the story, "owing to some oversight the caddies at East Lake were not paid at the usual hour." In turn, the caddies became disgruntled and "there was much commotion in the caddy house." Evans noted that the club paid little attention to the commotion because, as he explained, "the negro is very loquacious and nothing was thought of it." When the club did not take the caddies' grievances seriously, several of them descended upon the clubhouse carrying golf clubs, bricks, and other weapons. They entered the clubhouse—which they were forbidden from doing—and took up their case with the Black waiter working behind the bar. The caddies demanded their money and apparently threatened the waiter with a pistol. According to Evans' account of the event, the waiter then grabbed a gun of his own, yelled for help, and the "riot" ended.[238]

The story of the East Lake caddies' "riot" should be treated with some caution, but it also provides evidence of Black caddies' collective resistance. Evans wrote the article, at least in part, to entertain Northern readers, so his account may be somewhat exaggerated. However, a number of the details from the article are factually verifiable, including references to other real caddies, and the East Lake caddie master.[239] Even if Evans sensationalized his account, it still reveals the collective will of Black caddies to receive adequate treatment and compensation for their work. A few aspects of the story are revealing. Firstly, the caddies clearly struggled to have their grievances taken seriously when they voiced them. In this instance, commotion in the caddy house was put down to a racist stereotype of African Americans as "loquacious." Secondly, their subsequent steps were full of risk, yet they took action nonetheless. To collectively enter the clubhouse, from which they were banned, and to demand their compensation with a threat of violence was dangerous. The workers' actions were an act of collective protest against a lack of adequate compensation and respect for their labor. While their actions were risky, they also clearly planned the measures they took. The caddies did not demand their money from White management. Instead, they took their grievances to a Black waiter within the clubhouse. Going to a fellow Black worker within the White leisure-world reduced the risk that the club would respond with violence, firing, or arrest. Even when taking a united stand against their treatment, the caddies calculated the risks involved and acted accordingly.

Organizing Within Caddie Ranks

Caddie strikes occurred on a sporadic basis, and no evidence exists of any union for Southern caddies. Occasional rumblings of organization and unionization made it into the pages of the region's newspapers, indicating that the idea surfaced on a few occasions. In Pinehurst, for example, resort management kept tabs on a local named Amy Foster, who in 1942 was "talking unionization" to all Black workers in the town.[240] In Washington, D.C. in 1934, the golf writer for the Black newspaper, the *Washington Tribune*, advocated for the creation of an "organization within [caddie] ranks to look out for their welfare." Under such an organization, "every boy would have to work his own club and not travel to another club ... practically insuring their earning capacity."[241] Happy Walters, the proponent of the organization, claimed that such a system would stop the favoritism shown toward certain caddies who went between golf courses and would create a "well meaning band of caddies united for the common good."[242] The organization in Washington—or any meaningful caddie union in the South—failed to materialize. The nature of the work, each bag constituting a different employer, made unionization particularly unlikely.

Strikes created a significant headache for golf course management. First and foremost, the strikes reduced the rate of play on the course. While many players bore the inconvenience of carrying their own clubs, some might not have been physically able or willing to do so. When the caddies struck at the Hermitage Club in Richmond in 1901, "golf got a rest ... for a while."[243] Commenting on a strike elsewhere, a journalist in Charlotte, North Carolina noted, "it's a dead cinch that we wouldn't do what the golfers in Chattanooga are doing—caddy for ourself. Golf is the best game in the books. But only when you have a caddy to carry your bag."²⁴⁴ In all likelihood, when caddies chose to withhold their labor, the number of players on the golf course decreased. Fewer golfers on the course likely meant fewer golfers at the clubhouse purchasing food and drinks, and fewer golfers in the club professional's shop buying new equipment. Where there were no caddies, there was clearly less golf and less revenue.

Aside from financial concerns, country clubs curated a perception of order, control, and etiquette.²⁴⁵ Caddie strikes interrupted the perception of tranquility and proper conduct at a seemingly perfectly controlled private haven. The strikes reminded members and tourists that the country club or resort was not entirely detached from societal problems or economic exploitation. Strikes not only harmed the sense of order at country clubs, they also harmed the image of the club as a place of luxury, where members were waited on hand and foot. When golfers had to carry their own bags, they no longer experienced the boost to their self-importance that came with employing a caddie, as well as the four-hour display of social and racial hierarchies in the South.²⁴⁶ Club management sought to quash any strikes because such disruptions harmed their bottom line and harmed the finely curated image in the minds of members and onlookers.

Strikes among the South's Black caddies took on extra racial meaning compared to the strikes of young White caddies in the North. Accepting the demands of striking Black workers was particularly troubling to White Southerners. In the Jim Crow South, Whites continuously sought to discourage Black labor unrest.²⁴⁷ In their minds, accepting Black demands might encourage further protest or questioning of the status quo. Increasing Black wages in response to a strike might embolden other strikes or encourage Black dissent in other parts of society. It was a racial imperative for Whites to discourage unrest as much as possible. It is also possible in the Jim Crow South that the White management knew how badly the Black caddies needed the work, how few alternatives they had. Unsurprisingly within that context, the majority of recorded strikes failed to achieve their overall aims, not least because White golf course officials understood that accepting demands of Black workers might cause consternation from other Whites.

Ideally for clubs, caddie-masters ruled over their workers in such a way that discouraged any strike in the first place. In Southern Pines, North Carolina, the local newspaper boasted that the caddies in 1922 were controlled by a caddie-master who was in Seattle when the mayor "cleaned the city up and drove out the I.W.W. [Industrial Workers of the World] strikers."[248] Such experiences were listed as evidence that he would keep the caddies under strict control. If caddies withdrew their labor, the first action that management often took was to encourage the caddies to return to the course at their existing rate of pay. This approach did not often work, though newspapers reported some success using the method. According to a report from 1922, a caddie strike at Belle Meade Country Club in Nashville, Tennessee, ended when the head professional, a Scotsman named George Livingstone, asked the caddies if they would like to caddie for him. Stories like these should be treated with caution. The report quoted Black caddies using exaggerated dialect in their response to Livingstone: "I does, Mr. Jawge."[249] The story also fuels the common stereotype that Black workers only needed excellent bosses to be made into competent employees. As one Pinehurst writer remarked about Black laborers in Moore County, "the darkies will do the work if the White man can engineer the campaign."[250] It seems unlikely that caddies who had real grievances about their job would simply return to work upon the asking of their boss.

A more likely scenario is that caddies who quickly returned to work without achieving any of their demands were issued with threats from management. Such threats could range from warning caddies that strikebreakers could replace them, to threats of violence. No newspapers reported on threats of violence, but such tactics did occur. In Pinehurst, the only reported instance of caddie unrest did not make it into newspapers, but the story survived through word of mouth. The year of the proposed strike is unknown, but it must have occurred in the first half of the 20th century, and during the time when Donald Ross ruled the resort's golf courses. As reported by Lee Pace in *The Spirit of Pinehurst*, the story goes that discontent among the caddies led to whisperings of a potential strike. When the talk reached head of golf operations Donald Ross, he reportedly made his way into the caddy shack brandishing a golf club—a 5-iron to be exact—and quickly quashed any notion of a strike when he hit one of the caddies over the head with the club.[251] White management likely hoped that violence—or the threat of violence—toward one caddie might be enough to deter others from withholding their labor. Even if management did not explicitly threaten the caddies with violence, the looming specter of violence existed whenever Black workers asserted themselves in the Jim Crow South.

Violence was certainly not management's first choice in most situations. More often, they threatened caddies with firing and permanent bans from caddying at the country club or resort. In Shelby, North Carolina, in 1935, the all-Black caddie corps began a strike for higher wages. They wanted a raise from 25 cents to 30 cents for nine holes. To demonstrate their demands, the caddies placed placards around the course and near the clubhouse outlining their stipulations. When the club professional Jim Reed arrived at the course, he saw the signs and immediately issued an order for all caddies to leave the premises and never return. Upon hearing the demand, a number of caddies began their exit before one caddie asked, "Can't we stay on if we'll keep caddying for a quarter?" Reed withdrew his order for all caddies to leave and allowed all but the individual who supposedly "inaugurated the strike," to continue caddying at their old rate.[252] When golf course management threatened to fire the entire caddy corps, the strike often collapsed. Such threats were successful because the caddies' livelihoods were precarious. As Black workers in states with minimal workers' rights, they had no legal protection from firing if they struck. Caddies did not have a union and did not enjoy the benefits that unionization brought with it, such as professional, legal representation and collective bargaining. If the country club wanted to fire them for striking, they could.[253] Former caddie DeWayne Wickham noted, "the threat of being barred from [the golf club] was all that was needed to bring us in line."[254]

No More Trouble at the Golf Links

If immediate threats did not resolve the caddie strike, golf management often turned to strikebreaking labor to end the unrest. In many cases, they began by looking for strikebreakers within the existing caddie ranks. Management likely felt that if they could end the unity among the strikers, then the caddies would soon realize that their efforts would fail. Even if such tactics did not end the strike, it would still furnish some golfers with caddies to carry their bags. In July 1913, at the Washington Golf and Country Club, in the nation's capital, a strike broke out among the Black caddies employed there. The course was among the few that employed both White and Black caddies. The Black caddies—who comprised three quarters of the workforce—demanded an increase in their payment from 35 cents an hour to 50 cents. The White caddies did not join them in withdrawing their labor. The country club chairman immediately ordered the Black caddies to leave the premises. He also quickly planned for more White youngsters to be brought in to fill the gap. Once "50 white boys were brought to serve in place of the colored youngsters," play could resume at a normal rate. In turn, the chairman decided to exclusively employ White caddies in the future.[255] In Gainesville, Florida in 1937, a similar scenario occurred: the Black caddies "walked out in the middle of a woman's tournament." In turn, the management at Gainesville Golf and Country Club put in a call to the campus of the University of Florida, and some eager young White students arrived at the course as strike-breakers.[256] In these situations, White management saw White youngsters who were in search of extra cash as potential strike-breakers when Black caddies struck and could serve as a stop-gap for a short-term labor stoppage; these youngsters could be leveraged against the potential threat of future strikes. In the minds of management, Black men and White children occupied a similar tier in the hierarchy of labor in the region: an act of condescension that was not unnoticed among the Black caddies.

Strike-breakers—or even the simple threat of strike-breakers—made labor organizing particularly difficult for caddies. On numerous occasions, when management threatened to bring in replacement caddies, the strike quickly ended. Such tactics broke the strike at Hermitage Golf Club in Richmond, Virginia, in 1901. On the first night of the strike, the club briefed the newspaper that White caddies would likely be employed in the future.[257] As the newspaper reported at the time, "Nothing but negro caddies are employed according to the rules of the club, and all of the 50 caddies are very black." After the club president, Thomas Rutherford, refused to accept the caddie demands, "It was decided ... under no circumstances to employ any of the striking caddies hereafter at any price." The newspaper noted that "White boys will probably be employed in the future." The next day, the striking caddies returned to work. Likewise, in 1910, a strike at the Columbia Country Club, in Chevy Chase, Maryland ended in a similar manner. The caddies demanded a raise from 35 cents per round to 50 cents. According to the local newspaper, the "old dodge of threatening to bring strikebreakers, worked like a charm, and all the caddies have agreed to stay at the former rates."[258] Threats alone might have been enough to entice striking workers to return to work, shocked by the potential that they would not just be replaced, but that the course would ban any other members of their race from caddying in the future.

Early in the century, White management found success in threatening to bring in replacement caddies, but that tactic proved less effective as the century moved on. Increasingly, golf clubs turned to the power of the state to quell strikes as they occurred. Throughout the 1930s, the police played an active role in squashing caddie organizing, especially in the South when Black caddies would strike. In Columbus, Mississippi in 1932, the Black caddies at Columbus Country Club signaled their intent to strike, and the club brought in the police. That same day the police rounded up 30 of the striking caddies and took them to the police station. According to news reports, "The boys were given a curtain lecture by Police Chief John Morton, and dismissed with a warning that the larger boys must not intimidate the smaller boys." (A "curtain lecture" was a term typically reserved for a wife privately scolding her husband, as if behind a curtain.) Once he finished his lecture, Morton informed the newspaper that "he was satisfied there would be no more trouble at the golf links."[259] Likewise, during a sit-down strike in Birmingham, Alabama in 1937, the caddie master summoned the police. The United Press report of the incident claimed that "at the sight of a score or more of blue-uniformed cops," the caddies "forgot their determination and fled."[260] On other occasions, the police went further and arrested the strike leaders, such as in Tampa in 1929 and in Richmond in 1936.[261] In the former instance, the club manager boasted that the "officer's visit had put a quietus on the trouble makers and most of the striking caddies had returned to work."[262] The police would often help restore racial decorum in the Jim Crow South.

Turning to the police was a successful strike-ending tactic because the police held great power in the region. It is hard to overemphasize the freedom that Southern police forces held when it came to arresting African Americans. They could create trumped-up charges, including vagrancy and trespassing, which forced thousands of Black Southerners into the prison system and convict leasing.[263] Black Southerners also had little protection from police brutality and beatings behind the closed doors of the police station.[264] White golf course management understood the power that the police held, so when striking caddies disrupted play on the golf course, management often immediately turned to local police who could quickly arrive on the scene. Simply the presence of police officers forced caddies into a decision—to continue their strike and risk arrest, beatings, and the racially discriminatory judicial process, or to end their protest. Understandably, caddies often chose to avoid interacting with the police when possible and ended their strikes. That some caddies chose to continue their strike and take such risks underscores not only their collective belief that their labor deserved proper respect and compensation, but also their remarkable courage.

Why did golf course management go from finding replacement caddies to using police as the main tool to end strikes? The answer to that question cannot be found in the words of management. Club officials never explained why they called the police. Perhaps the answer lies in the changing nature of the job over the course of the first half of the 20th century. At the start of the century, caddying was viewed as a menial service job, one that almost anyone could do. The main tasks of the caddie were to carry their player's clubs and to keep an eye out for their wayward golf shots. As the decades progressed, the job became increasingly professional. Caddies added skills to their working capabilities including their knowledge of the course, an understanding of golf tactics, and expert judgment of distance and slope. Pinehurst advertising in the late 1920s even boasted that some of the caddies had carried "bags for more than 20 years and have developed caddying into a profession."[265] By the 1930s, a good caddie could do a great deal to improve the score that a golfer made on the course. World famous professional golfer Walter Hagen noted in 1929 that Black caddies in the South knew "golf from A to Z, and they quickly learn all there is to learn about a player's game." By Hagen's estimation, the caddies' judgment of slope and distance was "just as good, if not better, than that of an average boy in the north."[266] As workers, caddies added greater value to the experience of golf in the 1930s and '40s than they had done previously.

Taking the changing nature of the work into account, caddies were less easily replaceable as they became more skilled. Management seeking to break a strike in the 1900s and '10s knew that they could bring in replacement labor, because the replacements would not take long to learn the job's requirements. Whereas in the 1930s, a club official knew that striking caddies were skilled workers, and were also viewed by the members as such, and that finding adequate replacements might be difficult. In turn, it was more important to encourage the striking caddies to return to work by any means necessary. The increased use of police to break strikes might point directly to a growth in caddie power, or at least evidence that clubs knew caddies were skilled workers.

Country clubs also likely turned to police because of a societal shift toward using formal institutions to enforce Jim Crow norms and customs. During the first few decades of the 20th century, White Southerners used informal and vigilante forms of violence toward

African Americans to ensure that Black Southerners knew their prescribed place. From a single slap in the face to a lynch mob, many White Southerners took the task of enforcing racial hierarchy upon themselves. As the years passed, though, these informal methods of control became exceedingly damaging to the region's reputation and potential for economic investment from the North. In turn, the previously informal violence was increasingly institutionalized within the criminal justice system. Increasingly, Southerners looked to their police to do it. Police became a key tool for enforcing Jim Crow with their brutal treatment of Black Southerners.[267] Within this context of growing police power and responsibility to commit violence against African Americans, golf clubs turned to law enforcement to quell strikes. Where previously a manager might have threatened firing or brandished a 5-iron, he could now just pick up the phone. And when the armed officers arrived, caddies knew well the potential for violence that followed.

Struggling Against the Tide

Occasionally, a well-timed strike led to success. At Forsyth Country Club, in Winston-Salem, North Carolina in 1937, 100 Black caddies withdrew their labor on the day of an important tournament. Striking on "the day of the opening of the most important golfing event of the season" proved a successful tactic. The club officials at first laughed at the strike but "got serious when the boys refused to go on the course." The longer the strike went on, the more frustrated management became. As was often the case, the club turned to law enforcement, calling the local sheriff. On this occasion, the sheriff did not take any legal or extralegal action against the caddies, and merely stood by as the caddies argued with club officials. Perhaps his looming presence would be enough. When the club's players became "alarmed at the prospect of no caddies … the officials gave in," and accepted the demands of the caddies for a 15-cent raise.[268] In most instances, the police took a more active role in quelling the riot, but on the occasions that they stood by, clubs realized they had little option but to negotiate with skilled caddies. Police power often trampled the seeds of caddie strikes, but occasionally the green shoots of worker-power breached the surface and brought tangible gains for caddies.

Despite occasional successes, caddie strikes—regardless of race or age—more often ended in failure than victory. Among reports from 240 caddie strikes around the country from 1890 to 1960, only 24 strikes could be defined as ending in absolute success for the caddies, where the golf course accepted caddie demands in full. On seven occasions, caddies experienced mixed success, when some aspects of their demands were achieved. When newspapers reported that the striking workers were Black, the caddies were even less likely to succeed. Of the 18 Black caddie strikes with reported outcomes, only one was reported as an absolute success, and one more could be said to have achieved mixed success, while 16 ended in defeat.[269]

How can the somewhat limited success of caddie strikes be explained? The answer most likely lies in the precarious nature of labor for Black caddies and for all Black workers across the South. The legal, political, and economic structures were in the hands of Whites, which removed a great deal of power from Black workers. Black caddies knew that they had very little possibility of legal recourse for mistreatment in the workplace. Black workers also knew that their alternative employment options were slim. Returning to the farm or working the dirtiest and most labor-intensive jobs in the industrial sector were not appealing alternatives. For many workers in service jobs like caddying, they understood that, as Pinehurst caddie Willie McRae put it, "caddying would be their lives."[270] Black caddies, for much of the 20th century, were precarious workers. At the start of the century, caddies were particularly replaceable because their professional tasks were minimal. Over time they developed skills that made them more difficult to replace. Yet by the middle of the century, mechanization once again loomed over caddies who made demands for better wages or conditions.[271]

But replaceability was only one factor that contributed to caddies' tenuous and insecure position as workers: caddies also suffered from the system of payment on the golf course. As opposed to being salaried employees, caddies almost universally received their pay directly from the customer—the golfer. What this meant was that caddies had no guarantee of income on any given day. Of course, on weekends or during the peak golf season, caddies could feel confident that the course would be full, and that they would have a golfer to work for. But the system added unwanted uncertainty to a caddie's life. Because golf has always been a fair-weather sport, caddies were often at the behest of mother nature. A week of stormy weather or simply a quiet day on the course could keep golfers away, and caddies out of a paycheck.[272] Because caddies were not salaried employees, when they went on strike they lost all of their income for the time they were off work. The longer a golf course refused caddie demands, the less financially secure the caddies became. This dynamic gave golf course management a great deal of power.

All told, caddies faced a long uphill battle any time they sought better compensation or improved working conditions. Their unique occupation created specific conditions that made organization and striking difficult, but their experiences were also representative of a large swath of Black workers in the American South during Jim Crow. White management held the power to fire and ban employees, to call the potentially intimidating or violent police in to quell unrest, and also knew and exploited the financial fragility in which millions of Black workers lived. Detached from the financial, legal, and political systems of power, caddies constantly struggled against the tide, grasping small victories where they could find them, and reaching for larger ones when the opportunity arose.

FIGURE 10: Caddies started young and often made a career of it, as shown by these two colleagues at Pinehurst (Tufts Archives).

CHAPTER 5

From Caddies to Players

How Black Caddies Became Excellent Golfers and Changed the Game

One year in the early 1940s, as winter thawed into spring on a municipal golf course in Philadelphia, two of the most revered men in the history of Black golf met for the first time. "You Howard Wheeler?" asked Charlie Sifford, a 17-year-old recent transplant from Charlotte, North Carolina. Wheeler was tall at 6'1", but his slim build made him seem even taller. He sized up the North Carolinian, smiled, and replied, "Uh huh." Confidence was not in short supply for the young man who replied, "I'm Charlie Sifford, and I'm gonna whip your ass on that golf course." Without another word, Howard Wheeler—himself a recent arrival in Philadelphia from Atlanta—turned toward the first tee with his clubs over his shoulder, beckoning for Sifford to join him. On the tee, Wheeler asked Sifford how much money he had in his pocket—Wheeler was confident too. Sifford had 20 dollars, so they agreed to play for 10 dollars on both the front and back nine holes of the course. What followed was an exhibition of golf from the elder statesman, Howard

Wheeler, who used his experience and talents to, in Sifford's words, "systematically take me apart." Every time Sifford hit a good approach shot, Wheeler would outdo him by nestling the ball closer to the hole. If the North Carolinian hit a slightly wayward drive, the man from Georgia split the fairway. When Sifford made birdie, Wheeler made eagle. At the end of the round, as the younger man was licking his wounds, Wheeler put his winnings into his pocket and told Sifford that he should not feel bad about his loss. After all, he had just been defeated by "the best golf player in the world."[273]

Both Sifford and Wheeler spent the vast majority of their working lives up to that point as caddies, and it was their early exposure to the sport that helped them become such accomplished players. Sifford caddied at the exclusive Carolina Country Club in Charlotte, and Wheeler worked first at East Lake before carrying bags at Brookhaven in Atlanta. In Wheeler's early years in the Gate City, he caddied for Atlanta's White elite—and some of the greatest golfers in the world—including Bobby Jones.[274] Both caddies used their exposure to the game as a means of learning a new sport and, before long, became obsessive players.

Their talents for golf, and their desire to find quality golf courses (where they were allowed to play) brought them to Philadelphia, where they could use the desegregated public course in the city: Cobbs Creek. At the time they met, Howard Wheeler was the best Black golfer in the United States, having won the National Negro Open in 1933 and 1938, while he was still a caddie. Both men put their golf careers on hold when they were drafted into the military, but when the National Negro Open restarted in 1946, Wheeler won three consecutive titles. Sifford went on to match Wheeler's five titles as he became the dominant golfer on the Black professional tour—the United Golfers Association (UGA)—during the 1950s. The ever-young Wheeler took his National Open victories to six at the age of 47.[275] Sifford later became the first Black member of the previously "Caucasian-only" Professional Golfers Association (PGA) Tour—an achievement that earned him the moniker "the Jackie Robinson of golf" in many news outlets.[276] Wheeler and Sifford's careers as professional golfers made them stars in the Black press and pioneers in a sport with a lily-white reputation. Their journeys were extraordinary, yet their stories reflect the impact that the Southern practice of hiring only Black caddies had on the Black sporting scene. For many, caddying was only a job; for others it became a fulfilling hobby, a means of disproving racist assumptions; for a few, it could even become a viable path to professional sport.

Early in the century, most Black men who became caddies had never had any previous interaction with golf. In their worldview, golf was a sport for Whites. Golf's birth in the South coincided with the rise of Jim Crow in the region, and country clubs and resorts strictly forbade Black participation.[277] Most Black caddies came to the job knowing little about the game of golf, and even less about the mechanics of a golf swing, the strategy required to navigate a hole, or the touch needed for differing shots. They were drawn to the game for the chance at earning an honest wage in working conditions that were more favorable than other demeaning or backbreaking jobs in the region. But many stayed caddying because of the opportunity it afforded them to play golf.

Once they spent some time on the course, many caddies became infatuated with golf. Appetite for the game among caddies was vast. A 1932 survey of Black high school boys in Nashville found that more than 1 in 10 played golf on a daily basis, largely owing to their status as caddies.[278] While some caddies treated golf only as a means for a living, others made it their lives. The reasons why Black caddies chose to also pick up a club and play the game varied from individual to individual. Some caddies, including Charlie Sifford who caddied at the prestigious Carolina Country Club in Charlotte, North Carolina, felt an instinctual attraction to the game. Sifford remembered that he "was in love with the golf course," and that "there was something about it that appealed to me on a very basic level."[279] Walter Stewart grew up caddying in Norfolk, Virginia and found that he was so instantaneously fascinated with hitting the ball and seeing it fly that he had to learn to play.[280] Black caddies who worked at the most prestigious and beautiful golf courses of the South—including the courses at Pinehurst and in Atlanta—spent every day in picturesque and manicured spaces, designed to be attractive to the eye. It was little wonder that many became fond of the sport.

Some caddies likely wanted to play the game because it was a forbidden fruit. White society dictated that it was not something Black folks could do. Other White-only spaces—including segregated buses and separate drinking fountains for Whites and African Americans—became direct targets for political action. Likewise, golf's largely White-only status made the game attractive to Black Southerners who wished to signal their discontent with Jim Crow. Sports were particularly ripe for such demonstrations. Jim Crow's proponents believed that only Whites were capable of excelling in sports and that African Americans as a race were athletically inferior. Black caddies in the South who demonstrated their sporting capabilities were also showcasing Black sporting excellence and proving the great falsity of White beliefs about racial difference. Charlie Sifford remembered that people told him his entire life that he "can't play golf for a living—no blacks allowed here, Charlie." To which he always "asked them to move aside."[281] Playing golf in the South as a Black person was not simply another pastime, it was loaded with racial meaning.

A Poor Man's Version of a Rich Man's Game

Caddies were also drawn to play golf for the same reasons that anyone chooses to play sport. It offered exercise in the form of hours of walking every round, carrying a heavy bag, and swinging the club. Golf also appealed because of the sports' significant difficulty, the pleasure that comes with mastery over a skill, and the consistent promise of improvement. Golf also offered an avenue for camaraderie among friends. Caddies who chose to play together after they finished work experienced the ways that sport brings individuals together. Matches between caddies on the course gave these workers a place to prove their sporting capabilities and demonstrate their skills to each other. In turn, caddies used their freshly earned wages to gamble on their matches with one another. Willie McRae, a Pinehurst caddie who—in the aftermath of World War II—made the twice-a-week journey to the desegregated federally run course at Fort Bragg, remembered that caddies also used their golf matches to settle personal disagreements or disputes. McRae remarked that a few of the caddies disliked his close relationship with the resort's owner, Richard Tufts, and therefore they wanted McRae to play with them so that they could take his money.[282] One of the reasons that Ralph Dawkins Jr.—who caddied in Jacksonville, Florida—went to play every day was that by "becoming the best player among the caddies," he could "take the tip money of the other caddies."[283] The satisfaction of sporting victory coupled with the opportunity to earn even more money on the golf course made the game an obsession for many.[284]

Given the financial and racial barriers to entry to golf for Black Southerners, caddies had to come up with novel ways to play the game. In many communities, the easiest place to practice was on the streets where caddies lived. One report from Southern Pines, North Carolina, just a few miles from Pinehurst, noted that "it is not an uncommon sight to see boys playing golf on the streets of the Negro town."[285] Seeking a more authentic golf experience, and fewer broken windows, caddies took it upon themselves to build spaces where they could practice. At Pinehurst, a caddie known as "Swamp" built a set of miniature golf holes for caddies to use. The course totaled 12 holes and started and finished at the caddy shack. The need to be economical with space dictated the size of the courses that caddies could build in those years. Miniature golf courses like the ones at Pinehurst allowed caddies to practice their putting and other short shots but did not give them the full experience of golf. Nonetheless, the mini-golf course at Pinehurst pre-dated the first commercial course of its kind in the United States. The *Pinehurst Outlook* noted that the caddie course was "perhaps the original miniature golf course of the world—at least it's been in operation longer than any we know."[286] Black caddies in the South—in their attempts to play the game in whatever form possible—were pioneers in the creation of miniature golf—a game that gained worldwide popularity in the decades that followed.

The courses that caddies built for themselves were improvised and often ramshackle in nature. The caddies themselves had little experience in greens-keeping or course maintenance, nor did they have access to the technology and equipment required to keep their short courses in pristine condition. Rather, caddies hacked out holes through the overgrown areas around their caddy shacks or in their neighborhoods.[287] At Woodholme Country Club in Baltimore, the work was done by a single caddie who created a weaving short course that "wrapped around a few trees and laced through the bushes that covered much of the ground." Just as on the White course, the caddie dug holes into the ground "a few inches deep and nearly as wide."[288] DeWayne Wickham, who played on the caddie course at Woodholme, described the golf played on these courses as "caddie golf," as opposed to the "real thing." According to Wickham, caddie golf was "a poor man's version of a rich man's game," despite all the pleasure it brought him and his fellow caddies.[289] Although caddie courses did not resemble the lavish ones where the men worked, they served the purpose of giving Black caddies an entry point into playing the game. Over time, nature has reclaimed such courses, and country clubs have repurposed the land for differing activities. The spaces where many thousands of Black golfers around the country hit their first shots have been lost.

When caddies could not play on their own courses, they took calculated risks to play on White-only courses. As employees at the golf course, they knew the schedule of tournaments and the playing patterns of most of the members. In the early mornings and late evenings, when there was just enough light to see the ball, and just enough darkness to hide from members, caddies dashed around the courses of the South, playing as many holes as they could. Charlie Sifford took every opportunity he could to play at the Carolina Country Club in Charlotte, sneaking out in the late afternoons once the members were finished playing.[290] The game that caddies played when they snuck onto the golf course was different than the one played by members in the bright of day: White golfers had the luxury of playing at a leisurely pace, but these caddies—crunched for time and light—chased their ball around quickly to play as much of the course as possible. Their fast pace of play was also partly attributed to the need to stay out of sight—caddies did not know when the club officials or staff might be lurking around a corner.[291] At times, playing golf on White courses was a direct threat to their safety. One Virginia caddie remembered White men in cars driving by the course and shooting guns at Black caddies who had snuck on to play.[292] Their dedication to playing in the face of such risks was indicative of their desire not to be forced off the course because of their race.

Hungry to play the real and full version of golf, on the same courses where they carried the bags of White golfers, Black caddies took the occasional risk of hitting the clubs and balls of their employers. In moments when waiting for their player to arrive, or when a player gave them the opportunity to hit, Black caddies took great pleasure out of playing the courses they were forbidden from playing. On the 13th tee at Woodholme Country Club, DeWayne Wickham waited for his player to arrive for the start of play—the format of the tournament was a shotgun start, such that players started simultaneously from different tees around the course.[293] Wickham realized that his employer's long walk from the clubhouse to the 13th tee provided a window of opportunity to play on the course, out of sight of players and club management. "This was the chance I'd been waiting for," he remembered, "an opportunity to do what I had done so many times before in my mind." Wickham grabbed a ball and club from his player's bag, took a few practice swings, and then hit the ball as well as he could. His first shot was not good, so he hit another, and another, and continued until he had hit six balls. At that point he stopped just as his player arrived. The thrill of hitting full shots on the actual course was coupled with the relief that his player did not realize what had just happened.[294] Wickham had not only finally played proper golf, but he also pulled a fast one on his employer.

Born to Golf

At times, White golfers invited caddies to hit a few shots during a round. Why they chose to do so is unclear, but on occasion they stood back and let their caddies hit. That is what happened to Willie McRae on Pinehurst's No. 2: the most acclaimed and prestigious of the resort's courses. When McRae's player that day, Jim Hunter, invited him to hit a shot on the 11th tee, McRae was stunned. He knew that African Americans were not allowed to play but took the opportunity presented to him. The experience of being able to hit even a single shot had a profound impact on him. "Standing on that tee," he noted, "I felt the blood course through my veins so hard it seemed like it poured right down the shaft." In that instant, McRae realized that he "was born to golf."[295] In the fleeting moments when caddies hit golf shots on the courses where their official role was as workers rather than leisure-seekers, many caddies felt what it was like to play real golf. These brief tastes whetted their appetites for playing the game the way it was intended and stiffened their resolve to find ways to play on an equal standing to the White golfers.

The financial costs of golf equipment proved a further obstacle to Black involvement in the sport. Golf clubs were expensive. In 1910, a new Spaulding driver cost three dollars—almost a full week's wages for a caddie.[296] Over the next decade, newspapers complained about how the price of clubs was increasing at an unsustainable rate.[297] Caddies therefore had to find inventive ways to play the game. Willie McRae could not afford to buy his own set of clubs, so he made his own. Carrying a saw and a hatchet, McRae ventured into the woods just beyond his family's farm. He found a sturdy root of a blackjack oak tree and hacked away at it for about an hour before bringing it back to the family barn. In the barn, he cut and sanded the root to resemble a head of a driver, and he cut the club to the correct length for him. For a grip, he wrapped masking tape around the top of the stick.[298] Other players remember using coat hangers, broom handles, or any material resembling a club to make their equipment.[299] Through improvisation, ingenuity, and hard work, caddies like McRae built their own imitation golf clubs that allowed them to practice the game they desired to play.

Homemade golf clubs offered a temporary solution to golf's financial barriers, but they did not last like commercially produced equipment. Caddies who wanted to play consistently needed to find real golf clubs. To do so, they often turned to the players for whom they caddied. White members occasionally let their caddies borrow one or two of their clubs on the days when caddies were allowed to play. Members would rarely let caddies use the full set, but even a single club proved more useful than the homemade alternatives. Caddies also were able to find old clubs that White players no longer needed, and second-hand balls which they found on the course while caddying.[300] Playing a full-length golf course, though, is particularly challenging with only one club, so caddies pieced together full sets and shared them. Charlie Sifford remembered working with his fellow caddies to borrow particular clubs to complete a set; "Ralph would have the 7-iron, I'd have a wedge, somebody else would have a 3-wood. We'd play a round that way, trading clubs the whole time."[301] Golf clubs were a shared treasure for young caddies in the Pinehurst area. One former Pinehurst caddie noted that "whoever had a golf club shared it with everyone."[302] Early images of Pinehurst caddies playing golf show men sharing a handful of clubs for their round (Figure 11).[303] For golf balls, caddies would use balls they found on the course or steal old ones from the bags of their players. According to DeWayne Wickham, the balls he and his fellow caddies used were "the old, beat-up ones that wouldn't be missed," and not the new balls that members kept a good track of.[304] Using their ingenuity, cunning, and planning, caddies pieced together the clubs and balls that allowed them to play golf in their own leisure time. Black caddies cleared every hurdle between them and the golf course as they refused to have their leisure time be dictated by the racial and financial constraints of Jim Crow society.

FIGURE 11: Caddies at Pinehurst practice golf and share the few clubs they have (Tufts Archives).

In the Shadows and on the Move

The way that Black caddies learned how to swing a club had a lasting impact on their style of play. Unlike White youngsters who joined country clubs or had instruction from the local golf professionals, caddies learned through observation. It was not until the establishment of Black country clubs in the 1930s and '40s—which employed Black teaching professionals—that coaching was readily available to Black golfers. Instead, they watched the way their fellow caddies and the best White golfers handled the grip, positioned their feet, and swung the club. "Nobody gave me lessons," Charlie Sifford remembered, "I picked it all up by watching."[305] Howard Wheeler and other caddies on the Atlanta golf scene caddied for the likes of Bobby Jones and took great effort to observe the best of the best.[306] They also noticed the common mistakes from the bad members that made a ball veer off course. In turn, when caddies picked up their own clubs, they implemented the best of what they saw while caddying and avoided the traits of the worst players.[307] The lack of formal coaching meant that caddies also adjusted their game based on feel and consistency. When they found something that worked for them, they stuck with it, even if it may not have been found in the pages of conventional coaching manuals. Howard Wheeler, for example, held the club in a cross-handed grip: with his left hand below his right. Any golfer who received coaching would never be encouraged to play with such a grip, but Wheeler found what felt right to him and made a success out of it. The game was one of improvisation for Black caddies who strove to be the best players possible.

Other golfers developed their own unique styles of play as a direct consequence of circumstances in which caddies were able to practice. One Black golfer told Charlie Sifford that his "short, flat swing," was that way because "when he learned the game he had to hit the ball quickly and move on in order to avoid the marshals and club pros." Another former professional, Walter Stewart, blamed his unorthodox swing on the fact that he did not often have the right club for a particular shot so would have to manipulate his swing to make do with what equipment he did have. If a shot required a longer club, he would simply swing much harder.[308] Sifford heard the same story from "many Black golfers who learned to play in places where they were not allowed to play." The same conditions, Sifford argued, were a reason why many Black professionals struggled with their putting. Improving one's putting requires vast time and practice, and for Black caddies running around the course, "there wasn't any time for standing around on the green hitting 50 putts." The problem was confounded by the fact that the golf clubs that some club members gifted caddies were rarely putters. According to Sifford, Black professionals "rarely got to use a real putter when they were kids."[309] Between learning from feel and observation—and having to play in the shadows and on the move—Black caddie golfers in the South developed a unique style of play that differed from the White players who learned from professional coaches.

Playing golf on the courses where they worked gave caddies a new leisure activity, but it also took on a racial significance. Because Whites did whatever possible to block Black participation in golf in the early 20th century, the act of playing golf alone represented a refusal to accept racial hierarchy. In the opening decades of the century whenever White newspapers and magazines discussed the notion of Black golfers they wrote in disparaging and dismissive ways. After the opening of a Black golf club in Westfield, New Jersey in 1922, one progressive writer summarized the general White attitude toward Black golf: "Cartoonists will make funny pictures of it. Vaudeville artists will do sketches about it." White people, he continued, found it particularly funny when the Black population did "things which are ordinary parts of the day's work and play to white people," because "the white man does not think of his dark-skinned fellow traveler on the planet as a human companion."[310] In picking up a golf club and taking to the courses where Whites told them they could not play, Black caddies refused to accept the position prescribed to them in the South's racial hierarchy.

The fact that caddies who played golf covertly ran from shot to shot and did everything possible to avoid the sight of club officials demonstrates that they understood their actions were not without risk. Had they been caught by the White authorities, they risked losing their job or their favor with the caddie master. Yet Black caddies took such risks because they did not want to have their leisure pursuits defined by the color of their skin. To maintain their jobs and their safety on the course, the easiest option would have been to approach the golf course as a workplace only. By turning the course into a site for their own sporting practice, Black caddies also made the golf course a place where they contested Jim Crow. Thousands of Black men around the South learned to become talented golfers in the exact spaces where they were forbidden from doing so. Their golfing excellence was a testament to their desire to break free from their typecast role as attendants to White Southerners.

Seizing the Opportunity

In Atlanta, middle-class African Americans who became interested in golf decided that they wanted a course of their own. A place to play on their own terms, in the light of day, and without having to be employed by the course to gain playing rights. Abandoned by the municipal government, which refused to integrate the city's public courses until the 1950s, these Black men and women came together to form the New Lincoln Golf and Country Club in 1930. The course was set up in basic fashion, with only nine holes and a simple layout. But for those who had been denied playing rights on the courses in the city for the preceding decades, it was a sanctuary. New Lincoln was open to all those who could afford to join, and the membership was a mix of the city's Black professionals—doctors, barbers, and teachers—as well as former caddies who learned the game on the White courses like East Lake and Brookhaven.[311] It was at New Lincoln where Howard Wheeler, John Brooks Dendy, and other former caddies honed the skills they had learned in their years toting bags for wealthy Whites.

The caddies at New Lincoln who were, of course, all Black—Jim Crow's unwritten norms could never have condoned White caddies at Black golf courses—also played the game and learned on the job. Unlike their counterparts at White country clubs, however, the New Lincoln caddies did not need to hide their playing time under the cover of darkness or in their own back yards. Rather they were given consistent rights to play on the course where they worked. The Black members at New Lincoln also encouraged the caddies to play and improve their skills. In the summer of 1936, member A.L. Miller took note of the talents of a caddie named George Harris and gifted him a full set of clubs. In the fall of the same year, the members noted that the talents of the caddies were of such a standard that they organized a "big time" caddie tournament. The *Atlanta Daily World* even listed odds on the caddies who played that day. George Harris was third favorite at "2 to 1," behind Connie Johnson and the favorite, Olin Robinson. The paper also noted that a large gallery was expected to witness the matches.[312] At Black-owned courses such as New Lincoln, caddies were less defined by their subservient role and allowed more autonomy to explore their own golf talents.

As the first third of the 20th century progressed, it became more and more difficult for White country club members to completely deny Black caddies the right to play on their golf courses. In the years when Whites outrightly banned African American caddies from playing on their courses, the caddies had proven that the efforts to completely forbid them from playing were futile. By the 1930s, White golf course management changed its approach to caddie golf. Rather than forbid caddies entirely from golfing, caddies were allowed to play on the days when the course was closed for maintenance, usually Monday afternoons. In the new configuration, caddies were given some playing rights. Yet the restricted and segregated time slot was a consistent reminder to caddies of their prescribed place in the South's racial hierarchy. The change in policy was one that caddies forced into effect with their actions, and not an act of benevolent kindness from country club and resort authorities.[313]

White newspapers featured occasional coverage of talented Black golfers who played the courses during maintenance day. The *Atlanta Constitution*, in 1926, documented the exploits of the Black caddie master, Jack Thomas, who worked at the city's West End Golf Club. Thomas received particular attention because he achieved a remarkable level of skill and did so with only one hand, the other having been amputated when he was a child. Despite his disability, the report noted that Thomas "shoots the [nine-hole] course regularly around the 40 mark. Better than many of us can do with both hands, both feet and an eraser on our pencil."[314] Likewise in Washington, D.C., one White news reporter documented the talents of Black golfers who "can get around any good course like Columbia in figures that would make you turn green with envy."[315]

Alongside the decision to allow caddies some restricted playing rights, some White country clubs and resorts instituted caddie tournaments. Allowing caddies to play on the course on selected days and to compete in a caddie tournament did not indicate that White golfers viewed Black caddie golfers as equal to them. Rather, the segregated nature of the play remained in place and any time caddies played they were reminded that they were playing in their capacity as caddies rather than as regular players. Under no uncertain circumstances were other Black citizens allowed to play the course. Charlie Sifford felt that White members at the Carolina Country Club in Charlotte were dedicated to ensuring that Black caddies' identity remained tied to their service to Whites, regardless of their golfing talent. Sifford claimed that "it was okay for me to whack balls around the course when I was a Black caddy playing with other Black caddies, or when I was carrying a member's bag."[316]

Regardless of White justification for caddie golf, Black men and boys seized the opportunities. Tournaments offered caddies an official and organized event in which they could compare their talents. In Atlanta, the first caddie tournament for Black caddies was held for Ansley Park caddies in 1922, and White members used the event as a means of perpetuating racial stereotypes by offering a prize of a large watermelon to the victor.[317] Some caddie tournaments were open to not just the caddies who worked at that course, but also caddies from the local or regional area. In Florida in the 1920s, caddies would travel around the state to play at White courses on the one day a year that caddies were given full access.[318] Likewise, in the 1940s, a tournament for Black caddies in Charlotte attracted entries from four different states.[319] Occasional tournaments also pitted caddies from one city against those from another, such as the 1939 match in which Greensboro caddies bested their Durham counterparts.[320] In Atlanta, where White caddies worked the city's municipal courses, caddie tournaments were strictly segregated. White caddies played in one city-wide tournament, and Black caddies played in their own tournaments at the courses where they were employed.[321] Tournaments allowed caddies to distinguish themselves as talented players and measure their capabilities against each other.[322]

Caddie tournaments also offered an opportunity to prove that Black golfers—given proper opportunity to play and practice—could perform at the same level as White golfers. On rare occasions, caddies had even more direct opportunities to compare their talents to White golfers. For example, in Atlanta in the 1940s, two black workers at the Capital City Club course challenged the future mayor of the city, Ivan Allen Jr, and his friend Charles Dannals—who had won the Atlanta Amateur Championship—to a match. The workers were called Booker and John: one was the caddie master and the other cleaned clubs in the back of the pro shop. The club professional allowed the match to go ahead on the condition that it was played at dawn on a Monday, when the course was closed for maintenance. His stipulations likely stemmed from the fear that White members would find out that African Americans were given permission to play. He may also have harbored concerns that the Black workers might win. About 50 caddies showed up to support their colleagues, highlighting what it meant for caddies to be able to compare their talents to Whites. In the end, the White club members won the match by a tight margin: no shame for the workers who had far less experience playing on the course.[323]

The first Pinehurst caddie tournament was a major event for African Americans living in the North Carolina Sandhills. In May 1939, 94 out of the hundreds of caddies employed at Pinehurst took to the No. 1 course: the oldest and second most prestigious at Pinehurst. White members of the Pinehurst Country Club offered caddies temporary use of some clubs for the day. Few expected the level of excitement the event created. Coverage of the Pinehurst caddie tournament made it into national Black newspapers. According to a report in the *New York Amsterdam News*, the tournament received a larger gallery than attended the National Negro Open in Chicago the previous summer. Attendees arrived at the course in their finest attire and followed their favorite players around, or waited by the final green for each group to finish their rounds. Supporters, who "knew what it was all about as well as the players," were not to be disappointed. The caddies wowed the gallery with their golfing capabilities as the newspaper commended their "remarkable exhibition of skill, knowledge of rules, competitive spirit and sportsmanship." Many White tourists also attended the tournament and were surprised "to see how well these colored boys and men had picked up the fundamentals of the swing."[324] It was not uncommon for onlooking Whites to demonstrate their shock at the talents of caddies who learned to play the game in the shadows. According to one Florida caddie, "It amazed the white golfers" to see them play.[325] At yearly tournaments like the Pinehurst caddie event, Black caddies exhibited that their lives were not defined by the subservient roles that Whites prescribed for them in the Jim Crow economy. In their demonstrations of their golfing abilities, caddies undermined the flawed symbolism of talented White golfers and smiling and contented Black caddies.

The First Professional

From the very start of professional golf in the United States, African Americans caddies demonstrated their talents. John Shippen, a Black former caddie, was the first American-born professional golfer of any race. Shippen caddied at the Shinnecock Hills Golf Club in Southampton, New York. A son of an enslaved man from Virginia, Shippen found himself in the vicinity of Shinnecock Hills when his father—who had become a Presbyterian minister in Washington, D.C.—was assigned there on mission. The course employed mostly Native American caddies—the practice of employing predominantly White schoolboys had not yet been established in the North—but Shippen joined their ranks and quickly learned to play golf with greater skill than most of those who he caddied for. By 1896, when the United States Golf Association (USGA) decided to host the second U.S. Open at Shinnecock, the members encouraged him to compete. At that time, Shippen's race was not a common reason to refuse his entry. Black participation in other sports occurred fairly frequently prior to the turn of the century, and White golfers held the amateur game in higher esteem than the professional one, so Black professionals were more acceptable than Black amateurs in elite sport. However, the Scottish and English professional golfers who competed in 1896 attempted a last-minute boycott to have Shippen and his Native American colleague, Oscar Bunn, removed from the field. Their boycott did not last long, as the USGA president Theodore A. Havemeyer rejected their appeals and allowed Shippen and Bunn to play. In the end, Shippen finished tied for sixth place and received a cheque for 10 dollars, the first prize money ever collected by an American-born golf professional. Over the next two decades, Shippen would compete in a total of five U.S. Opens but never matched his high finish in 1896.[326]

The somewhat racially liberal worldview that allowed Shippen to compete in professional golf in the late-19th century did not last. Professional golf settled into the same racial exclusionary pattern as other major sports in their unspoken rejection of Black athletes. Black professional golfers knew that their presence was not accepted in the national tournaments organized by the USGA and the PGA in the 1920s and '30s, and few challenged the status quo. They understood the ever-present threat of racial retribution. The example of two golfers who did challenge the unspoken ban on Black players demonstrates the steadfast desire for White-only professional golf in the major national golf organizations. Former Atlanta caddie Robert "Pat" Ball and his fellow Black professional, Elmer Stout, qualified for the 1928 USGA Public Links Championship in Philadelphia. Having qualified for the final, all seemed well until the organizing officials informed the two Black competitors that they had been disqualified for scoring errors. The two men objected and filed an injunction at a local court. In the hearings that followed, it was found that not only had the men done nothing illegal, but some officials of the USGA had planted individuals posing as reporters in the crowd to follow both players and find any infraction possible to disqualify them. The court threw out the USGA's case and ruled that the men had been incorrectly disqualified. Yet some of the USGA officials' attempts to remove them from the tournament proved successful because, by the time the court made their ruling, the tournament had advanced to a stage where reinstating the players would be almost impossible. In turn Ball and Stout withdrew themselves from the event. Their example illustrates the ways that Black golfers were discouraged from ever attempting to enter professional tournaments organized by the nation's largest White-run governing bodies in the first third of the 20th century.[327]

Unwritten agreements that banned Black golfers from competing with the best White players also extended to elite amateur events. As noted, the amateur game was held in high esteem in the first third of the century and tournaments like the U.S. Amateur Championship were seen as the pinnacle of golf—a combination of skill and gentlemanly conduct. In 1915, the USGA implemented an update to the rules that redefined the status of amateurs. In doing so they noted their main responsibility as a governing body, "to safeguard the interests of golf; to preserve it as it has always been, a dignified recreation and gentlemanly pastime."[328] In their interpretation of "safeguarding the interests of golf," they ruled that anyone over the age of 16 who collected payment for services as a caddie would be in violation of amateur status.[329] Of course, the USGA was entirely aware that the vast majority of caddies over 16 in the United States were African Americans working in the South. Almost all White child caddies in the North turned to other more profitable occupations as they reached adulthood. Howard Wheeler and other Atlanta caddies who continued to carry bags well into adulthood were ineligible for amateur competition. The redefinition of amateur status banned all Southern Black caddie golfers from seeking to compete in prestigious national amateur tournaments.

By the 1930s, golf's governing bodies moved from unspoken bans on Black golfers to a clear color line. The USGA still claimed to be race-neutral in its governing but hid behind the segregation of the golf clubs that hosted their events. In 1942, when Robert "Pat" Ball and others—including former Northwestern University golfer Horace McDougal, and other UGA players Clyde Martin, and former boxer Joe Louis—tried to play in the 1942 Hale America Open tournament in Chicago, the president of the USGA claimed that the players could not play because who was allowed to play was up to the host club, Ridgemoor Country Club, noting that "the USGA merely respected the rights of the member club."[330] The PGA was more forthright about their stance on Black golfers when, in 1934, they instituted a "Caucasians-only" clause into their rules, ratifying the informal ban that had been in place for years. The clause stated that only "professional golfers of the Caucasian race," could become members of the PGA.[331] In the four decades between John Shippen's performance in the 1896 U.S. Open and the institution of the "Caucasian-only" clause, golf had transitioned from a sport with potential for racial inclusion, to one of the most segregated sports of all.

The United Golfers Association

It is perhaps of little coincidence that the PGA formally instituted the "Caucasians-only" clause at a time when former Black caddies around the country proved themselves as excellent golfers in a segregated Black golf tour. In the mid-1920s, Black golf became organized for the first time on a national scale. The few Black golf clubs around the North hoped to create tournaments that would allow African Americans, who were unable to compete in White-only USGA and PGA events, to test their skills against each other. The interested golfers came together to create the United Golfers Association. The star in the UGA's crown was the National Negro Open, which was the biggest prize available to Black golfers. The first and only national tournament open to Black golfers, it was played for the first four years in Stow, Massachusetts. The inaugural tournament in 1926 was won by Harry Jackson of Washington, D.C. The champion in 1927 and 1929 was Robert "Pat" Ball, who lived in Chicago. In 1928, the last year that the event was played in Stow, Porter Washington won on his home course. On the face of it, golfers from northern states—where Black golfers could play at private Black country clubs—seemed to have the edge over their southern competitors. In 1930, the *Chicago Defender* noted that "heretofore the northern boys have held sway ever since the inception of the tournament."[332] However, the National Open took some time to garner the prestige it eventually would achieve, meaning players from the South did not travel to the event in great numbers until the 1930s. Categorizing the winners by where they lived at the time of their victories also underplays the South's influence. Robert "Pat" Ball was born in Atlanta, caddied at East

Lake, and was an assistant clubmaker at the Druid Hills Club before joining the Great Migration and settling in Chicago at the age of 16. By the time he won the National Open, the newspapers of Chicago claimed him as one of their own, but his time as a caddie in Atlanta was foundational to his golfing excellence.[333]

Ball's victories were the opening notes in a crescendo of dominance for southerners in the National Open, almost all of whom learned the game caddying. Ball's second victory was followed by back-to-back championships in 1931 and 1932 by Edison Marshall of New Orleans, who learned to play during his time as a caddie in his hometown's private White country clubs.[334] John Brooks Dendy who grew up caddying in Asheville, North Carolina won the event three times, in 1932, 1936, and 1937. Howard Wheeler, who caddied at East Lake and at Brookhaven in Atlanta, won in 1933 and 1938. Robert "Pat" Ball added his third National Open title in 1934, followed by Solomon Hughes of Gadsden, Alabama. The only non-southern champion in the 1930s was Cliff Strickland of Los Angeles, who won on his home course in 1939. In fact, Strickland was the only person who did not grow up caddying on a southern golf course to win the UGA National Negro Open between winners Porter Washington in 1928 and Richard Thomas in 1959.

The achievements of Black Southerners on the UGA at the time are even more impressive when the locations of the events are considered. It was not until 1954 that the National Open was held in the South, when it was hosted in Dallas, Texas, and it did not return until 1962 in Memphis, Tennessee. The North, with its comparative racial liberalism that tolerated Black golf infrastructure failed to compete on the national stage with the caddies and former caddies of the South.[335]

The reasons behind the South's depth of professional talent were not entirely clear at the time. Logic would suggest that northern players who faced less racial barriers to golf course access, should have held the edge over their southern counterparts. One writer from the *Chicago Defender* suggested that climate was the cause of the South's success noting that "perhaps warm weather in the southern states, which permits all year play, gives the Dixie boys an edge."[336] The most likely reason for southerners' dominance in the 1930s through 1950s, was the early exposure to golf for Black Southerners as caddies. The region was flush with private White courses that almost exclusively employed Black youngsters as caddies. "There is no doubt," read the sports pages of the *Atlanta Daily World* in 1939, "about the greatest golfers being for the most part mere graduates of caddy lists on exclusive white golf country clubs."[337] In the North, where White youngsters caddied, African American boys had less direct exposure to the sport, so fewer played the game at an early age. The racial hierarchy of labor in the South—and White desires to fill subservient roles with Black workers—created a glut of great Black golfers.

The Capital of Race Golf

Introduction to golf through caddying was not enough on its own to create quality golfers, of course. Many thousands of Black caddies in the South enjoyed playing the game leisurely rather than competitively. But the depth of southern talent was undeniable, and the southerners who excelled and eclipsed northern players the first half of the 20th century tended to reside in towns and cities where a healthy Black golfing infrastructure complemented and supported the ranks of Black caddies. In towns and resorts where Black-owned private courses did not develop, golfers who learned the game growing up as caddies found themselves bereft of opportunities to play golf. Once they left the caddie ranks, they were no longer able to play in caddie tournaments or have playing rights as employees. In cities like Atlanta, players who grew up caddying could join Black private clubs such as New Lincoln Golf and Country Club and play their entire lives, regardless of their employer, as John Brooks Dendy demonstrated. Dendy grew up caddying in Asheville, North Carolina but moved to Atlanta to study at Morehouse College. It was there where Dendy honed his golf on the New Lincoln course and won the UGA Southern Open before winning the biggest prize of all—the National Open—Indianapolis in 1932.[338] Had Dendy stayed in Asheville, where there was a less-organized Black golf scene, he may not have reached such heights. Another noted advantage of living in a town where Black golf infrastructure was well developed was that Black country clubs could provide funds for talented players to travel to UGA events. In the early 1930s, the New Lincoln Golf and Country Club hosted qualifying tournaments for the city's caddies to decide who from Atlanta would travel to the National Open. In 1934, Zeke Hartsfield and Howard Wheeler qualified and as a result the club covered the expenses of their travel to the National Open in Detroit.[339] Such official preparation and funding undoubtedly helped the players who took part and was only available in the places where Black private courses existed.[340]

The importance of strong Black golf infrastructure in combination with early exposure to the game as caddies perhaps helps to explain why so few Pinehurst caddies featured on the UGA leaderboards. It was not that Pinehurst lacked talented Black golfers. Quite the opposite: a reporter from the *New York Amsterdam News* who witnessed the first caddie tournament at Pinehurst noted, in 1939, how remarkable it was that "among the Pinehurst caddies there were players capable of winning" the National Open.[341] Black caddies who worked at Pinehurst and other Sandhills courses played golf on course maintenance days and on the short courses they built themselves, and they formed a Pinehurst Golfers Association for Black players in the town. The Pinehurst Golfers Association organized occasional tournaments for the area's Black players in the 1940s and made attempts to build a course of their own in 1954, but their efforts appeared to run short of the funds required to construct the site.[342] Pinehurst caddies did not have a private course like New Lincoln, where they could hone their skills and consistently play competitive golf on a full-length course, or the institutional support to send a vast number of players north to the major UGA events. Atlanta's golf officials even turned to Pinehurst to round up Ralph Richardson and Jimmy Steed—two of the best Pinehurst caddies—to play in the 1941 National Open.[343] Pinehurst caddies had the skill to compete, yet the lack of Black golf infrastructure in the area hampered their progress toward national competition.

Unlike Pinehurst, Atlanta became a hub for professional Black golfers who rose up through the caddie ranks. During the 1930s, Atlanta's golf scene flourished as the New Lincoln G&CC helped develop a pipeline of former caddies. John Brooks Dendy and Howard Wheeler's championships spoke for themselves. Others who learned golf as caddies in Atlanta included Zeke Hartsfield and, of course, Robert "Pat" Ball. The appetite for golf among African Americans in Atlanta at the time was staggering, given the lack of access Black Atlantans had to courses. In a survey of Black boys in Atlanta's First Ward conducted in the early 1930s, almost three quarters (72%) responded that they had either taken part in golf or wished to do so: a higher number than for basketball, and only just behind baseball.[344]

As the epicenter of golf in the South, Atlanta played host to the UGA's Southern Open and Amateur tournament hosted annually from 1932 on the New Lincoln course. The Southern Open proved to be an early predictor for the men's National Open as Dendy and Wheeler both won the event in the same year of their first national triumph.[345] Local sportswriters took great joy in the Southern Open's prestige as one writer pointed out that over the first ten years of the tournament "every national golf champion, with the exception of two, competed first in the Southern Open."[346] Atlanta's dominance of the Southern Open was never greater than in 1946, when six of the top nine finishers were locals.[347] The city became the "capital of race golf," because it had both a steady supply of Black youngsters introduced to the game as caddies and the strong Black golf infrastructure to prop up such talent.[348]

Players who made their journey from the caddie ranks to the top of the Black professional game eventually pressured golf's major governing bodies to remove their racial barriers to entry. Howard Wheeler, John Brooks Dendy, and Robert Ball's generation were already past the peak of their talents when the Civil Rights Movement combined with the glaringly obvious talents of Black golfers to break the color line. According to Charlie Sifford, the players of Wheeler's era had to settle for a career combining incomes from multiple jobs and playing on the Black tour. Sifford "never questioned Wheeler about why he didn't try to match his game up against the Hogans and Sneads and Byron Nelsons of the world ... it was still too early for that."[349]

The End of the Official Color Barrier

By the late 1950s, the tide began to change. The best Black male professionals—Sifford, Bill Spiller, and Teddy Rhodes (a former Nashville caddie)—received invites to PGA Tour events such as the L.A. Open and the Canadian Open, but they were still not allowed full membership on the tour because of the "Caucasian-only" clause. Their invites only applied to events in the West, Midwest, and Canada. They were forced to miss the tour's southern swing, where racial barriers to golf remained as strong as ever. Black professionals also could not compete in a number of important events that required full PGA membership. In 1960, after years of attention on the issue in Black press and from Black golfers, public officials in New York and California threatened to ban PGA events in their states if the rule did not change. When the PGA met for their annual meeting in November 1961, they felt the full pressures from a combination of evident Black talent, negative stories about the tour in nationwide media, and the threats from state officials. The PGA voted to permanently remove the "Caucasian-only" clause and allowed Black membership.[350]

The end of the official color barrier in men's professional golf offered Charlie Sifford and others the chance to play in tournaments that had been previously unthinkable. But his first PGA tour event in the South, in his home state of North Carolina, showed the stubborn racist attitude that governed golf in the region. On the first day of the 1961 Greater Greensboro Open at Sedgefield Country Club, Sifford shot a 68 to lead the tournament. That evening as he prepared for the following day, he received a phone call: "You'd better not bring your black ass out on no golf course tomorrow if you know what's good for you," said the anonymous voice on the other end of the line, "we don't allow niggers on our golf course." On the course the next day, he received abuse from some members of the gallery. One shouted out to him from the side of the 12th fairway, "Hey, boy, carry my bag."[351] He finished fourth in the tournament—a remarkable achievement given the conditions. Three years later came the first Black victory on the tour when Pete Brown, a former caddie from Jackson, Mississippi, won the 1964 Waco Turner Open in Texas. In 1967, Sifford had his own day in the sun when he won the Greater Hartford Open in Hartford, Connecticut at 44 years of age. Two years later, he won the L.A. Open for his final victory on tour. His success marked the culmination of a journey from the caddie ranks to the heights of professional golf.[352]

For every Charlie Sifford or Howard Wheeler, though, there were thousands of other Black caddies whose stories have been lost to history. Information about talented players who appear only briefly in the historical record never to appear again reveals the depth of Black golf skill in the caddie ranks of the early 20th-century South. Take, for example, the story of James C. Hamilton, who caddied in Bradenton, Florida in the 1930s. An account of his talents appeared briefly in a 1938 issue of the short-lived magazine, *United Golfer and Other Sports*. A letter to the editor from a White tourist who witnessed Hamilton's play detailed his remarkable talent: "without doubt he is the longest driver in the world and his short game is not far behind." One White golf professional who saw him play said, "I never happened to get a chance to watch Sammy Snead but I'll back this kid against anyone I have ever seen hit." His talents were so remarkable that the White tourist who alerted the magazine to Hamilton's ability attempted to enter him into the USGA-run U.S. Open but, "due to him being a Negro," the application and fee were returned.[353] There were likely many other caddies like Hamilton who possessed a wealth of golfing talent, expertise, and execution, but who did not pursue a golf career.[354] Their names may only have appeared in brief magazine articles or newspaper reports on caddie tournaments, but their existence should not be forgotten in the long history of African American golf.

By becoming excellent golfers, former caddies like Charlie Sifford and Howard Wheeler rebuffed the notion that they were only fit to carry the bags of talented White players. Southern Black caddies reached a skill level that could more than compete with White professionals. That they could become such accomplished players despite the challenges and barriers they faced was a testament to the dedication, commitment, and talents of Black golfers in the Jim Crow South. While their styles may not be encouraged by any modern professional, their golfing excellence reflected the ways that Black Southerners continuously undermined the mindset that saw African Americans as talentless and subservient workers in the region's racial hierarchy.

Almost three quarters of a century after Charlie Sifford carried his last golf bag as a caddie in Charlotte, North Carolina, he went to the White House to receive the Presidential Medal of Freedom from President Barack Obama. A few months later, in February 2015, when Sifford died aged 92, Obama noted that he "was honored to award Charlie the Presidential Medal of Freedom last year, for altering the course of the sport and the country."[355] Perhaps the greatest golfer of all time, Tiger Woods, added to the tributes: "Thanks Charlie for inspiring Pop, who then in turn inspired me and others like us."[356] The "us" who Woods referred to was people of color. Woods' father had learned to play in the 1970s, when public golf courses around the country could no longer ban Black participation in golf. The rising tide of the Civil Rights Movement and the excellence of Black golfers like Sifford threw open golf's gates to all. Yet Sifford's past as a golf caddie in Charlotte received relatively little attention in obituaries or tributes.

Black boys and men who worked tirelessly as bag carriers in the Jim Crow South, then painstakingly honed their golf games, were a vital part of the evolution of golf, which made it possible for Tiger Woods to win 82 official PGA Tour events, 15 major tournaments, and become a global sensation with a net worth of more than $1 billion. Those former caddies—Charlie Sifford, Howard Wheeler, Zeke Hartsfield, John Brooks Dendy, Ralph Richardson, J.C. Hamilton, and thousands of others—deserve proper recognition for turning golf from a game of Black subservience into a game of Black excellence.

FIGURE 12: A young caddie prepares the bag for Pinehurst CC professional Bert Nichols in the 1940s (Tufts Archives).

CHAPTER 6

Cart Path Only

Caddies, Mechanization, and the Search for Profit

One morning in March 1975, Gene Haywood—a caddie who worked at Carolina Country Club in Raleigh, North Carolina—laid back inside a golf cart: the machine that threatened to end his career. "Might stay 'til after lunch, but it doesn't look too good," he said to his colleague, Henry Jones, lounging in an adjacent cart. Neither man seemed convinced that they were likely to see any work that day. "Well, you never know what you're gonna get if you don't show up," said Jones. Years earlier their day would have been filled with two full rounds carrying bags, maybe two, for golfers who walked the course. Only a couple of decades earlier, the course employed dozens of caddies, all of whom showed up on a daily basis, expecting rather than hoping for a day's work. "You couldn't get out here for all the caddies," Haywood remembered. But times had changed and caddying was not what it used to be. By the 1970s, they were lucky to get a single bag in a day. "They sometimes sit out all day and don't earn a dime," said the club professional at

Carolina Country Club. Caddying was no longer a chance at a healthy cash payment for tough but novel outdoor work. Save for at a small number of golf resorts around the country, caddying was an inconsistent wage, rendering it a part-time job best suited to youngsters in search of extra pocket money. On that warm spring day in Raleigh, Henry Jones summed up the mood among many of the nation's long-term caddies in the 1970s, "This is the first time I've come back in years. I don't think I'll be coming back."[357]

It was the same story around the South. In Atlanta, the private courses that once relied on Black men and boys now used golf carts to carry players around their lush fairways. In 1978, the *Atlanta Constitution* marked the end of "an era of golf," with the passing of the last few long-standing Black caddies who had worked the city's country clubs for decades. Roy Jones, the African American caddie master at the city's Ansley Golf Club, passed away that year after a career of almost 65 years as a caddie. He caddied first at the Capital City Club in 1914, where Atlanta's White elites played, and then at Lincoln Golf Club: the one place where Black golfers could play in the city prior to the 1955 ban on segregated facilities. During those years he built a reputation as one of the best Black amateur golfers in the region and the country, winning numerous local prizes and competing in the Southern Amateur championship for Black golfers.[358] Later in his career, he became the caddie master at Ansley Park, and he came to symbolize the dying cadre of Black caddies in the South. Over his final decades as caddie master, he noticed a marked decline in the number of caddies under his command. A few years before he passed, he remarked that "pretty soon, the guy who comes along after me is gonna just put a bag on a cart."[359]

What explains the rapid decline in caddie numbers in the three decades after World War II? While many workers who clung to caddying throughout those years placed the blame solely on the golf cart, the question has never been properly addressed.[360] To those men, the caddie was another victim of the machine age and the continued drive toward automation. Certainly, the popularity of the cart played a significant role, but the decline of caddying as a significant occupation for thousands of Black men in the South cannot be reduced to one single factor. Such a simplistic answer promotes a false sense that the golf cart's ascent was entirely inevitable. Framing caddies as victims of machines also removes the human decisions that brought about the replacement of labor with golf carts. Likewise, the narrative also removes the agency from many Black workers who chose to leave the profession of their own volition. And even if golf carts were the sole reason for the caddie's demise, it's important to understand exactly why the new invention took such a hold. The next two chapters will address the complex decline in the number of Black caddies working the South's fairways and greens, starting with the most commonly cited cause: the golf cart.

Curiously, the story of the decline of caddying in the South actually begins with the mass mobilization of the United States workforce at the onset of World War II. With millions drafted into military service—and millions more employed in industrial manufacturing to fuel the war effort—caddie ranks around the country became increasingly thin.[361] Golf courses and resorts had a problem: a caddie shortage. As one Washington, D.C. journalist pointed out, "The Selective Service Act has taken a good many [caddies] but most of them are working in connection with the defense drive." Defense jobs were "easier to get than they expected and which pay at the lowest more than the tops in caddy wages."[362] At Pinehurst, the caddie master Jack Williams brought in the elderly and those deemed unfit for the Selective Service. In Jekyll Island, Georgia, new caddies were recruited from a local orphanage and housed in nearby barracks.[363] Without plentiful caddies, golf clubs needed an alternative way for their players to traverse the course with ease.

While the golf world initially conceived of temporary solutions to the war-induced problem, it soon became clear that the war had permanently changed the landscape for caddying in the United States. The shortage of caddies that existed during the war never fully ended. Clubs around the country complained that they were unable to furnish all players with caddies, as they had done prior to the war.[364] In the North, where White children still dominated the caddie ranks, the strict adherence to full-time education meant that caddies were in short supply in any season other than summer. In the South, the same problem applied to young Black and White caddies, but southern courses were also hit by a lack of adult Black caddies. Having experienced more fulfilling work during the wartime industrial boom, African American workers were disinclined to return to service labor.[365] As one writer noted, "The old caddies returned from the wars and chose other means of making their dollars."[366] At Pinehurst, the resort treasurer even floated the idea of using White boys to fill the shortage of Black men. Jack Williams, the club's caddie master, responded that he was "not certain if White boys could be used" and that he should "let it go for the time being."[367] The trend created a void in the caddie ranks around the country and "younger boys did not take to caddying," creating a "sad gap due to lack of experience and competence."[368] The shortage that was only meant to last a few years became an almost permanent issue.

The Crisis of Carrying Your Own Clubs

Without plentiful caddies, golf courses devised an alternative way for players to continue playing without carrying their clubs. By the 1940s, golf bags were still fairly heavy and golfers had grown accustomed to playing without the burden of lugging their equipment around for four hours. An early attempt to alleviate the issue came in the form of a push cart, or what was called at the time the "caddie cart." Caddie carts—which later became known as bag carts—were the first invention to allow players to transport their golf bag around the course on their own without carrying it. The first incarnation of the caddie cart appeared during the Great Depression. A golfer named Herbert Strong (not to be confused with the course designer of the same name, who died in 1944) wanted to create an alternative to caddies given the financial difficulties that much of the golf playing population encountered at the time.[369] The depression led many golfers to save money by avoiding employing caddies. In Atlanta, the financial woes of golfers were such that some who continued playing paid their caddies with "I.O.U.'s scribbled on the back of business cards."[370]

Multiple manufacturers entered the caddie cart market in the early 1940s, but the designs of early models remained fairly consistent: they usually had two wheels on the sides, a central area to rest the golf bag, and a long handle. Caddie carts were usually made using sturdy metal and were finely balanced to allow the golf bag to remain in an upright position. Golfers would push and pull the caddie cart around the course between shots. Such early incarnations of the caddie cart did not widely catch on, however, and employing a caddie remained standard throughout the 1930s.

It was not until the 1940s that golfers began to use the caddie cart more widely. Many clubs around the country turned to caddie carts out of necessity. One 1941 article asked, "How long will members of private clubs continue to support a club where they cannot play unless they carry their own clubs?"[371] In response to the crisis, golf clubs turned to caddie carts that allowed golfers to continue playing despite the caddie shortage. Amid the spirit of sacrifice throughout the war, golfers too had to sacrifice the luxury of employing a caddie.

A shortage of caddies did not alone guarantee the long-term adoption of caddie carts—it was the popularity of the new invention that ensured its success. Despite initial skepticism, golfers appreciated that they could continue playing golf without having to carry their own bag throughout the caddie shortage. According to one article in the magazine *Golfdom*, "First a player will timidly try one and may feel a little self-conscious rolling the little cart along the fairway." After the round, though, golfers felt fresher than when they carried their bags and noticed that their shoulders did not ache, and their play also benefited. Players preferred pulling a cart to carrying their own bags.[372] Some also found reasons to choose caddie carts even when caddies were available. Individuals who lacked golfing talent and who were self-conscious about their abilities realized that the use of the caddie cart meant they could avoid embarrassing themselves in front of others. One writer even claimed that some women golfers chose to use caddie carts because the presence of caddies curtailed their free speech on the course.[373] Frugal golfers also found reason to turn to the bag cart over the use of caddies. At most courses the cost of renting a caddie cart was lower than hiring a caddie, and many individuals bought their own bag carts, cutting down on caddie fees permanently. *Golfdom* reported that "reduced expense with light bags and bag carts is getting play from plenty who might curtail their play because of caddie costs."[374] The convenience and affordability of caddie carts, coupled with continuing shortages even after the war, ensured that the invention was a widespread addition to golf courses around the country.[375]

Golf courses and country clubs were delighted to fulfill the demand for push carts when they realized the increased revenue that the invention brought. "These carts have come to my course to stay, and boy they sure do add to my income in days when income is not too easy to increase," said one professional employed at a country club.[376] When golf courses first felt the strain of the caddie shortage, they filled the gap by investing in fleets of push carts and renting them out to members and visitors. What courses quickly realized was that the carts soon paid off the initial investment, and once the costs were covered, every subsequent rental represented pure profit for the golf course. One Chicago course found that in the first month of use, the rental fees recuperated almost half the price the club paid for the entire fleet of bag carts.[377] By 1947, revenues from rentals and sales made bag carts a multimillion-dollar industry. And golf courses felt the benefit of encouraging the use of caddie carts. Public and private courses around the country could leverage the caddie cart boom by offering incoming club professionals a share of the profits from rentals. In turn they could attract the best professionals to their club. Around the country, clubs also undertook much-needed improvements to their courses and facilities on the back of the newfound revenue from cart rentals.[378] The important difference between caddies and carts—in the eyes of golf course management—was that caddies pocketed the entirety of the caddie fee, and the club saw no direct financial benefit from the arrangement. Of course, the courses' finances benefited indirectly from caddies, as caddies allowed players to play more golf than they could on their own. With bag cart rentals, however, the golf industry found an entirely new revenue source that generated a passive income over decades. For municipal courses starved of investment and private courses in search of added profits, the promise of increased revenue from caddie carts made the two-wheeled bag carriers an appealing alternative to the employment of caddies.

Although golf clubs were quick to adopt bag carts, the change was not without growing pains. Golf courses who ordered fleets of push carts needed to find space for their new apparatus. One writer in 1950 noted that "cart storage is proving to be a problem," and "carts in some instances must be taken from a storage room that in most clubs is still makeshift."[379] Even by 1953, according to a report in *Golfdom*, very few clubs had "adequate storage for bag carts."[380] A similar survey of golf professionals employed at clubs around the country found that the "greatest single factor contributing to the shortage of storage space," was "the increase in the popularity of the caddy cart."[381] Those in the golf industry highlighted the need for push carts to undergo repairs, and for courses to employ individuals dedicated to administering bag carts during peak playing times.[382] What became clear was that manual bag carts had changed the way that country clubs and resorts thought about the game, yet the golf industry had only just begun to realize the longer-term effects. A writer named Verne Wickham prophesied in 1946 about the potential wide-ranging impacts. He argued that golf course designers would have to add "bag-cart traffic" to the traditional considerations of "topography, direction of prevailing wind, or type of golf course desired," when conceptualizing their plans.[383]

Not every country club or resort welcomed the push cart as a replacement for caddies. As a sport that places great importance on tradition and custom, golf often changes at a glacial pace. Caddies had been a part of the game in the United States since the game was first played in the country, so it was unlikely that they would be removed from the landscape quickly. Some golf professionals who oversaw operations at country clubs felt the need for a mixture of caddies and bag carts, allowing for individuals to make their own choice. One superintendent at a course in Illinois argued in 1956—more than a decade after the start of the caddie shortage—that "it is a must to have experienced caddies and good caddy carts."[384] At some courses caddies and bag carts went hand in hand, and bag carts even helped to solve the caddie shortage as smaller and weaker child caddies who could not carry large bags were able to use a caddie cart when working. Clubs found that allowing caddies to use bag carts meant that the club could "use many smaller boys who otherwise would be ruled out because of their size."[385] Some players also preferred it when their caddies used caddie carts, because it reduced the guilt of having the caddie carry such a heavy bag full of equipment. When a caddie used a bag cart, the player could bring all his clubs with him, as opposed to leaving some behind to "make the load easier for the lad."[386] At least in the early years of caddie carts, it did not seem a foregone conclusion that mechanization would replace caddies.

Elite private clubs were the most reluctant golf courses in the country to replace caddies with caddie carts. Many of the most exclusive clubs—steeped in their traditions and storied pasts—hoped to avoid the adoption of bag carts in lieu of caddies. One writer described a "prejudice against pulling bag carts … at numerous 'prestige' clubs," where "they wouldn't have thought of pulling carts."[387] The reasons for their reluctance for change were unclear, but a few likely scenarios exist. Firstly, many old golf clubs have historically been slow to adapt to changes on all fronts. Caked in tradition and custom, change moves slowly at such institutions.

Finances likely also played a part in some courses' reluctance toward caddie carts. Elite private clubs hardly needed to concern themselves with chasing the next dollar in profit from bag carts—they had plenty of income from their expensive membership rates and green fees. Wealthy members of elite private clubs also did not have the same cost concerns as other golfers who chose bag carts over caddies for their cost-saving benefit. Some members of prestigious courses likely appreciated that hiring caddies was a sign of their wealth and their status in society. Just as hiring servants had been a tangible symbol of an individual's social class earlier in the century—hiring caddies while others used bag carts—offered some players a means of conspicuous consumption. In the early 1950s, at least at the most elite clubs, it seemed unlikely that caddie ranks around the country were set for a rapid decline.

The Contraption Found on Courses From Coast to Coast

A continuing caddie shortage and the success of the caddie cart led directly to another invention that revolutionized the game of golf: the golf cart. With an electric or gas engine, seats for two players, and enough space on the back to hold two golf bags, the golf cart made it easier than ever to traverse the nation's courses. Initially known as "golf cars," to distinguish them from manually pushed or pulled bag carts (also known as caddie carts), motorized wagons that carried golfers and their equipment quickly became known as "golf carts."[388] Exactly who invented the motorized golf cart or where it first appeared are matters of dispute. Lyman Beecher, a member at Biltmore Forest Country Club in Asheville, pioneered an early forerunner to the motorized cart in 1935 at his home club. His invention resembled a rickshaw, with two large wheels running alongside a chair for one golfer and a shelf on the back for their golf clubs. A long wooden handle extended from the front of the cart, which required two caddies to pull.[389] In the rugged terrain of Biltmore Forest CC, the caddies likely had a torrid time pulling the device around the course. The early cart may have appealed to some of the game's lazier players, but—given that it required two caddies to operate—it did nothing to solve a caddie shortage.

Beecher's pull cart did not receive widespread adoption, but the motorized vehicles that followed certainly did. Some accounts claim that the electric cart first appeared in Texas, where players started converting Jeeps and Crosley cars into vehicles that could carry four players and their equipment.[390] Another origin story claimed that the first model of golf cart "rolled up to the first tee of an Oak Park,

[Illinois] golf course," in the early 1940s. A few years later, a motorized cart known as the "Arthritis Special" was said to have been used in Houston, and another adapted car was used by a California cardiac patient.[391] These first sightings of golf carts were sporadic and undertaken by individuals who sought to ease their round and add a bit of novelty to the game. It was not until 1953 that companies began selling golf carts on the market. The first golf courses to adopt the motorized carts were on the west coast and in the southwest. A Long Beach, California company named Autoette Inc. may have been the first to popularize the invention. In fact, golfers were not the original target audience for the invention—some accounts claim that the vehicle was meant to make transportation easier for those with disabilities. Nonetheless, by 1953 the company was selling three-wheeled electric vehicles to golf courses. That same year, President Eisenhower used electric golf carts in both Palm Springs, California and Augusta, Georgia, and soon the contraption could be found on courses from coast to coast.[392]

The golf cart swept through the game and into every corner of the country at an astonishing pace. In 1950, not a single course in the United States used motorized vehicles to move players around the course, yet only eight years later in 1958, more than three quarters of private country clubs in the country used golf carts.[393] By 1962, there were more than 100,000 golf carts on the country's 5,000 golf courses.[394] In a 1966 survey, 92% of golf professionals employed at golf courses around the country reported that golf carts were available at their course, and that only 59% of those courses had caddies available to players.[395] The golf cart's unceasing rise continued, and by 1969 the total golf carts in the United States reached 205,700 and was projected to rise to 243,800 only one year later.[396] In a sport that usually adapts to change at a snail's pace, no other novel innovation or product spread as quickly as the golf cart. In 1950, the thought of riding a vehicle over the lush fairways of America's golf courses would likely have been met with laughter in the nation's clubhouses. Within only two decades, playing golf without a cart was unusual.

The motorized golf cart became so widespread, in part, because of demand from golfers. The 1950s and '60s witnessed a rapid growth in consumer demand for products that harnessed the newest advancements in technology, and golf was not spared from the trend. The prosperity of White suburban families in the post-war era allowed them to afford the latest home goods, cars, and toys. In all areas of society—whether that be the workplace, the home, or the golf course—consumers demanded products that made their lives easier or more enjoyable. As one manager of a golf cart manufacturing company put it, "In an era of two cars for every suburban garage, the attitude of the entire golfing family is 'why walk, even on the golf course.'" Where previously golfers played for exercise, he noted, by 1960 they played for fresh air and therefore "approve, even demand, golf cars."[397] Golf carts enabled some players to continue playing the game well into their older years, when previously they might have been forced to give up the sport if they could not walk the course. The invention also opened up golf to those with disabilities who were previously kept from playing.[398]

Demand also increased due to the widespread visibility of the carts in the national media. Celebrity golfers, none greater than President Eisenhower, endorsed the golf cart and soon the product became associated with luxury and prestige: a phenomenon that did not follow the bag carts that preceded motorized golf carts.[399] One phrase more than any other dominated the discussion around golf carts in the golf media of the 1950s and '60s: it was the notion that carts were "here to stay."[400] Previously cynical golf stakeholders slowly realized that the golf cart was not a fad. T.M. Baumgardner, the course superintendent at the Sea Island Golf Resort in coastal Georgia summed up the mood in 1963 when he noted that "whether we like it or not, I think we all agree that golf cars are here to stay and that their use will probably greatly increase rather than decrease."[401]

While the culture of automation in golf appealed to players because it promised to make the game easier, it appealed to those in the industry because of the financial benefits. The golf cart was one of several changes that promised to "cut costs far beyond the figure that resourceful and experienced [superintendents] have been able to reach by rigorous economy."[402] Manufacturers who sold golf carts directly advertised profit potential as much as the comfort or ease of their products. An early advert for golf carts made by a company called Victor, led with the tagline "Make More Profit Renting 1956 Victor Electri-Car."[403] A similar ad for Pargo golf carts, manufactured in Charlotte, North Carolina, encouraged golf course managers to buy the electric carts "For Personal Fun.... Or Profitable Fleet."[404] Just like with the earlier invention, the caddie cart, country clubs and resorts around the nation understood that the electric golf cart offered profit-making potential through rentals to their members and guests.

Golf courses that sought to make as much money as possible saw the golf cart as a gold mine. As one superintendent noted, "so far as income is concerned, golf cars are the best things that happened since slot machines."[405] At golf courses that existed to make profit like semi-private and public courses, the rental fees from golf carts were an easy way to pad their yearly accounts. Over the seven years from 1963 to 1968, Pinehurst reported more than half a million dollars of profit from golf carts alone.[406] A 1966 survey of golf professionals found that more than two-thirds of country clubs generated more than 10 percent of their income from golf car rentals, and about one-quarter of clubs made 25 percent of their income from rentals.[407] The profit came from both receiving rental fees and attracting new golfers who previously played at courses that were yet to adopt the cart. For golfers who were not members at private courses, choosing where to play might be dictated by the attraction of the cart. At private country clubs that existed "not for profit but for the pleasure and relaxation of its members," the course management still saw the benefits of a new avenue of revenue generation to alleviate any budgetary issues elsewhere.[408] Firstly, they needed to attract the best golf professional to work at their course, and offering professionals a share of rental cart profit made them an attractive workplace. Secondly, they realized that the revenue could be used to make improvements to the course and the facilities which would, in turn, benefit the membership.[409] Likewise, municipal courses that existed for public recreation were often saddled with minuscule budgets and low investment. The use of carts aided in making them self-sufficient. Even if the carts were not used to produce profits, golf clubs certainly benefited from the newfound revenue.

The Marvels of New Technology

The replacement of caddies with bag carts and electric golf cars in the 1950s and '60s was part of a wider societal trend toward automation and mechanization. Technological advancements combined with mass consumption left the country flush with cutting-edge gadgets that promised to make life easier for Americans.[410] If a task could be made easier and/or give people more free time, inventors and corporations tried to harness new technology to do so. Golf was not spared from the craze for automation. Herb Graffis—a consistent writer in the golf business magazine, *Golfdom*—pointed to a "New Frontier" of "revolutionary changes" in the industry in the '60s. Chief among the golf revolution were the "radical changes in the caddy situation," caused by the golf car and bag cart. But that was only part of a wider culture of automation according to Graffis; other areas of the sport, he believed, were set to benefit from the marvels of new technology. Clubhouses—where golfers ate and drank after playing—were set to "have automatic food machine service that will provide a quality and variety of menu." Likewise, course maintenance would feel the tangible benefits of advancements in "methods, materials, machines, and grasses."[411] Amid the nationwide craze for harnessing modern technology to make life easier, the golf industry did not want to be left behind.

The golf cart only truly prevailed because those in the golf industry built a new interconnected economy around it. In the mid-to-late-1950s, it was not guaranteed that the golf cart would become ubiquitous, even if demand was high. Golf management around the country could have banned golf carts in favor of bag carts or caddies. Yet when clubs made the decision to adopt golf carts, they placed themselves into a web of codependent corporations and financial institutions that was almost impossible to escape from.

An economic and infrastructural system made golf carts irreplaceable at most courses in the country. The costs of buying and operating a fleet of bag carts or motorized golf carts brought the golf industry closer to financial services in the United States. Many country clubs and resorts could not afford the initial investment required to buy and service dozens of golf carts outright, so the golf cart companies offered financing schemes that allowed cash-strapped golf clubs to purchase their fleets over time with monthly payments and interest.[412] This was especially true for courses where the on-site golf professional operated the fleet, because they often had to furnish the carts with their personal money.[413] When golf courses paid for their fleets in installments, the full payments could take years. Other companies rented their carts to golf courses that were perhaps less convinced by the long-term viability of the new technology.

Even courses that could afford to purchase carts outright understood that the carts had to operate for years to return a profit on the investment. An average cart in the early 1960s cost around $1,000 to purchase outright—roughly $10,000 today, adjusted for inflation.[414] By 1963, the Athens Country Club in Georgia operated 20 golf carts. The club superintendent noted that the operating costs totaled $7,350 per year. Spread over the 150 uses that each of the 20 carts got each year, the operating costs came to $2.45 per usage. Given that the club bought the carts for roughly $20,000, and that they rented them out for $6 per usage ($3.55 profit per usage), it would take almost two full years for the club to begin making profit on their initial investment.[415] This conservative calculation presumes that uptake from golfers started at the level of 150 rounds per year. It also does not take into account the associated costs of constructing the facilities and paths needed to house the carts and to prevent them from damaging the course. Athens Country Club spent $5,000 alone on building storage facilities exclusively for their golf carts, and one superintendent in California claimed it took $10,000 per year in labor and materials to maintain paths.[416] While clubs that invested in motorized golf carts made money eventually, they had to make a long-term commitment. Likewise, golf professionals and golf clubs that turned to banks to finance their investment in golf carts became tied to the revenue that the carts generated as a means of paying back the loans they had taken out. Finances and the search for profit ensured that carts were "here to stay."

Carts became irreplaceable in the two years that it took for them to begin producing profit, because their use required vast infrastructure investment. Existing facilities and courses were not designed with the cart in mind. In 1969, Pinehurst's head of golf operations, Peter V. Tufts, succinctly summarized the double-edged sword of carts when he stated that "the electric golf cart operation at the club is a thriving, growing, leaping, profitable monster that now might be best described as an Excedrin headache #264."[417] One superintendent noted that carts brought with them the need to "construct car stables with expansion in mind," while also ensuring space for "good ventilation (for battery fumes), adequate electric power, adequate room for car rotation, areas for repair, washing and painting, an office, and plenty of storage for spare parts."[418] At Pinehurst, the need for a cart-storage basement could "not be postponed any longer as the servicing of carts … reached unmanageable proportions."[419]

Alongside clubhouse changes, management redesigned their courses around the golf cart to prevent (as much as possible) the damage that carts did to the fairways. Country clubs and resorts around the country began constructing blacktop paths throughout their courses that protected the grass. Of course, any golf hole that crossed small rivers or creeks required a new bridge that could hold the weight of a golf cart. These infrastructural investments came at a cost. One superintendent noted that "cart paths are costly," and "bridges in their cheapest form are expensive."[420] Having made such vast changes to their buildings and landscape, and at substantial costs, golf courses tied themselves into a certain future in which removing the golf carts would reverse years of investment of time, labor, and changes to the landscape.

By the middle of the century, the golf cart was a primary concern when constructing new golf courses. A country club in Jacksonville, Florida, centered golf carts in their planning of their clubhouse and course. Early in the club's plans, the architect was made aware of the electrical charging needs and was tasked with ensuring that the "membership and their fleet of cars can grow."[421] In many ways, golf carts were only "here to stay" because the golf industry made drastic infrastructural changes that made carts an essential part of the game's operation.

The adoption of motorized golf carts spawned a flowing river of money that brought a wide array of stakeholders into the game of golf and created an entire industry around the cart. Alongside the financial sector, the insurance industry soon joined the golf cart boom as golf course management sought to protect themselves from legal disputes over injuries caused by golf carts. Of course, it was rarely the carts that caused injuries—it was the drivers that did. Pinehurst president Richard S. Tufts neatly summarized the painful mix of golfers and carts on the course. "One of the great problems," he proclaimed, "is that you have to anticipate what the golfer will do, and you can be sure that whatever it may be it will be stupid."[422] By 1966 it was commonly accepted that golf clubs "must and should carry insurance," because "if the brakes fail on a golf cart and a user runs into a tree or stone wall … who pays the bill?"[423] Quickly, the scale of investment in golf cart insurance policies spawned another new financial interest in golf: specialized country club insurance consultants. One consultancy agency offered "not to sell clubs insurance, but to advise them on proper insurance they require on a fee basis."[424] The transportation and hauling sector industry also cashed in on the golf cart boom. Moving companies advertised in golf trade magazines. The Trans-American Van Service, which previously specialized in worldwide moving services, saw an opportunity to make money in shipping golf carts. They claimed to offer "the logical way to ship golf cars," removing the country club's headache of collection and transporting the carts.[425] Companies that previously had nothing to do with golf became widely invested in the success of golf carts.

Just as with the caddie cart, though, some old and elite golf clubs were resistant to adopting the golf cart. The old guard at historic resorts and clubs shouted into the wind in their fight to maintain caddie ranks. "For gosh sakes, lets [sic] not buy golf carts," wrote Richard Tufts to his brother, years after he handed over control of the club, "I have hollered for years about doing more for our caddies."[426] On courses of historical significance, the damage and infrastructural changes required for carts made them undesirable too. At Pinehurst in 1975, 12 years after carts were introduced to the resort, management banned their use on the famed No. 2 course, citing the need "to preserve the quality which Pinehurst No. 2 has become so famous for."[427] But these old and storied courses were the exception to the rule. For the most part, the golf cart's spread was as fast as it was sprawling. By the mid-1970s, the country's golf courses were grassy highways.

Where golf carts went, money followed, and the widespread promises of the golf cart's financial spoils created a behemoth of an industry that became self-sustaining. Golf cart producers actively promoted the cart on its potential to generate profit for a wide range of industrial interests, and tied the newfound industry to perceived American greatness. William Freund, the manager of the electric cart division of Adding Machine Company, proclaimed that "In America—land of opportunity—industrial growth has made our nation great." He claimed that those who cooperate with the growth of the golf cart "have every opportunity of participating in the benefits it brings."[428] Golf cart manufacturers even formed a trade association that further entrenched the cart in the fabric of the game.[429] From manufacturing to infrastructure to financial institutions, insurance, and transportation, the golf cart spawned an interconnected industry that survived on the continued growth of the motorized bag carriers. According to William Freund and others in the golf cart industry, the growth of motorized golf carts "brings more business and more activity for everyone related to the game of golf."[430] His definition of "everyone" forgot one important and historic individual: the caddie.

Those who stood to benefit from the introduction of carts saw no reason to stop the flow of money that the carts created. It was a newfound system that spawned a previously unfathomable sustained income. Importantly, the money that created this industry was the same money that used to go into the pockets of golf caddies around the country. When country clubs, resorts, and municipal courses began diverting that money into their own accounts, they started a chain of events that made many people rich at the expense of caddies. The funds that formerly paid caddies now went to the golf course, and then onto cart companies, construction companies, transportation companies, insurance firms and consultants, and into a wide range of corporate interests. For those who stood to benefit from the new golf cart industry, the demise of caddying was a just another consequence of automation and mechanization's profit-making potential. The replacement of caddies with carts was fueled by the search for profit and efficiency in the boardrooms of country clubs, manufacturers, and financial services.

CHAPTER 7

"Not a Man's Job"

The Decline of Caddying Amid Social Change

One evening in April 1953, along Sand Bar Ferry Road in Augusta, Georgia, the lights from the nightclubs and bars added a neon glow to the mild spring air. Rich's Club hummed with anticipation. The White folks at Rich's that evening—most of whom worked at the hydrogen-bomb plant over the river in South Carolina—were there to see a local band. At around nine o'clock, as they lined the oval bar and sipped their drinks, two of the three-piece band made their way onto the stage: a singer and a pianist, both Black men, dressed in blue jackets, white shirts, and black ties. The crowd took note of the absence of the drummer. Murmurs of discontent among the revelers at Rich's spilled over: "We want Cemetery!," came the cry from one impatient audience member. "Where's that boy?," another shouted. At quarter past nine, the man known as Cemetery walked onto the stage, his outfit ever-so-slightly disheveled as if he had gotten dressed in a hurry. His huge presence in the room did not match his modest stature at only 5'6", 135 pounds, and his face showed evidence of his age, 53. As the crowd cheered his arrival, Cemetery took the microphone in one hand and held up his other to silence the crowd. "I apologize to you folks for being late 'cause I knew you all been waiting for me to play," he explained, "but, ladies and gentlemen, I been unavoidably detained by the President of the United States." As he took his place behind the drums the crowd cheered and applauded. With a nod from the pianist, the trio burst into their version of "Chattanooga Choo Choo."[431]

For a period of time in the 1950s, Willie "Cemetery" Perteet was famous for being a golf caddie rather than a musician: drumming was simply his passion, not his profession. On that day, he had been "unavoidably detained" by President Dwight D. Eisenhower on the golf course at Augusta National, the home of the Masters Tournament. Every year, in the week after the tournament, Eisenhower vacationed in Augusta. The tradition started in 1948 when Eisenhower made his first visit to the course. Caddie master Henry Williams knew that someone of Eisenhower's importance needed a first-class caddie; Eisenhower was not yet president, but his reputation as the Supreme Commander of the Allied Expeditionary Force during World War II made him a celebrated national figure. Williams remembered

FIGURE 13: Willie "Cemetery" Perteet and Eisenhower at Augusta National in 1953 (Getty Images).

why he chose Perteet as Eisenhower's caddie: "Cemetery—now he's mature. He's got sense ... knows the course and he knows his clubs." From 1948 to 1957, Perteet was Eisenhower's only caddie at Augusta National, and it made him a relatively well-known figure. In 1953, just months after Eisenhower's inauguration, *Life Magazine* ran a four-page feature about the President's caddie.[432] His name and image (Figure 13) appeared in newspapers around the country when Eisenhower made his trips to Augusta—and the President made plenty of them; some estimates suggest that he played more than 700 full rounds of golf (and 300 practice sessions) around the country during his eight years in office.[433] Eisenhower became so associated with Augusta National that they named a tree there in his honor—a tree he lobbied to have removed from the course that he often hit with his tee shot. As Eisenhower's dedicated Augusta caddie, Perteet became a minor celebrity.[434]

More Important Things Than Toting Golf Bags

"Cemetery" rose to fame at a time of rapid racial upheaval in the United States, and his position as a caddie to the president became a point of interest to many commentators, Black and White. The Civil Rights Movement was gathering pace, and questions about Black labor went hand-in-hand with calls for equal rights. For most of the preceding half-century, the racial hierarchy of the Jim Crow South largely restricted Black workers to jobs in servile positions, including caddying. By the late 1950s, however, discontent among African American workers spilled into outright demands for equality in hiring practices. Amid the hotbed of political action, Black leaders and commentators questioned whether African Americans should continue working in service jobs for White employers. The movement demanded better and more dignified jobs for African American workers.[435]

Perteet, the most visible caddie in the country, became a point of discussion. He was a Black man, well into the second half of his life, who served wealthy and powerful White men as they went about their leisure pursuits. A few years after he made an appearance in

Life, Augusta National replaced Perteet as Eisenhower's caddie with a younger and fitter worker. The *Baltimore Afro American*—one of the biggest Black newspapers in the country—reported the change with an accompanying editorial titled, "Not a Man's Job." The editors commented that "We like to think that there are important things in this world for a grown man besides toting golf bags around a course even for the president of the United States."[436]

The golf cart alone does not explain why caddying collapsed. The changing attitudes toward caddying and the upheaval happening around the South certainly played a significant role in the decline of caddying as a profession for Black workers.

The end of World War II ushered in debate about service jobs. Black men who served in the United States armed forces around the world expected to return to a country that offered them more opportunity than when they left. The so-called "Double-V" campaign focused on fighting racism abroad and racism at home. By sacrificing themselves for the good of the country, the defeat of fascism, and the protection of democracy, Black Americans hoped to demonstrate that they deserved absolute freedom and equality.[437] Such hopes extended to the job market.

During the war years of the early '40s, caddie ranks around the South had been greatly depleted, as Black youngsters enrolled in the war effort.[438] On their return, they hoped for well-paying and skilled jobs that moved them out of service labor. One report warned that "there would be trouble" if the cities of the South continued to offer Black workers only the same employment opportunities they had when the war started.[439] Many returning Black veterans found that the jobs they wanted were not available. In a 1947 pamphlet entitled "Our Negro Veterans," the American Veterans Committee noted that in more than two-thirds of cities, the number one desire among Black veterans was for better jobs. The pamphlet stated that "in most places Negro veterans found only menial old-line Negro jobs" in service and unskilled occupations.[440] The differences between the "old-line" and the new-line jobs were clear: African American workers wanted to use the skills they had, to be fully and fairly compensated, and to avoid menial and service labor at the behest of Whites.

After the war ended, Black leaders and writers encouraged African American workers to look beyond service labor. Industrial development opened doors to Black workers that did not exist in the first third of the century. W.E.B. Du Bois noticed the structural changes that the war had accelerated in 1945, noting that "We have for the first time in modern history practically full employment in the United States with high wage." The new phenomenon, he pointed out, meant that "The members of the laboring classes are getting away from menial service," because they did "not want to work under social stigma."[441]

No longer confined entirely to service jobs, African Americans found work in unionized industrial occupations, government jobs, and less-menial service roles. Such jobs offered better pay and career stability than previous work.[442] In Augusta, Georgia, where Willie Perteet had been caddying for a number of years, the labor landscape was also changing. Take, for example, the hydrogen plant across the Savannah River, which employed most of the White folks who came to watch Perteet play drums in Rich's Club. When it first opened in 1951, the local Black leadership complained of discriminatory hiring practices that confined Black workers to only menial tasks, if any.[443] However, less than a year later, the site employed 5,000 Black workers with around one in five in technical or skilled roles.[444] While secure, well paying, and fulfilling jobs were certainly not plentiful for Black workers, the outlook in Augusta was better than it had been prior to the war. The best jobs also took Black men out of occupations in which one of their key duties was to demonstrate subservience to White Americans.

Amid national changes to the labor market, golf mainly appeared in the Black press during discussions of Black professional golfers, and the push for desegregated golfing facilities. The coverage of successful Black athletes highlighted the skills and talents of players like Charlie Sifford, Bill Spiller, and Teddy Rhodes, and promoted the notion that Black golfers were as good as White golfers. Newspapers acknowledged that such players came from the caddie ranks but, by the 1950s, papers emphasized their skills as players over their caddying capabilities. After Jackie Robinson broke the color line in baseball in 1947, the Black press demanded the same rights for the best Black golfers. Once the barriers in baseball and football were behind them, asked one reported, "what about professional golf?"[445]

In many of the articles that explained the history of Black golf in the United States, writers charted an almost rags-to-riches storyline. In this narrative, caddying was seen as a means to an end, as opposed to a worthy occupation in itself. The best Black golfers in the country were discussed as "graduates of the caddy lists on exclusively white country clubs."[446] One writer in Atlanta noted that the mission of the local Black golf club—Lincoln Golf and Country Club—was to help youngsters "come up from the ranks of caddies and develop into full stature golfers."[447] Stories that framed caddies as less than "full stature" golfers helped create a narrative of Black golf, in which caddying was seen as something of the past. A 1951 article in the *New York Amsterdam News*, which told the long history of golf in the United States, discussed the progress of Black golf from a time when "Negro youths ... picked up the fine points of the skill while serving as caddies," to now when "a lot of ground has been gained by Negroes in the way of integration."[448] In the post-war era, when African Americans wanted equality in leisure and sports, the Black press relegated caddying to the rearview mirror and demanded that Black golfers—professional or amateur—be given access to golf courses as human beings rather than employees.

In the eyes of many, caddying represented some of the more undesirable aspects of Black work in the first half of the 20th century, not least subservience to White bosses. In 1964, a satirical article in the *Mississippi Free Press* highlighted the opinion that caddying as an African American was synonymous with acquiescence to White demands. The piece listed parody job postings at Mississippi governor Ross R. Barnett's mansion. "HELP WANTED:" began one listing, "Employer looking for Negro policeman. Applicants must have past experience as a caddy for a city official, and should not expect to arrest white people."[449] The fake job listing suggested that the stereotyping of Black caddies as Uncle Toms had become conventional in the Black press. At times, the press framed caddying as the opposite end of the spectrum from the kinds of jobs that Black workers deserved. In one such piece, a writer argued that President Eisenhower would be capable of understanding certain issues "even if he had no more intellect than a golf caddy."[450] In many such instances, writers performed some disservice to the caddies who performed their work with dignity, talent, and without caricaturing themselves as Uncle Toms. The widespread reputation of Black caddies in the Black press did not accurately reflect the reality for those who performed the job on a daily basis. Black caddies may have professionalized their work, but it did not spare them from criticism. Since caddying in the South was a job tainted with the region's racial structures, it became easy for Black writers to dismiss it as an unwelcome holdover from the darkest days of Jim Crow.

As African Americans increasingly occupied industrial and professional jobs in the mid-20th century, the clichéd Black service worker became more of a stereotype than a reflection of reality. The Black press and media intensified their criticism of White typecasting of Black workers as a monolithic servile group. One 1961 investigation into the appearances of African Americans on television explicitly referred to Black caddies as a White stereotype. The report noted that if one added the appearances of African Americans as performers to the "percentage of domestics and caddies in sports," then more than half of all appearances of Blacks on television were in "traditional roles assigned to the Negro, namely performing or personal service."[451] In their claims that Black caddies were a demeaning stereotype, these reports revealed a belief that Black workers should not choose to occupy such roles. Why, one might ask, would someone want a job that was traditionally assigned to African Americans, when they could choose something different in the newfound job market of the mid-century? Over the course of the 1940s, '50s, and '60s, the popular Black opinions about caddying and other service jobs changed from begrudging acceptance of such labor as a symptom of the racially segregated labor market, to a belief that such roles were holdovers from a previous era.

Black liberation movements abandoned the theory that African Americans could progress by dedicating themselves to work. In turn, Black service labor for White bosses was seen as a relic of the past.

The End of Cemetery

Amid the changing attitude toward caddies was Willie Perteet—the most famous caddie in America. His fame peaked in the months after Eisenhower's inauguration in 1953, and he was featured in a number of articles in the White and Black press. One piece received particular attention. The article was written for the Associated Press and was therefore disseminated widely in the country's newspapers. The *Chicago Daily News* ran the story with the headline "'Cemetery,' Ike's Caddy, Is a Live One, Yassuh." The article dripped with offensive dialect that portrayed Perteet as a dimwitted and forgetful-but-loyal worker. Unsurprisingly, Black leaders found the article in poor taste. The leader of the National Association for the Advancement of Colored People (NAACP) at the time, Walter White, printed part of the article without comment in a column that cast doubt over whether Eisenhower was really likely to support racial equality. How could African Americans expect such a President, who still hired Black men to carry his golf clubs, to usher in racial change, was White's insinuation.[452] Harvey Lee Moon, the press secretary for the NAACP, saw the article and immediately wrote to the president of the Associated Press. "Evidently," Moon wrote, "there is no policy against the release of offensive dialect stories about Negro citizens." He also demanded that the Associated Press "not repeat this kind of misrepresentation of any group."[453] Moon or White did not criticize Perteet as an individual, yet they bemoaned the fact that Black workers still served in roles that allowed the White press to misrepresent the entire race as dimwitted and menial service workers. One concerned reader wrote to the Black newspaper, the *Pittsburgh Courier*, convinced that "white America should have some concern and even shame that the environment and educational climate of Georgia are still producing 'Cemeterys.'"[454] To some, the continued existence of Black caddies was a sign that the United States had much work to do in the pursuit of racial equality.

Perteet found himself in the headlines again in 1957 when he lost his job as Eisenhower's caddie. The Augusta National club professional felt that Perteet was getting too slow for the president, who supposedly played the game at a rapid pace.[455] Usually the firing of a Black worker with little cause would be fuel for Black leaders and newspapers to scorn the offending employer—especially if the employer happened to be the president. In this case, writers could have highlighted Augusta National's hypocrisy in claiming that Perteet was too old to caddie for a man at least a decade his senior. But for Perteet, there were no voices in the press calling for him to be reinstated. Instead, the *Baltimore Afro-American* used the story as a platform to deride those who chose to work in such roles. "It would seem to us," the editorial noted, "that even in Augusta a grown man should find a more important job these days than caddying on the golf course." In emphasizing the point, the article likened caddying to butlering and barbering—professions that "may have grown into professional status."[456] To the Black press in the 1950s, caddying no longer represented simply another example of one of the many service jobs available to Black men, as it had done earlier in the century. The image of a Black caddie for a White player, no matter how professional or skilled the caddie, was incongruent with the idea of Black liberation. The Civil Rights Movement demanded that African Americans become central characters in the nation, and not the supporting cast. On the golf course, this manifested as golfers, not caddies.

As winds of racial change blew over the country, doubts about the value of service labor combined to portray caddying as a historical relic. In 1960, the great poet and writer Langston Hughes dreamed up a potential future for the United States. His satirically-named character Jesse B. Simple—who Hughes framed as an everyman and folk philosopher—imagined his platform if he was running for president that year. "Me, Jesse B., for president of the United States," he began, "champion of free beer and equal rights for all in Harlem or Houston, Manhattan or Mississippi." From the "golf links of Augusta, GA., to the number pads of New York," said Simple, "regardless of race, let there be white caddies for black golfers and black writers for white numbers players."[457] During the Civil Rights Movement of the 1950s and '60s, Hughes highlighted the alternative country that was possible: a nation where African Americans were equal participants in society. A nation where African Americans were golfers in their own right. A nation where individuals like Willie "Cemetery" Perteet could walk down the storied fairways of Augusta National and employ a caddie of any race to carry his bag. In this new United States, the Black press asked: Was caddying a job still worth doing?

Black caddies were caught at a crossroads in the 1950s and '60s. Their role was simultaneously as skilled as it ever had been, and also disparaged as a relic of Jim Crow America. With other job opportunities available, it made sense for Black workers to avoid the roles that were tarred with the brush of the nation's troubling racial past, regardless of how much they liked the work.

It was also not coincidental that Black caddie ranks shrunk at the same time that the Civil Rights Movement achieved monumental victories for Black Southerners. Early in the 20th century, White employers reserved the most subservient jobs for Black workers. Restricting Black workers to such jobs reinforced racial hierarchy and was intended to keep African Americans from finding dignity in their work and demanding equality in other aspects of society. As much as restrictive labor practices kept Black workers poor, it also kept up the façade of racial difference between Black and White Southerners.[458] Minimizing Black self-respect was a common tactic of Jim Crow proponents to discourage Black Southerners from demanding equality in all areas.[459] When White leisure-seekers and Black workers met on the color line, everyday enforcement of racist norms served as a soft power that upheld and maintained the key economic, legal, and political structures of Jim Crow. After the victories of the Civil Rights Movement, many White Southerners chose to remove themselves as much as possible from the areas of society that African American now had equal access. They retreated to the suburbs—far from the inner cities—and relied on the financial advantages of generational wealth and economic advantages that uplifted millions of working-class Whites into an affluent middle class by the mid-century.[460] By the late '60s, employing a Black caddie to enforce racial etiquette or to display racial difference held less utility than it had during Jim Crow's hold on the South.

At the tourist resorts where White Northerners played, the decreasing demand for Black caddies differed slightly from the courses where White Southerners played. Earlier in the century, White tourists desired Black caddies as part of an authentically Southern vacation, where they could play out their fantasies of the imagined South, in which smiling Black helpers waited on their every need.[461] Tourist demands for luxury and leisure while on vacation meant that they wanted to use golf carts, which saved them time and conserved their energy on the course. Where previously they would have used a caddie—and therefore sought caddies that fulfilled their perception of the South—by the mid-century they did not want to walk the sweaty courses of the South, so they rode in a cart instead. Similar declines in the use of Black service workers occurred in other tourist-industry occupations such as the use of Black men to push visitors around in luxury transportation wagons on Florida's coastal resorts. There, the rise of the automobile created a new standard of luxury and convenience.[462]

Integration for Everyone But the Rich, High, and Fancy

The golf cart's monumental rise also coincided with the sweeping changes that occurred in southern cities in the mid-century. Black golfers waged tireless and sustained efforts to desegregate municipal golf courses. At those courses, where White caddies were the norm, Black golfers had long been denied the right to play. In Atlanta, all five of the city's courses were open only to White golfers, while Black golfers were restricted to the one Black private course: New Lincoln

Country Club. After five years of sustained political pressure and legal battles, the city desegregated the courses in 1955. One significant outcome of the battle over desegregation was that White working-class golfers who played municipal courses felt abandoned by wealthier Whites. Working-class White golfers argued that the city's rich did little to oppose desegregation, because the courses where the powerful played were privately-owned and therefore still segregated. One angry White Atlantan summed up the discontent: "integration for everyone but the rich, high & fancy."[463] Black presence on any golf course in southern cities in the 1950s and '60s created growing discontent among White working classes. They were combative to racial closeness in all forms, and had been for some time. A few decades earlier, working-class Whites in Atlanta called for the end of employment of Black caddies.[464] For them, the symbolism of Black servitude mattered less than complete separation of the races. In the mid-century, when absolute resistance to desegregation became central to White working-class politics, private golf clubs likely recognized that their closeness to Black caddies on the golf courses was unwelcome. White demand for an increasingly separate society at that time likely hastened private clubs' adoption of the golf cart and shunning of Black caddies.

Changing locations of golf courses in the South and the phenomenon of White flight likely also contributed to the decreasing numbers of Black caddies on golf courses in the 1960s. The burgeoning White middle-class moved out of inner cities at a staggering pace in the '50s and '60s. The exodus can, in part, be attributed to the growing rights of African Americans in southern cities; previously, Whites enjoyed exclusive access to the city's municipal facilities and had the ability to exclude non-Whites from their neighborhoods. In the '50s, federal courts squashed the notion of "separate but equal," and Black Southerners began using public facilities, as was their right. Some Whites felt affronted by the intrusion of African Americans into parts of society that were previously "theirs," and in turn fled to the suburbs. Because African Americans were excluded from many of the benefits of the G.I. Bill and could not access federally backed mortgages, the suburbs became new sites of White exclusivity in the aftermath of desegregation.[466] Golf courses followed the White exodus to suburbs.[467] In Atlanta, the famed Atlanta Athletic Club, which had built the nationally famous East Lake golf course in 1906, sold the property in 1965, citing the changing demographics of the area and the club's increasingly suburban membership.[468] They moved to Duluth, far from the inner city, and far from predominantly Black neighborhoods. While all courses were well on their way to adopting golf carts, moving far away from Black workers made it increasingly difficult to employ Black caddies.

In the late 1950s, the writing was on the wall for caddying as a viable long-term career in most of the country. In a sign of things to come, the first golf course in the United States to officially replace all caddies with motorized golf carts—as a matter of policy—was the Tam O'Shanter Club, just north of Chicago, in 1960. The change in their policy made headlines around the country, in no small part because their previous policy required golfers to use caddies. In one fell swoop, the club management moved from mandating caddies to removing them entirely. The club's management cited the dramatic increase in golf cart usage. In 1959, "two and one-half as many members used cars as in 1958."[469] When Tam O'Shanter made their decision they had 65 golf carts in operation. In the same year, the East Lake golf course in Atlanta had a fleet of 85 carts, and the membership had grown so accustomed to their usage that they chastised the superintendent on days when carts were locked up due to weather.[470] Although clubs like East Lake and other southern golf courses had not yet mandated carts, by the early '60s caddies must have been discouraged by the outlook for the future.

The Winds of Change

In the '60s, many courses around the country closed their full-time caddie ranks, and caddie numbers dwindled around the nation. In Raleigh, where Gene Haywood awaited a bag on that warm spring day in 1975, some clubs had begun hiring caddies on an appointment basis and many of the caddies were now White high schoolers from affluent neighborhoods and suburbs.[471] By virtue of their financial comfort, such youngsters were relatively well-suited to the sporadic nature of employment as a caddie. The occasional employment served as a welcome boost of spending money for White teens, from families who did not need to lean on caddie income to get by. Such an arrangement simply was not viable to those seeking full-time work or steady weekend jobs. By the 1980s, the only courses in the South left that employed dozens of full-time caddies were some of the most elite resort courses including Augusta National and Pinehurst Country Club. While the occupation has never died and continues as a full-time job for thousands in the United States, it never recovered to anywhere near the numbers of men and boys who did the job prior to World War II, when caddies could be found on almost every public or private course nationwide.

The fate of caddies mirrored the fate of Black workers in other industries caught up in the rapid mechanization of the mid-century. Pullman Porters, for example, found their work in diminishing demand, as passengers flocked to air travel. Airlines did not hire Black stewards and opted to hire White women to serve passengers. In fact, airlines presented their White stewardesses as glamorous employees who worked for enjoyment, in contrast to Pullman Porters who they portrayed as tired and kowtowing servants in search of tips.[472] Likewise, Black agricultural workers in the South followed a remarkably similar path to Black caddies. War mobilization took workers off fields and into industrial manufacturing jobs, and the ensuing shortages of field hands increased labor costs. The agricultural industry found a solution, just like the golf industry did, in newfound technologies that could replace labor.[473] The winds of change that blew across the nation in the '50s and '60s touched every part of the country, and they gusted through the tree-lined fairways of southern golf courses. For all of these reasons, Black labor in 1940 was unrecognizable 30 years later.

Taking a quick glance at U.S. golf courses today, with their vast distances between holes, extensive path systems, and large cart barns, it is easy to quickly dismiss the decline of the caddie as an inevitable outcome. Another of technology's gifts to modern life, the golf cart might be deemed as a natural replacement for the caddie, and one that streamlined the game for players and course management alike. However, very little about the decline of caddie ranks around the South was inevitable, nor was it entirely attributable to the marvels of modern technology. The change from burgeoning caddie ranks before the war to full cart barns in the '70s and '80s was a result of various human decisions. It was in part attributable to the golf industry's desire for profit and financial return that spawned a self-sustaining industry around carts. And it came down to the rapidly changing social and political circumstances of the mid-century that diminished the symbolic importance of hiring a Black caddie in the eyes of Whites. It had also become a job that the many in the South saw as a relic of Jim Crow—a symbol of a more troubling time in the region. Last, but certainly not least, it was also a consequence of increasing Black demand for better-paying and less-demeaning jobs in a society that provided greater opportunity for African Americans than ever before.

FIGURE 14: Pinehurst caddies awaiting their golfers (circa 1920s, Tufts Archives).

CHAPTER 8

Getting to Par

Caddies and Civil Rights

On the eve of the final round of the United Golfers Association's 1939 Southern Open, the leaderboard was tight. The quality of play at New Lincoln Golf Course—the only course in Atlanta for Black golfers—was of the highest standard. In the professional field, John Brooks Dendy and Howard Wheeler led the way, followed closely by Zeke Hartsfield. All three would have been popular winners, given their close ties to the city. But for Hartsfield, the stakes were higher. The other two men had succeeded where he had not in their victories in the National Open and the Southern Open. In the amateur field, defending champion Alfred "Tup" Holmes was favored to reclaim his title.

The final round saw Hartsfield produce perhaps the finest round of his professional career. He scored an astonishing 62 to win the tournament by 3 shots over Howard Wheeler and best John Brooks Dendy by 6. In his ninth attempt, Hartsfield had finally won the UGA's Southern Open, and on home soil too. On the same day Alfred "Tup" Holmes defeated Howard Gay to complete consecutive successes in the tournament's illustrious amateur stakes.

Hartsfield, a professional golfer, and Holmes, a businessman with a love of the game, represented the each represented the two paths to golf for Black Southerners. The former made his way into golf through labor and the confines of the caddy shack. The latter, a son of a physician, hailed from the Black middle class and picked up the sport as a pastime. Off the fairways they belonged in different circles. Yet, they shared one common grievance; on account of the color of their skin neither had access to public golf courses in their city, Atlanta.

That same year—1939—Hartsfield quietly sought to test the shackles of Jim Crow segregation on the city's public links. A local White baker who Hartsfield worked for at the time (combining odd jobs with professional golf to make a living was commonplace among Black pros) encouraged him to try to play a round on the White-only Candler Park municipal course. This was almost two decades before challenges to segregation became commonplace. Hartsfield claimed that he was able to complete two holes before he reached the third tee where members of Atlanta's police department awaited him with handcuffs. Hartsfield was released only after some convincing from the White baker who had encouraged him in the first place.[ii]

For Hartsfield, Holmes, and other Black Atlantans seeking golf on the city's courses, their time would have to wait. Holmes graduated from Tuskegee Institute and built a career for himself while continuing his success in Black amateur golf. Yet 15 years later it was he, not Hartsfield, who found himself at the center of the battle for equal rights on the golf course.

A Skeptical Public

For caddies and other Black Southerners in the first half of the 20th century, access to affordable golf courses was limited. Starting in the 1920s and '30s, municipal governments around the South began building golf courses for their citizens to play on. In Atlanta, for example, municipal golf started on the city's Piedmont Park Course in 1920 to a "skeptical public," but within two years the course facilitated almost

4,000 rounds per month.⁴⁷⁴ But, as with almost all public facilities in the South, only White citizens were allowed to play. Cities such as Atlanta, Houston, and Charlotte had public courses for White golfers only.⁴⁷⁵ In the 1940s, other municipal governments had designated golf courses assigned to Black golfers, segregated from the White courses. Such was the case in Birmingham and Greensboro, where the White courses were of a higher standard and in better condition than the lone Black course.⁴⁷⁶ Another common policy was to segregate courses by the day of the week. In Miami, for example, Black golfers could play the municipal course only on Mondays. Whites could play on Tuesday through Sunday.⁴⁷⁷ Regardless of the specifics in each city, the discrimination was obvious. No city in the South offered anything near equal golf opportunities for Black and White citizens.

Cities practiced outright discrimination under the protection of federal law. Since 1896, when the U.S. Supreme Court ruled in *Plessy v. Ferguson* that segregation was legal on the condition that public facilities were "separate but equal," White Southerners held almost a monopoly on all the best public facilities in the region. Everything from parks and recreational spaces to public restrooms, schools, and train station waiting rooms were segregated based on race. And the standard of facilities for White Southerners far exceeded those for African Americans.⁴⁷⁸

Without widespread access to public facilities, Black golfers had few ways to play golf. One of the peculiarities of Black golf in the South was that more Black golfers played on elite, White-only private courses than on public municipal ones. Country clubs and resorts often allowed their Black caddies to play on days when the course was closed for maintenance, and on annual "caddie days." Black workers also snuck onto the course early in the morning and late at night to play as often as they could.⁴⁷⁹ Municipal courses, on the other hand, did not allow their Black caddies the same playing privileges. In fact, many municipal governments employed White child caddies on public courses. In Atlanta, for example, the caddies at the municipal courses were all White, at least in the 1940s.⁴⁸⁰ The same was the case in Washington, D.C., where 85 percent of caddies at country clubs were "older colored boys," while municipal courses used White schoolboys.[481] No public officials went on record to explain why the municipal courses employed White rather than Black caddies, but one plausible reason is that working-class and lower middle-class Whites who played the city's municipal courses demanded priority for Whites in all occupations.[482] Another explanation is that public officials employed White caddies to avoid having any Black presence in public parks and recreation spaces, which were strictly segregated. Cities that employed White caddies avoided having to allow Black caddies the right to play the course on maintenance days. Regardless of their reasoning, the fact remained that across the South the vast majority of African Americans had severely limited access to the game of golf.

In the 1930s and '40s, new opportunities emerged for Black Southerners to play the game, despite racist municipal policies. Black private courses developed in select cities—including Atlanta and Jacksonville—where Black middle-class and elite golfers played. Starting with the Tuskegee Institute in 1927, some Black colleges built golf courses, offering another route to the game.[483] But as with Black private clubs, college golf catered only to those with the wealth and background to attend institutions. Most southern cities did not have private Black country clubs or university courses, meaning that prior to World War II, African American playing opportunities were largely confined to those who worked as caddies.[484]

One unexpected outcome of the war was an explosion of Black interest and access to golf. Military experience exposed thousands of African Americans to the game. At bases around the country, Black golfers learned to play in record numbers. More than 14,000 Black soldiers stationed at Fort Huachuca, Arizona had access to golf lessons in their spare time. In Washington, D.C., the Army made golf clubs available to 500 Black soldiers stationed at a recreation camp. And just a few miles from Pinehurst, at Fort Bragg, Black soldiers competed in golf events.[485] Through Black private clubs, college golf, and military service, African American interest in golf had never been higher than it was in the late '40s. In 1949, a commission in Greensboro, North

Carolina found that there were "more Negroes who play golf than anyone can imagine."⁴⁸⁶ Yet the most affordable golf courses around the South remained largely closed to African Americans who wanted to play.

"We Just Want to Play Golf": The Knoxville Negro Golf Association

In cities around the South, Black citizens demanded the right to play but were met with fierce opposition. The efforts in Knoxville, Tennessee illustrate the difficult task Black golfers faced. In March 1952, a group of Black golfers known as the Knoxville Negro Golfers Association—led by Reverend R.E. James, the pastor at the local Mount Zion Baptist Church—petitioned Mayor George Dempster for access to the city's single municipal course: Whittle Springs. The course was reserved for Whites only. Initially the mayor responded positively to their request and said that the course would be desegregated pending discussions with the association to work out the specific details.⁴⁸⁷ However, when Dempster submitted the request to the city council, and specifically asked Welfare Director Arthur Atkin to investigate the possibility, pushback began. The local newspaper reported that White residents in the neighborhood began calling the council to protest any desegregation. The *Knoxville News-Sentinel* even published an editorial opposing the opening of the course to Black golfers, describing the request for access as "unreasonable and unworkable." The editorial made unsubstantiated claims that no more than a dozen Black locals would actually want to play, and that "recreation interests in the area are confined largely to playground sports such as football and basketball."⁴⁸⁸ Hundreds of African Americans signed petitions demanding access to the course, belying the editorial's claims.⁴⁸⁹

While the *Knoxville News-Sentinel* and many local Whites opposed opening the course to Black locals, many readers voiced their support in response. In doing so they also referenced the history of Black caddies in the region to make their argument. One White woman who wrote to the paper took the editorial team to task on their assertion that Black demand for golf was low, noting that Black locals might be just as interested in golf as their White counterparts, should they be given the opportunities to play and not just work at golf courses. "Perhaps the fact," she noted, "that [African Americans] have had no chance to visit local courses except as caddies may have something to do with this."[490] At least some of Knoxville's White residents supported opening courses to African American golfers.

Amid the public debate, Welfare Director Arthur Atkin began sharing details of the golf course's expenses. According to Atkin, the course "lost" more than $26,000 between 1948 and 1952. Mayor Dempster subsequently commented that the facility had been "operated like a country store." Of course as a public good—as with all taxpayer-funded facilities—the municipal golf course was not necessarily expected to turn a profit.[491] The mayor and welfare director likely published the golf course's financial costs to promote their plan to lease it to a private operator. By doing so, the city could avoid addressing the desegregation of the facility entirely. Private golf courses could openly discriminate against whomever they wanted, while public facilities needed to at least appear to provide separate but equal facilities for Black and White citizens.

Perhaps in response to the mayor's threat to lease the course, the Knoxville Negro Golf Association retracted their request for open access to Whittle Springs. In a letter to Mayor Dempsey, the group altered their demands and offered two options. The first was a proposal that the city construct a separate 18-hole golf course for Black golfers, in line with the principle of separate but equal. Alternatively, the group proposed that Black golfers be given permission to play the course three-and-a-half days per week—equal time for Black and White golfers. At a heated city council meeting on April 25, a local Black golfer who was growing frustrated at the inaction threatened to test his constitutional rights by playing the course. Other members of the Knoxville Negro Golf Association present at the meeting voiced their displeasure at the welfare director's assertion that the city did not have funds for a separate clubhouse at the course for African Americans; they did not want facilities, "we just want to play golf," the man said.[492]

Despite the protests of Black locals, less than two weeks later the council offered Whittle Springs up for lease.[493] The council claimed their decision was based on the course's financial burden on the city, but both the *Knoxville News-Sentinel*—which had vehemently opposed allowing Black golfers access—and local Black golfers felt that the council leased the course to prevent having to open it to African Americans.[494] By May 20, the course was under the operation of local businessman Charles Faust, who could freely discriminate against whomever he wanted.[495] Cities around the South adopted similar tactics when Black golfers demanded access to municipal golf courses. Mayors and councils delayed wherever possible, leased courses to private operators, or closed courses entirely. At every stage, White officials did whatever possible to avoid desegregation of the game.[496]

A Civil Rights Battleground

Although city governments opposed desegregation, Black golfers never gave up hope. In fact, golf became an early battleground in the legal battles of the Civil Rights Movement, and caddies played a prominent role in the fight. In the late 1940s and early '50s, civil rights groups such as the National Association for the Advancement of Colored People (NAACP) began formally challenging the legality of segregation around the South. Following World War II, as Black Southerners returned home from serving their country and fighting oppression and intolerance abroad, visible signs of their discontent and opposition to segregated spaces at home grew.[497] In turn, so too did the number of legal challenges that sought to end segregation.

The first golf desegregation case to make it all the way to the U.S. Supreme Court occurred in Miami. In the spring 1949, a black golfer named Joseph Rice and a small group of friends—a few of whom were caddies on nearby courses—went to the White-only municipal course, Miami Springs Golf Club. Officials denied Rice and his fellow players access to the course. In response, Rice filed legal proceedings. Over the next two years, the case made its way through various courts before the Florida Supreme Court ruled that the arrangement of one day of golf per week for Black golfers fit the legal precedent of "separate but equal." Rice and his legal team appealed to the U.S. Supreme Court, who ordered the Florida Supreme Court to reconsider their original ruling but stopped short of overruling them entirely. Local golfers in Miami, including Joseph Rice, felt sure that the order to reconsider would force the State Supreme Court to change their ruling. Unfortunately for them, it did not. The Florida Supreme Court upheld their original ruling, claiming that one day per week of golf for Black golfers constituted "separate but equal" accommodations, on the basis that White demand for golf exceeded Black demand. Miami's Black golfers waited until 1957 for full access to the course.[498]

Rice v. Arnold galvanized the local Black community in the struggle for civil rights, and the man who started it all was a former caddie. For Black Miamians, the case meant more than simply playing golf: it represented a struggle against White control over their lives, the spaces they could occupy, and the pastimes they could enjoy. Once Joseph Rice opened legal proceedings, a group of Black locals banded together to start the Cosmopolitan Golf Association, which raised awareness of the case and generated funds to support the legal battle. They held fundraiser events and demonstrations in the name of supporting Rice. At the same time, the local Black newspaper, *The Miami Times*, became a vocal advocate for desegregating the city's golf courses and framed the case as symbolic of the wider struggle for Black freedom in Miami and the nation.[499] Both the *Times* and the Cosmopolitan Golf Association urged Black Miamians to take up golf, and to fill the course on the day allotted for the Black community to play. They did so in the hope of disproving the court's claim that low Black demand for golf justified the existing so-called separate but equal arrangement. These efforts, which resulted from Rice's legal battle, challenged existing beliefs that Black involvement in golf was consigned to the South's caddy shacks.[500]

Although it is unclear whether Joseph Rice was still a caddie when he tried to play at Miami Springs in April 1949, he certainly learned to golf as a caddie.[501] The 1940 federal census listed Joseph Rice as a "caddy" on a "private golf course."[502] Two years later, when the United States entered World War II, Rice signed his name onto his military draft card and listed his employer as "Normandie Isles (Golf Course)."[503] Although he did not appear in the 1950 census, his older brother, Festus, did. Festus Rice worked as a caddie that year, the same year that Joseph's case made its way through the courts.[504] Even if Joseph Rice had retired from caddying and changed occupation, the fact that his initiation into the game came from his time in the caddy shack should not be overlooked. His experience as a caddie indirectly led to the first major legal challenge to segregation of golf courses in the South.

Holmes v. Atlanta

In the aftermath of the Miami case, similar battles took place in cities around the South, many of which built upon the legacy of Black caddies in the region. In Houston, Texas, five members of the Lone Star Golf Club—the city's Black golf society—sued the city for access to the public golf courses in 1950 in *Beal v. Holcombe*. Houston had three golf courses, and all of them were reserved for White golfers only. Although the five men who sued the city were not caddies—they hailed from the contingent of middle-class and wealthy Black golfers who played the game in private clubs—their legal battle had roots in the actions of former caddies in the city. It was four former caddies who—after returning from military service in 1945—came together to form the Lone Star Golf Club. In 1948, the club held a demonstration at one of Houston's public golf courses to demand desegregation. After a two-year legal battle, a federal judge ordered the mayor of Houston to make plans to desegregate city courses, but the ruling afforded the mayor time to make such changes.[505] By 1954, Black golfers had access to Houston's municipal links. Former caddies also led the charge in Beaumont, Texas. In 1955, Booker T. Fayson and six of his friends—who all learned the game growing up caddying at Beaumont's private clubs—sued the city for the right to play the one local municipal course. When their case reached the U.S. District Court, the judge ordered the city of Beaumont to immediately open their public courses to all citizens.[506]

The prospects for Black golfers changed in May 1954, when the U.S. Supreme Court handed down the most significant ruling on racial segregation since *Plessy v. Ferguson*. In the case of *Brown v. Board of Education* (1954) the Court ruled that the Board of Education in Topeka, Kansas could not continue the practice of segregated schools. The case overruled "separate but equal" doctrine, noting that separate educational facilities were "inherently unequal." The Court also declared that segregated school districts denied children the equal protection of the laws guaranteed to them in the 14th Amendment.[507] Prior to 1954, golfers seeking playing rights on municipal courses appealed on the basis of *Plessy*—that municipal governments were not providing separate-but-equal facilities—and on the 14th Amendment. With *Brown*, golfers had a new tool: cities could no longer hide behind loose interpretations of what constituted equal, segregated facilities.

The most influential golf desegregation case—and one of the first segregation cases in the country decided after *Brown*—took place in Atlanta. In 1951, three Black golfers—Alfred "Tup" Holmes, Oliver W. Holmes, and their father Dr. Hamilton M. Holmes—petitioned the city of Atlanta to allow them to play the Bobby Jones Municipal Golf Course. City officials denied their request. Atlanta at the time boasted six municipal golf courses and all were strictly Whites-only. None of Georgia's 15 municipal courses allowed Black golfers.[508] The Holmes family grew discouraged by the lack of playing opportunities in Atlanta, so they often travelled hundreds of miles every weekend to play high-standard golf courses.[509] After two years preparing for a legal challenge with the support of both the national NAACP and the local chapter, the three men sued the city for denying them equal opportunity to use public facilities. By late 1954, the case of *Holmes v. Atlanta* made it all the way to the federal district court. The judge ruled in favor of the plaintiffs, but only on the basis that the arrangement at the time did not fit the definition of separate but equal. In the judgment, the court told the city to construct a new golf course for African American use, or to open one of the other facilities for segregated play. In response, the city of Atlanta set aside two days for Black golf: Monday and Tuesday.[510]

The Holmes family dismissed the district court decision as inadequate, because the ruling largely ignored *Brown*.[511] Tup, Oliver, and Hamilton wanted to play whenever and wherever they wanted. Meanwhile, prominent members of the NAACP voiced their disinterest in continuing this particular desegregation case. Thurgood Marshall, the NAACP's chief lawyer and a future Supreme Court judge, believed that civil rights groups should focus on education rather than golf. "We are not going to spend any money on a golf course case because we could not justify spending money for a few doctors in Atlanta to play golf," he claimed. "We are going to use the money to get black kids admitted to White schools."[512] The Holmes family ignored Marshall's opposition and pressed ahead for equality on the course with support from Atlanta donors and the local chapter of the NAACP.[513] In November 1955, the U.S. Supreme Court ruled in favor of the three men and ordered the city to desegregate the municipal golf courses completely. *Holmes v. Atlanta* was the first case that truly tested the implications of Brown beyond the realm of public education. The court's intent was clear: the doctrine of separate but equal was unconstitutional. In the ruling, the court cited the *Brown* case and made clear that future cases regarding segregated public facilities would be judged on the same basis.[514]

Holmes v. Atlanta was a landmark case in the early Civil Rights Movement. Not only did it reinforce the importance of *Brown*, but it also signaled that the tide was turning against desegregation in all spaces. The South's segregationist politicians recognized the case's importance as the sign of things to come in other areas of society as well. Georgia Governor Marvin Griffin noted that "[*Holmes v. Atlanta*] is but a foretaste of what people can expect," while a Kentucky politician lamented that the Holmes ruling would likely "end all segregation cases" in that state.[515] After all, if the growing Civil Rights Movement could usher in equality in golf—a sport inextricably tied to Whiteness in the American imagination—then what could it achieve in other sectors of society?

Closing the Gates

Although the *Holmes* case had long-term implications for the snowballing Civil Rights Movement, neither that decision nor the *Brown* decision brought about the immediate desegregation of the South's public facilities. Municipal governments around the South took various measures to avoid desegregating. Some cities tried the old trick of leasing the course to a private operator. In Fort Lauderdale and Jacksonville, Florida, Black golfers won the right to play municipal courses in 1958 and 1961, respectively. In response, the municipal governments in both cities sold the courses at knock-down prices to private parties. Other cities, including Birmingham, Alabama, closed the gates to their courses and allowed the fairways to grow into wild parks.[516] Clearly, many White Southerners preferred the idea of ending public golf in their cities than integrating public golf. Regardless of the Supreme Court decision, in the decade that followed, on a city-by-city basis, municipal governments determined whether they would open their golf courses to Black players on terms of equality with White players.

During the years of litigation over golf course segregation, Black caddies were not always the ideal plaintiffs. In the eyes of the NAACP, the Holmes family were the ideal candidates to front a case; the family counted themselves among the city's Black elite. Alfred "Tup" Holmes, was a leading amateur golfer in the city, having played during his years in college at the Tuskegee Institute. Oliver Holmes was a minister at a local church, and their father, Hamilton, was a well-respected physician.[517] Hamilton's wife was a nurse and a founding member of professional association for nurses at the turn of the century.[518] Although caddies fronted a few of the golf course desegregation cases from the 1950s and '60s, in most cases it was middle-class and elite African Americans who sued for equal access. In Greensboro, North Carolina—just days after the *Holmes* decision was handed down—a highly respected Black dentist named George Simkins Jr. began the struggle of bringing integration to golf courses in his city. Likewise in Charlotte, several Black business owners—including a pharmacist, a doctor, and a barber—petitioned the city.[519]

Elite Black men fronted the campaigns for a number of reasons: they were keen golfers, active members of local civil rights groups, and they were likely to command more respect than those in the working- and lower middle-classes, such as caddies. In the many cases that caddies did not lead, they still likely had an indirect impact. In the Atlanta case, for example, Alfred "Tup" Holmes, "learned the game of golf from caddies … during his formative years," before he honed his game at Tuskegee. In other cities around the South, golfers took inspiration from former caddies who had become stars on the United Golfers Association tour. George Simkins Jr. was a fan of Charlie Sifford and even financially supported the UGA's Gate City Open in Greensboro, which Sifford won twice in the three years before Simkins began his desegregation case against the city.[520]

Even when caddies were not plaintiffs, their symbolism lingered in the background. When desegregation cases made it into the headlines of local newspapers, editors and readers noted the hypocrisy of encouraging Black participation as caddies, yet discouraging their participation as players. "To some whites there is no objection to touring a golf course with Negroes as caddies, but there is if they tour the course as ordinary golfers," wrote the editorial team of the Black newspaper, the *Louisiana Weekly*, in response to the ongoing battle to desegregate in New Orleans. "In other words," they continued, "some whites have no desire to segregate Negroes as long as they are in the servant or menial role, but do want to segregate when Negroes are cast in roles as human beings."[521] During the height of the controversy in Knoxville, one White resident wrote to the local White paper that there had been "no instance on record of a golfer's life, liberty, or pursuit of happiness having been curtailed or injured by his having a Negro caddy." She continued that "we can assume that no more serious consequences would result if the caddy paid his green fee and walked on the same acre of grass with us, swinging a golf club of his own instead of carrying ours."[522]

Occasionally, lawyers used the example of Black presence on public courses as caddies in their arguments in court, as was the case in Palm Beach, Florida, in 1957. The plaintiff attorney William Holland highlighted the hypocrisy of allowing Black caddies but not Black golfers. Holland asked the city's attorney if "negro golfers would come in closer contact with White golfers than the Negro caddies working on the course." He declared that he "couldn't see why the presence of Negro golfers would create violence if the presence of Negro caddies has not."[523] The purposeful inclusion of Black caddies and the strict exclusion of Black golfers offered as clear an example as any of the racial inequality in municipal facilities in the South.

With Gusto

When the South's golf courses finally desegregated, caddies were among the chief beneficiaries. Thurgood Marshall's statement that desegregation cases served only to allow "a few doctors" to play golf proved wildly off the mark. Black doctors and other elites were joined by caddies and former caddies on the course. In Atlanta, on the day that courses officially opened to Black golfers—Christmas Eve in 1955—Oliver and "Tup" Holmes played the North Fulton Public Golf Course.

Caddies in other cities around the South took full advantage of the freedom to play public courses. In June 1954, the first African American to play on the newly desegregated public courses of Houston was former caddie Charles M. Washington, quickly followed by Dr A. W. Beal—the face of the desegregation battle there—and three of his friends.[524] Over the six weeks that followed, many "caddies and other employees from the country club courses" played consistent golf on the city's municipal facilities.[525] Likewise in Charlotte in 1957: the first Black golfer on Bonnie Brae Municipal Golf Course was 17-year-old James Otis Williams, who worked as a caddie at the nearby Eastwood Golf Course.[526] The superintendent of Charlotte Parks and Recreation commented that "some of our own caddies pick up 75 cents for carrying another golfer's bag and then turn around and spend the money to go around themselves."[527] When Charleston finally desegregated its courses in 1961, Black caddies availed themselves of the opportunity to play. The manager of the Charleston Municipal Golf Course said he knew most of the Black players because they "were or had been caddies."[528] Across the South, from Houston to Charlotte, Charleston to Jackson, and on down to Sarasota, the men who had carried bags in the region's cities took to municipal courses with gusto.[529] The desegregation of public golf courses around the South liberated Black caddies from a life of playing on maintenance days, or from taking the risk of sneaking onto White-only courses under the cover of darkness.

When cities opened their courses for Black and White golfers, some paid particular attention to the caddie situation on those courses. In Atlanta—where for the most part White schoolboys and young men caddied on municipal courses—the city changed the caddie policy when the course desegregated.[530] One newspaper reported that the city "does not force caddies to carry bags for any of the players," in an attempt to rule out the possibility of an "adult White caddie and a Negro player clashing." The city also likely understood that many White golfers, caddies, and members of the general public would be uneasy with the optics of a White caddie serving a Black golfer. The explicit reason the city gave for implementing new policies was "to ease whatever tensions it could."[531] Such a scenario represented an inversion of the racial customs in the golf world that had existed in Atlanta for the previous 50 years. A similar situation occurred in Alabama, when Birmingham finally reopened its golf courses on a desegregated basis in 1963. For almost two years, Birmingham closed the courses to avoid having to abide by a federal court order to desegregate. When the courses opened as integrated facilities, they decided against supplying bag carriers, and golfers had to supply their own private caddies.[532] Similarly to Atlanta, their decision avoided the potential for White caddies and Black golfers—which would have been a powerful, symbolic inversion of the South's racial past.

For the most part, Black golfers who wanted to employ a caddie on newly desegregated municipal courses used Black caddies. A 1957 study of Black golfers in Atlanta explicitly asked them about their use and opinion of municipal caddies. The study surveyed 21 members of the Pioneer Golf Club, a social golf club that did not have a home course but played events and golf outings on municipal courses. Most of the members of the Pioneer Club were former New Lincoln Golf and Country Club members, and—as suggested by the name—the club was the brainchild of members of the Holmes family and other individuals who served to desegregate the city's courses. Of the 21 respondents, only one reported ever having used a White caddie; the other 20 golfers exclusively used Black caddies.[533] In general, the Pioneer Club members found White caddies to be substantially less friendly than the Black caddies. All the respondents rated the general attitude of Black caddies as "friendly," while 90 percent felt that White caddies were "tolerant," and 10 percent thought White caddies were "hostile."[534]

In the years that followed, caddies—both White and Black—quickly disappeared from public courses. Tension over the potential interactions between White caddies and Black players was relatively short-lived, as caddies made way for bag carts and golf carts on municipal courses. But for a short time, the potential symbolic power of White caddies for Black golfers troubled White officials, golfers, and onlookers.

* * *

In 1973 Gladys Knight and the Pips released their now-famous hit, "Midnight Train to Georgia." The song's protagonist, having failed to make a life for himself in Los Angeles, embarks upon a physical and metaphorical return to the South. To him, Georgia was home, and his journey back to the South symbolized a retreat to a place he once abandoned.[535] Knight's masterpiece speaks to the complexities that came with the Great Migration of millions of Black Americans from the South to the North in the 20th century. They ventured north in search of better lives and a more equal treatment, yet in doing so they left the place that they and millions like them called home for generations.

Unbeknown to Knight, one of the great Black golfers of the 20th century took his own Midnight Train to Georgia in December 1955. Sixteen years earlier, Zeke Hartsfield had quietly attempted to play the Whites-only Candler Park golf course in Atlanta. At that time, Jim Crow segregation remained strong. Hartsfield had migrated to New York after World War II, in search of a better life away from Southern segregation, and equal playing rights on Northern courses. On December 23, 1955, news came over the wire to New York that Black golfers would be admitted for play on Atlanta City courses the next day. Hartsfield knew that he had to be there. He had to be one of the first Black golfers to play the courses that he had so long been denied. He boarded an overnight train for Atlanta. "I got in town about 10 o'clock the next morning, and I didn't stop," he remembered, "I grabbed a cab, went to Adams Park, and ran until I was standing at the first tee." Unlike Gladys Knight's protagonist, the Georgia that Hartsfield returned to was not the one he left behind—but an entirely new one.[536]

FIGURE 15: Braving the rain at Pinehurst in the 1950s (Tufts Archives).

CHAPTER 9

Green Jackets, White Coveralls, Black Caddies

A Complex End to a Southern Tradition

In April 1983, Augusta was the center of America's sporting attention, just as it was every year for the Masters Tournament. Greenskeeping and maintenance teams pruned Augusta National's fairways to perfection. Newspapers waxed lyrical about the beauty of the course. It truly was a cacophony of color. "Green is the color of the Masters, the bright green fairways that seem to stretch forever," commented one reporter, "and the darker green of the Georgia pines and magnolia trees."[537] The flowering azaleas and the dogwood trees received the attentions of another writer, who delighted in the course "ablaze in red and pink." In the center of the golf course sat the clubhouse, a grand white building trimmed in green. The architecture was "right out of *Gone with the Wind*."[538] The other color that attendees discussed that year was the skin color of the caddies. "You just made history," yelled one of Augusta's African American caddies at a Masters competitor and their White caddie, "you're the first white man ever to caddie here."[539] 1983 was the first year that the tournament committee at Augusta National allowed the players at the Masters Tournament to bring their own caddies. In the first four decades of the tournament's existence rules dictated that the golfers had to use local caddies. At that time, all the local caddies were Black.

The changes at Augusta marked the end of the symbolic image of Black caddies serving White golfers across the South. "All those black caddies," one journalist reported, "were part of the image Augusta National presented ... as America's last plantation."[540] Yet the men who caddied at Augusta National year round—who prided themselves on their expertise and guidance that they provided to the nation's best golfers every year—did not rejoice. In a complex contradiction, many across the country applauded the end of a tradition of Black servitude rooted in centuries of oppression, while the Augusta National caddies lamented the closing of one of the few opportunities for African Americans to prominently display their skills and talents in the golf world on television.

Just 14 years after the first White caddies walked the fairways at the Masters, Tiger Woods became the first African American to win the Masters. Woods' victory marked the symbolic triumph of racial progress in one of the Whitest sports in the United States. Yet his victory owed much to the legacy of caddies, like those who trod the fairways and greens of Augusta National and other southern courses. With a passion for the game, and dignity in their work, those men toiled for the best part of a century to receive equal opportunities to not only work on golf courses, but to play them as well. The story of struggle for equality on the links cannot be told without caddies.

As the battle over public golf waged on across the South, Black professional golfers continued their fight to gain access to the White-only Professional Golfers Association (PGA). Early in the 1950s—thanks to pressure from Black celebrity golfers including Joe Louis, and the consistent efforts of elite players such as Charlie Sifford and Bill Spiller—the PGA stopped strictly enforcing the "Caucasians-only" clause in their rules. Black professionals began playing events that accepted their participation in the North, Midwest, and West, but could not participate in events in the deeply segregated South.

However, by 1960, state officials in New York and California threatened to ban PGA Tour events in their states if the organization did not drop the White-only rule that still existed. Finally in 1961, the PGA dropped the rule, and Black golfers began competing as full members of the tour, playing events around the country.[541]

While the main battle to desegregate the professional golf ranks concluded in 1961, with the end of the PGA's "Caucasian-only" clause, the symbolic fight against the game's stubborn Whiteness continued for decades. The Masters Tournament held firm as the last bastion of lily-white professional golf. Held annually at Augusta National Golf Club—the most recognizable course in the country—the Masters occupied a place of unmatched prestige in the American golfing public.

The tournament committee at Augusta differentiated the Masters from any other tournament through the creation and maintenance of unique traditions. Most famously, the club gave every winner of the tournament a green jacket, a symbol of the exclusive club of past champions. Each year, on the evening before the tournament, those past champions gathered for the traditional champions' dinner, when the defending champion chose the menu and the guests shared notes on their Masters victories. Tradition also dictated that every year, five selected amateur players were invited to play the Masters, and they were allowed to stay in the tiny bedrooms in the top floor of the manor clubhouse, known as the Crow's Nest. The crowd—or patrons as the Augusta National officials referred to them—partook in their own Augusta habits, including eating pimento cheese sandwiches and walking—never running—around the property. The annual return to Augusta for the Masters Tournament reinforced these customs and elevated the status of the tournament in the national imagination.[542]

Tradition also dictated that the players at the Masters were White, and that those who carried their bags were Black.[543] Perhaps this tradition was more of an unwritten rule than it was an annual habit. Clifford Roberts, cofounder of Augusta National and chairman from 1933 to 1976, reportedly once said, "as long as I am alive, all the players will be white and the caddies will be black."[544] While the provenance of the statement is unclear, and no written record of such a statement exists, the sentiment rang true.⁵⁴⁵ Between 1934 and 1974, not a single Black player competed, and not a single White caddie carried a bag. The Augusta caddies became symbols for the club in a number of ways. Their uniforms—white coveralls with bright green numbers—became famous over the years for the way they contrasted not only with the luscious green grass and bright pink azaleas that lined the fairways, but also the color of their skin (Figure 16).⁵⁴⁶ The white coveralls also strictly differentiated the workers from the White golfers and the White patrons in the crowd. Augusta's caddies symbolized the club's image as the last bastion of southern golf's Jim Crow image.⁵⁴⁷

When the tides of change washed over professional golf in the 1950s and '60s, Augusta National stood firmly in place. Officially, the

FIGURE 16: Arnold Palmer surrounded by Augusta caddies in 1965 (Getty Images).

Masters tournament had no rules against the inclusion of Black players. Prior to 1972, players qualified for the Masters on any one of 14 criteria, usually related to performance in previous major championships, or selection for team events like the Ryder Cup or the Walker Cup. In theory, all the criteria were race neutral. But two of the criteria—being a past Masters winner, and placing in the top 24 in the previous year's Masters—only really applied to White golfers, because no Black golfer had ever competed in the Masters.[548] In 1972, the rules changed. That year, the Masters committee began inviting the winners of the previous year's PGA Tour events. Had that rule been in place before, Charlie Sifford would have qualified. Of course, all qualification criteria meant that no Black player could possibly qualify until the desegregation of the PGA Tour in 1961. No Black professional fulfilled the Masters criteria from 1961 to 1974, but the committee still had the option to invite a player like Charlie Sifford or Lee Elder. An invite might have helped the club shed some of its image as a stronghold of Jim Crow. Yet the club held firm until Lee Elder won at the Monsanto Open in April 1974, a victory that, according to their own self-imposed rule, qualified Elder for the Masters. Soon after, Elder received a call from Clifford Roberts congratulating him on his victory and informing him that he was invited to compete in the Masters Tournament. Almost a year later, Elder joined the Masters field as the first Black player ever to compete, breaking one of the last race barriers in American professional sports. For the all-Black caddie corps at Augusta National, the day was a long time coming.[549] Even when the first Black players appeared in the Masters, the color line in the caddie shack was as strong as ever. The official rules of the Masters dictated that all competitors had to use local caddies. At Augusta National, local exclusively meant Black.

In the middle of the 20th century, caddying in the professional game underwent changes that had far-reaching consequences for the Augusta National caddies. For much of professional golf's existence, players did not have consistent personal caddies as they do today. Golfers travelled from event to event and used local caddies. As the game became more lucrative and competition purses increased in the 1950s and '60s, professionals could afford to employ their own caddies. Having a personal touring caddie—someone they knew and trusted, and who knew them and their game well—was beneficial because it brought consistency to their performance. Over the course of several tournaments, a player and a caddie could develop a rapport. The caddie learned the distances that the player could hit each club in the bag, knew which clubs the player was most comfortable with, and understood when to offer advice or stay silent. While it was possible for local caddies to develop this understanding over the course of a single tournament, they could not match the relationships that touring caddies formed with their professional.

Augusta's corps of Black caddies, though, continued to receive acclaim from golfers. In 1959, Art Wall credited his caddie, Henry Hammond, for helping him toward victory at the Masters. On the 15th hole of the final round, Wall initially decided to use his 3-wood for his second shot onto the green. "But Hammond my caddie," Wall explained, "who really knows this course, said 'I think a 2-iron.'" Wall followed his advice and ended up making a birdie on the hole: a moment he claimed gave him "the biggest charge" toward winning the event.[550]

As the number of touring caddies grew, so too did discontent among players about having to use local caddies at select tournaments. Augusta National was not the only course to insist that professionals used local caddies. Other major tournaments, including the U.S. Open, mandated that professionals used the caddies provided by the course that hosted the event. Professional tournaments brought a big pay day for local caddies, since the rate to caddie for a pro was far higher than for an average club member, and professionals often gave caddies a cut of their winnings if they ended the week at the top of the leaderboard.[551] While no golf course ever officially said so, the cash windfalls that caddies received during tournament week helped offset low wages paid to caddies during the rest of year.[552] Augusta National caddie master Fred Bennett noted that he prioritized the caddies who worked tirelessly at the club throughout the season. "They're not going to sit around and starve all winter then miss this chance," he said ahead of the tournament.[553]

When other tournaments began loosening the mandates on usage of local caddies, Augusta National held firm. The U.S. Open allowed touring caddies to work starting in 1976, leaving the Masters as the last of the tournaments where local caddies were the rule.[554] Augusta National's stubbornness may have been construed as a commitment to their local African American caddies, yet the club's snail-pace approach toward desegregation only served to strengthen the perception of Augusta National as the last bastion of White exceptionalism in golf's troubling racial past. Few onlookers saw the club's insistence that players used local caddies as anything other than the club swimming against the tide of change. Once the color line among the players fell, all that was left of Augusta National's "plantation image" was the Black caddies in their white overalls.

The Dying Embers of Racial Hierarchy

The monopoly of Black caddies in the Masters Tournament came to an end in 1983. That year, the tournament committee made the decision to allow the players to bring their own touring caddies to Augusta. In the years running up to 1983, a sentiment grew among the players that the caddies provided by Augusta National were not all of equal standard. Some players received caddies who had decades of experience of caddying at Augusta National, while others were assigned caddies recruited by the caddie master for that week only. In the end, pressure from professional golfers made the decision inevitable. A year earlier, in the 1982 edition of the tournament, several players were left without caddies to complete their opening round. Torrid weather disrupted the first day of play, and 36 players could not complete their first round that day. The tournament arranged for players to come to the course early the following day to complete their opening round in time for the second round to begin. However, owing to a breakdown in communication between the club and the caddies, many of the caddies were not told about the early start. When play resumed at 7:30 the following morning, a few players had to scramble for a caddie to complete their round.[555] Growing increasingly frustrated with the varied standard of caddies, the competitors seized upon the caddies' tardiness as their opportunity to force Augusta National's hand on the issue. Shortly after the tournament a number of players, including two-time champion and national star Tom Watson, wrote to Hord Hardin, the tournament committee chairman. They implored him to allow the use of touring caddies during the Masters. Augusta National bowed to the pressure and confirmed the change in a memorandum issued in November 1982. "We have concluded," Hardin noted in the statement, "that it is very important to the player competing in one of golf's four 'major' titles that he be comfortable with his caddy; that it is unfair to him to require a person in that vital capacity as to the selection of whom he has no choice."[556]

As the last major tournament to admit a Black golfer, and with the long tradition of Black caddies for White golfers, the Masters came to represent the dying embers of visible racial hierarchy in the South. Two years before the tournament committee decided to allow touring caddies to work the Masters, one journalist summarized a common view of Augusta National: "To many of the millions in the television audience this weekend, the Masters' all-black caddy corps may serve as an unfortunate reminder of the race's subservient past in the South," he wrote.[557] Throughout the 1970s and early '80s, Black journalists continuously pointed to the ways that Augusta National resembled the Antebellum South. Black sportscaster Frank Bannister commented in 1975 that the Masters "typifies an old plantation myth that Blacks are supposed to serve whites."[558] That same year, the *Chicago Defender* noted that "all caddies are black on the plantation-like Augusta National."[559] Upon the announcement of the rule change, the *Augusta News-Review*, the city's only African American newspaper, ran an editorial entitled "Shameful policy ends." The editorial team celebrated the downfall of the caddie policy at the Masters, which produced a "plantation image" of African Americans. The tournament, they commented, "projected Blacks as servants in an international event. It was strictly Old South. To the few black spectators at the tournament it was both striking and humiliating."[560] The Augusta National members certainly did not praise the end of the tradition, and they criticized Hord Hardin for making the change. "My members gave me the devil," he remembered. "They thought I was turning my back on long-time friends of ours." The end of the club's long-term policy was difficult for some to swallow.

It is important to point out that Augusta National's caddies themselves did not view the policy change as a victory in the fight against outdated racial practice. Those men—especially the ones who worked all winter on the golf course only to be denied a high-paying week during the Masters—had to be more concerned about their own livelihoods than their symbolic position in the nation's racial landscape. Caddie master Fred Bennett voiced that the Augusta National caddies were upset, but that "rules are rules."[562] Leroy Schultz, who caddied every Masters from 1963 to 1983, summarized the discontent: "I didn't like [the change]. That took a lot of money from the guys that live around here and work here year-round."[563] Other caddies felt not only a hit to their wallets, but also to their dignity. They hailed from a long tradition of Black caddies who treated their work as skilled labor and saw themselves as expert professionals. Jariah Beard, a caddie who helped Fuzzy Zoeller to Masters victory in 1979, lamented the change: "At one time, we prided ourselves on being the best caddies in the world," Beard noted a decade after the change, "We worked at it. It wasn't a matter of just picking up a bag and carrying it around. It really hurt when they did that to us. We lost a lot of pride."[564]

Hard Even to Get a Bag

In the years after Augusta changed their local caddie policy, some players stayed loyal to the caddies who helped them in previous years. Ben Crenshaw continued using his Augusta National caddie, Carl Jackson, from 1976 until his final Masters appearance in 2015. Most players quickly replaced their local caddie with their regular touring caddie.⁵⁶⁵ Willie Peterson, for example, caddied for Jack Nicklaus one final time in 1983 before being replaced the subsequent year.⁵⁶⁶

Some of the more famous caddies, like Peterson, took to the road to become touring caddies themselves. They joined other Black caddies who followed the PGA Tour from course to course, picking up the bags of players who did not have regular caddies. Yet they joined at a time when the caddies on the tour were becoming increasingly White. The very first touring caddies who appeared in the 1960s were Black, as most Whites still viewed the job as beneath them. However, with increasing prize purses over the course of the '70s, previously disinterested Whites began seeing professional caddying as a respectable occupation.⁵⁶⁷ In turn, the friends and relatives of professional golfers—the majority of whom were White—became interested in caddying. Slowly but surely, White caddies with connections to professional golfers displaced Black caddies with longstanding histories in the game. Reflecting on his career as a touring caddie, an aging Black caddie named Lawrence Swanson summarized the change:

> "[Golfers] are playing for so much money nowadays that everybody will caddie. ... Many years ago it was a disgrace for a White man or a White woman to caddie. I remember the times when we could almost choose the bag we wanted to work for. Long time ago. But nowadays it is hard to even get a bag unless you know somebody."⁵⁶⁸

The end of Black caddying was bittersweet in many ways. It marked an end to the plantation image of Black servants for White leisure-seekers on the South's golf courses, so it made sense that some chose to celebrate it. Yet a long line of African American men who worked the golf courses of the South were instrumental in transforming the job from a menial one to a skilled profession. Their dedication to their craft, and the skills and knowledge that they passed on from one generation of caddies to the next was a point of pride. The job created a generation of Black golfers who played on a burgeoning Black golf tour, and a generation who followed and smashed the color line in professional golf. In their absence, the pipeline to Black success in professional golf is in the nation's college golf programs which, owing to lack of financial access to the game for millions of Black children, are overwhelmingly White in racial make-up.[569] Since the 1983 Masters, Black caddies have all but disappeared from the golf courses of the South and from the national consciousness. Their withdrawal from the region's fairways is a contradiction: their absence is simultaneously a sign of racial progress, and the end of a racial monopoly over an occupation which brought pride, dignity, and a means to play golf to thousands of African American men.

In many ways, the fate of Black caddies reflected the messiness and superficiality of desegregation in many aspects of society. The promise of the Civil Rights Movement—of Rev. Dr. Martin Luther King Jr.'s dream society, where "every valley shall be exalted, every hill and mountain shall be made low, the rough places will be made plain, and the crooked places will be made straight"—never truly came to pass.[570] Desegregation of the South was undoubtedly one of the movement's most righteous and glorious victories, but it came with a number of unintended consequences. Many storied Black schools—that were the pillars of communities for generations—shuttered their doors as school districts consolidated, and future Black students had to compete with White students for resources and access to the best education, in a system that for many decades would clearly underserve its Black population. The educational curriculum across the country largely did not evolve to accommodate their integrated classrooms, and instead promoted a method of education that elevated most aspects of White culture, downplayed historical injustices by Whites, while catering more to White students than Black ones. Black teachers—mentors to thousands—lost their jobs, and the esteemed position of the school in Black life suffered.[571] After the Civil Rights Act, Black business districts across the South entered a long decline as their clientele availed themselves of newfound freedom to spend at previously White-only establishments. Black Main Streets in cities from Durham to Atlanta to Hattiesburg fell apart as segregation crumbled.[572] As the world of golf opened its doors to Black golfers in the '60s, the number of Black caddies around the South declined just as the job began receiving the widespread recognition and financial compensation it deserved.

With the passing of the Black caddie, there is a feeling among those who did the job that something has been lost. Nostalgia tinges their recollections of the past. Augusta National caddie Jariah Beard remembered that he and his fellow workers "knew that golf course, and we loved what we were doing. Those were the best moments in our lives."[573] Another former Houston caddie looked back on his "beautiful memories as a caddie" and the "happiest days of his life" when he played with other caddies on Monday mornings.[574] For many years, Willie Peterson's daughter originally could not understand her father's gratification in his time as a caddie." "I thought, 'How can he be proud of carrying a real big bag of golf clubs around for some guy?'" Only years after Peterson's passing did she recognize the contributions a caddie made.[575] Like those Black Southerners who looked back on segregated schools and Black businesses with a hint of sadness at what was lost, former caddies knew that their job was not a simplistic manifestation of racial hierarchy.[576] It was a means to make a living. A space to build community. An opportunity to demonstrate their talents and develop skills in a storied sport.

The South's Black caddies lived full, important, and varied lives, and their passing is not a linear tale of racial progress from sporting servants to expert golfers. They were a collection of dignified and talented workers who graced Tennessee tee boxes, Florida fairways, Georgia greens, and the woods and bunkers in between. The caddy shacks of the South may now be largely empty, but their memory marches on.

Epilogue

Writing about caddies in 1997, famed essayist John Updike claimed that

> "The fact is, most Americans are uneasy with servants. In our democratic fashion we keep thinking of them as people. The French nobles were surrounded by servants through every detail of their morning toilette; this was possible because servants weren't people, they were human artifacts, constructed to serve. Not that golf is quite as private an activity as the morning toilette, but it is toward the intimate end of the continuum, somewhere between making love and writing a poem. Imagine writing a poem with a sweating, worried-looking boy handing you a different pencil at the end of every word."[577]

Updike's pronouncement on America's unease with servants, while perhaps true of the 1990s—and truer among his more progressive brethren in Massachusetts—was certainly not the case for the majority of the 20th century, especially in the South. Rather, Updike's statement perhaps represents the general discomfort that many White Americans felt over the nation's racial past when he was writing. During that same year—1997—Tiger Woods became the first man of African American descent to win one of golf's major tournaments. Tiger's victory at the Masters in 1997 symbolized the promise of a racially tolerant nation. If a Black man can win at Augusta, the reasoning went, then racial equality was on the horizon. In the late 1990s and early 2000s, it was undoubtedly easier for White Americans to focus on the potential for a racially tolerant future than to linger in the discomfort of the nation's Jim Crow past. The history of Black caddies reminded the nation of the ways that race had defined who was allowed to enjoy leisure time and who was enlisted to facilitate it. Amid the spirit of racial optimism at the turn of the century, the notion of servants made many like John Updike uneasy.

Three years after Updike penned his thoughts on caddies, the movie *The Legend of Bagger Vance* opened in theaters around the country.[578] It is certainly the best-known piece of popular culture depicting an African American golf caddie. Set in the 1930s in Savannah, Georgia, the movie features Will Smith as a Black caddie named Bagger Vance. Vance helps Rannulph Junuh, a World War I veteran suffering from post-traumatic stress disorder, to overcome his demons and become a successful golfer once again. *The Legend of Bagger Vance* received widespread criticism, not only over its meek screenplay, but also because of the ways that the movie presented its one Black protagonist. Vance arrives in the dead of the night: a rogue traveler carrying a suitcase, with no back story and no explained reason for his presence at Junuh's grand plantation home. Through a mix of folk wisdom and seemingly otherworldly powers, Vance helps Junuh rediscover his golf swing, and in turn get his life back on track.[579] In the aftermath of the movie's release, the award winning Black director, Spike Lee, commented that movies like *The Legend of Bagger Vance* "have these magical mystical Negroes who show up as some sort of spirit or angel but only benefit the White characters."[580] A number of movies in the 1990s and 2000s had supporting Black characters whom film critics and cultural commentators deemed to fit the mold of the "Magical Mystical Negro." Like other characters, Vance used his magic to help the White protagonist, worked in a service role, demonstrated "folk wisdom" rather than intelligence, and did not use any magic for his own benefit.[581]

The depiction of a Black caddie in the clichéd "Magical Negro" typecast was—just like Updike's unease with caddies—representative of the racial moment. White filmmakers likely saw characters like Vance as an improved representation of African Americans in film. After all, Bagger Vance was the expert guiding the alcoholic and lost White golfer back to success. This was surely better than Hollywood's historic stereotyping of African Americans as Sambo, Mammy, Jezebel, or Uncle Tom, right? While Vance may have been the expert, he was also an entirely incomplete and one-dimensional character. His abilities were not rooted in his intelligence or physical skills or golfing knowledge, but rather in his mythical powers: nothing earned, practiced, or learned, just magic. He arrives on the scene as if from thin air in the dead of the night, and then departs literally into the sunset once Junuh has been saved. His own life story is entirely unknown. What's more, the daily issues of racial intolerance, Jim Crow policies, lynching, segregation, racial etiquette, or fraught race relations in any way are wholly missing in the movie's depiction of 1930s Georgia. Vance is better understood not as a depiction of Black caddying in the '30s, but as an early 2000s utopic imagining of a post-racial American society. The movie imagines a colorblind world of interracial friendship. Why dwell on the past? It wasn't so bad, it is behind us now, and we can now all get along.

While *The Legend of Bagger Vance* may seem harmless, it distorts the reality of what life was like for the thousands of Black men who worked the golf courses of Georgia and the rest of the South. Unlike Vance, these were men who had real skills, not mythical ones. They could judge distances and match the yardage to a club in their player's bag. They could read the slope of the green and accurately assess the impact of the grass's grain on the ball's movement. These were skills rooted in mathematics and physics, learned from years of honing their knowledge—not unexplained powers. Unlike Vance, these men had lives outside of caddying, with families to help and leisure pursuits of their own to fulfill. They suffered hardships and faced adversity far worse than a golf slump. Unlike Bagger Vance, real Black caddies had rich, real back stories, real lives, real feelings. They did not appear on the course from thin air to help White golfers—rather they hailed from a long trajectory of Black service workers, factory workers, and servants: without whom the South could never have functioned and developed as a region.

With Bagger Vance as the most famous representation of Black caddies in popular culture, few people have been exposed to their vast contribution to the game. The custodians of golf's history have largely celebrated the successes of the 20th century's White golfers without fully accounting for the African American caddies who helped considerably along the way. Perhaps they did so because of the same unease that plagued John Updike. Or maybe they shied away from the topic because Black caddies personified the game's long-standing racial intolerance. In many ways, as one *New York Times* article from 2012 put it, the caddies "stood as a striking symbol of the sport's segregated state."[582] Dealing with a powerful symbol like that takes a level of introspection that many in the golf world were uncomfortable with in the 1990s and 2000s. Country clubs and golf resorts—corporations with a consistent eye on public perception—would rather not draw attention to the potentially troubling images of racial hierarchy that existed on their fairways.

It is little surprise that Updike's essay on caddies and *The Legend of Bagger Vance* appeared as the 20th century came to a close. Americans wanted to progress beyond the beating of Rodney King and the racially charged case of *The People v. O.J. Simpson*. President Bill Clinton launched "One America in the 21st Century: The President's Initiative on Race." Golf entered the new millennium riding a wave of inclusion. Tiger Woods's rise to stardom coincided with—and largely represented—a belief that the United States was becoming a post-racial society. African American athletes from Tiger Woods to Michael Jordan starred on the sports fields, Black celebrities like Oprah Winfrey and Will Smith were among the nation's best known and most rewarded cultural figures, and Black politicians made strides into local and national office. In the aftermath of Barack Obama's presidential election in 2008, many commentators across the political spectrum claimed that his victory was the final indication that the country had become a "post-racial" society.[583] In all the ways that Black caddies symbolized a troubling past, Tiger Woods promised a better future. It is easy to see why the golf industry focused on the latter rather than the former.

Since Tiger Woods' rise to prominence, it has become clear in golf, as it has in wider society, that the United States is not enjoying a post-racial moment. The success of Black sports stars or the election of a Black president did not usher in a racial utopia like the one dreamed up in *The Legend of Bagger Vance*. Golf remains one of the Whitest sports in the country, with fewer Black golfers on the PGA Tour now than in the 1960s, when former Black caddies from the South joined in force. While there is no simple answer to golf's race problem, it is clear that avoiding the history of Black caddies in the South—or ignoring the racial politics that put them there—achieves little.

There is no need for today's golf establishment to feel ashamed that those who held their positions 100 years ago built a region defined by racial hierarchy. Yet by ignoring or incompletely telling the story of Black caddies, we inadvertently accept the flawed notions of what constituted good work and what constituted bad work. Caddies themselves defied those prescriptions and turned their jobs into a profession, became skilled workers, and grew into talented golfers. Black golfers, writers, and scholars have long foregrounded the history of caddying as a proud beginning to a rich story of Black golf. Framing the story of Black caddies as one of Black dedication, pride, and excellence—while acknowledging and condemning the Jim Crow power structures that put Black caddies on the course—is a challenge. But for a truly inclusive future, it is a challenge worth facing.

There are signs that Black caddies are beginning to get the recognition they deserve. Every April, as the greenskeepers at Augusta National prune the azaleas and rake the pine straw in preparation for the Masters, newspaper articles appear highlighting the history of Augusta's Black caddies. Some of the most famous caddies—including Willie Peterson, who caddied for Jack Nicklaus, and Nathaniel "Iron Man" Avery, who caddied for Arnold Palmer—finally received adequate headstones on their graves, which sat unmarked for more than two decades. The Pinehurst Caddie Hall of Fame honors caddies whose contributions to the club's storied past were previously ignored.

And yet, outside of the most famous and wealthy of the South's golf courses, little has been done to remember the lives of the thousands of Black caddies who roamed the region's fairways. In time, they will be remembered. Men and boys of skill, dignity, and pride, these Black caddies made an indelible mark on the South's sporting landscape.

Acknowledgments

This book is the culmination of seven years of work, from the first green shots of an idea during a class as part of my Master's at the University of Glasgow in 2017 all the way to publication with Back Nine Press today. Along the journey I learned that many golfers are nothing without their caddies, just as I am nothing without those who have helped this book become reality. W. Fitzhugh Brundage was a reassuring and caring dissertation advisor during my PhD at the University of North Carolina at Chapel Hill. I had the privilege of working with a wonderful committee comprised of Matt Andrews, Jerma Jackson, Bryant Simon, and William Sturkey. I am also indebted to the many folks who read chapter drafts, heard conference papers, and probed my ideas including Ryan Anderson, Ashley Brown, Lane Demas, Eric Hall, Erik Gellman, Bob Korstad, and Katherine Turk. I want to especially thank Marina Moskowitz who told me I was capable of doing a PhD and encouraged me to apply to schools in the United States. Without her I would not have ended up at UNC and so I owe her a great deal.

The staff in the UNC Department of History deserve great credit for helping me navigate various deadlines and hurdles, while always searching for more funding for me and my fellow graduate students. Amanda Mills and the folks at the UNC International Student and Scholar Services were invaluable in guiding me through the complexities of visas, taxes, and funding. The staff at Tufts Archives, the United States Golf Association library, and at UNC's Wilson Library were generous with their time and resources in my various trips to the archives.

Along the way I have received generous funding and support from numerous parts of the University. I am thankful for the Department of History's summer funding and Clein summer internship. Ashley Melzer and the Humanities for the Public Good program gave me two wonderful opportunities to apply historical training in fulfilling ways. The Center for the Study of the American South provided me with summer funding that kickstarted my doctoral research. Finally, the Richard Brooke scholarship from the office of Scholarships and Student Aid was a welcome and helpful surprise as I pushed towards the end of my dissertation.

A few key individuals helped me navigate the muddy waters of publishing and turn my dissertation into a book. Thank you to Kenny Pallas and Jim Hartsell who connected me to Back Nine Press. Jim Sitar has been an encouraging and thoughtful editor, and I most appreciative of his belief that this project should reach an audience of golfers.

I am forever grateful to my family for their support and dedication. My eternal thanks go to my mother and father, Heather and John, for their generosity and love as I continued to explore my studies. Scott and Emma have served as a model for keeping sight of the important things in life and have always been there when I needed them.

I reserve my final and most important thanks to my partner, Stephanie, and our dog, Luna. As chief research assistant, Luna was by my side as I typed every word of this book. My partner in life and in PhD, Stephanie, is both my greatest inspiration and my most caring cheerleader. Without her encouragement this story may never have made the jump from a dissertation on a dusty shelf to a published book.

Bibliography

Primary Sources

Government Documents

Ancestry.com. 1900 United States Federal Census [database on-line]. Provo, UT, USA: Ancestry.com Operations Inc, 2004.

Ancestry.com. 1910 United States Federal Census [database on-line]. Lehi, UT, USA: Ancestry.com Operations Inc, 2006.

Ancestry.com. 1920 United States Federal Census [database on-line]. Provo, UT, USA: Ancestry.com Operations, Inc., 2010.

Ancestry.com. 1930 United States Federal Census [database on-line]. Provo, UT, USA: Ancestry.com Operations Inc, 2002.

Ancestry.com. 1940 United States Federal Census [database on-line]. Provo, UT, USA: Ancestry.com Operations, Inc., 2012.

Ancestry.com. 1950 United States Federal Census [database on-line]. Lehi, UT, USA: Ancestry.com Operations, Inc., 2022.

Hoover, H. Conrad. The President's Reemployment Agreement. Office of National Recovery Administration Division of Review, 1936.

US Bureau of the Census, 1940 Census of the Population, vol. 3, The Labor Force, part 2. Alabama-Indiana, Washington, D.C.: Bureau of the Census, 1940.

US Bureau of the Census, Negro Population, 1790-1915, Part 6 Economic Statistics, Washington, D.C.: Bureau of the Census, 1918.

US Bureau of the Census, Reports of the Thirteenth Census Vol. 6 Agriculture Reports by States, with Statistics for Counties—Alabama-Montana, Washington, D.C.: US Bureau of the Census, 1914.

US Bureau of the Census, Reports of the Thirteenth Census Vol. 7 Agriculture Reports by States, with Statistics for Counties—Nebraska-Wyoming, Washington, D.C.: US Bureau of the Census, 1914.

US Bureau of the Census, Sixteenth Census of the United States, Reports on Agriculture, irrigation and Drainage Vol. 1 Statistics for Counties, Part 3 South Atlantic Division Washington, D.C.: US Bureau of the Census, 1942.

"Statement on the Death of Charles L. Sifford," February 4, 2015, DCPD201500079, Administration of Barack Obama, https://www.govinfo.gov/content/pkg/DCPD-201500079/pdf/DCPD-201500079.pdf.

Films

Pinehurst, Pictoreel Sportscope 1938.
The Last Colored Caddy, 2005.
The Legend of Bagger Vance, Dreamworks, 2000.

Legal Cases

Southern Grocery Stores Inc. et al. v. Herring, 11 S.E.2d 57 (Ga. Ct. App. 1940)
Claremont Country Club et al. v. Industrial Accident Commission 163 P. 209,174 Cal. 395 (1917)
Andrews v. North Shore Country Club, 258. A.D. 1017 (1940)
Essex County Country Club v. Chapman, 173 A. 591 (N.J. 1934)
Indian Hill Club v. Industrial Com. 309 Ill. 271 (1923)
Piusinski v. Transit Valley Country Club, 259 App. Div. 765 (N.Y. App. Div. 1940)
Meyer v. North Hills Golf Club, 238 A.D. 752 (1933)
Duck v. D'Angelo, 32 Misc. 2d 164, (N.Y. Sup. Ct. 1961).

Newspapers and Magazines

Alabama Tribune (Alabama)
American Federationist (District of Columbia)
Anniston Star (Alabama)
Arizona Gleam (Arizona)
Asheville Times (North Carolina)
Atlanta Constitution (Georgia)
Atlanta Daily World (Georgia)
Atlanta Georgian (Georgia)
Augusta Chronicle (Georgia)
Augusta Herald (Georgia)
Augusta News Review (Georgia)
Baltimore Afro-American (Maryland)
Baltimore Sun (Maryland)
Bangor Daily News (Maine)
Birmingham News (Alabama)
Birmingham Post-Herald (Alabama)
Birmingham Reporter (Alabama)
Black Enterprise (New York)
Brooklyn Times (New York)
Buffalo Commercial (New York)
Butte Inter Mountain (Montana)
Carolina Times (North Carolina)
Charlotte News (North Carolina)
Charlotte Observer (North Carolina)
Chicago Daily Tribune (Illinois)
Chicago Defender (Illinois)
Cincinnati Enquirer (Ohio)
Cinecaste (New York)
Cleveland Star (Ohio)
Country Life in America (New York)
Covington Virginian (Virginia)
Davenport Democrat and Leader
Decatur Herald (Illinois)

Durham Sun (North Carolina)
Eagle River Review (Wisconsin)
Florida Star and News (Florida)
Fort Myers News Press (Florida)
Fort Worth Star-Telegram (Texas)
Golf Course News (Ohio)
Golf Digest (New York)
Golf Illustrated (New York)
Golfdom (Virginia)
Greensboro Daily News (North Carolina)
Greenville News (South Carolina)
Hartford Courant (Connecticut)
High Point Enterprise (North Carolina)
Jackson Clarion-Ledger (Mississippi)
Jonesboro Weekly Sun (Arkansas)
Kingston Daily Freeman (New York)
Knoxville News-Sentinel (Tennessee)
Life (New York)
Los Angeles Express (California)
Los Angeles Herald (California)
Los Angeles Sentinel (California)
Los Angeles Times (California)
Los Angeles Tribune (California)
Louisiana Weekly (Louisiana)
Macon Telegraph (Georgia)
Messenger (New York)
Miami New Times (Florida)
Miami News (Florida)
Mississippi Free Press (Mississippi)
Nashville American (Tennessee)
Nation's Business (New York)
National Magazine (New York)
New York Age (New York)
New York Amsterdam News (New York)
New York Tribune (New York)

Newsday (New York)
Norfolk Journal and Guide (Virginia)
Norfolk Landmark (Virginia)
Owensboro Messenger-Inquirer (Kentucky)
Oxnard Courier (California)
Palm Beach Post (Florida)
Philadelphia Public Ledger (Pennsylvania)
Philadelphia Tribune (Pennsylvania)
Pinehurst Outlook (North Carolina)
Pittsburgh Courier (Pennsylvania)
Pittsburgh Post-Gazette (Pennsylvania)
Raleigh News and Observer (North Carolina)
Richmond Dispatch (Virginia)
Richmond News Leader (Virginia)
Richmond Times (Virginia)
Roanoke Times (Virginia)
Robesonian (North Carolina)
Rochester Democrat and Chronicle (New York)
Rock Island Argus (Iowa)
San Bernardino County (California)
Sandhill Citizen (North Carolina)
Saturday Evening Post (Indiana)
Southern Pines Pilot (North Carolina)
Sports Illustrated (New York)
Tampa Tribune (Florida)
The American Golfer (New York)
The Atlanta News (Georgia)
The Golf Course Reporter
The Golfer (New York)
The New York Times (New York)
The Southern Golfer (New York)
The Voice of The Negro (Georgia)
Time (New York)
United Golfer and Other Sports
USGA Golf Bulletin (New York)

Wall Street Journal (New York)
Washington Evening Star (District of Columbia)
Washington Herald (District of Columbia)
Washington Post (District of Columbia)
Washington Times (District of Columbia)
Washington Tribune (District of Columbia)

Online Databases

"NCAA Demographics Database." Accessed February 8, 2023. https://www.ncaa.org/sports/2018/12/13/ncaa-demographics-database.aspx.

"Pinehurst, Moore County, North Carolina, September 1920." 1:600. New York: Sanborn Map Company, September 1920. North Carolina Collection, University of North Carolina. https://dc.lib.unc.edu/cdm/compoundobject/collection/ncmaps/id/6783/rec/4.

Nelson, Robert K, LaDale Winling, Richard Marciano, and Nathan Connolly. "Mapping Inequality." Accessed February 21, 2023. https://dsl.richmond.edu/panorama/redlining/.

Seamheads Negro Leagues Database. "J. C. Hamilton." Accessed December 20, 2022. https://www.seamheads.com/NegroLgs/player.php?playerID=hamilo1jam.

Published Primary Sources

Du Bois, W. E. B. *Darkwater: Voices From Within The Veil*. New York: Harcourt, Brace, and Howe, 1920.

King Jr., Martin Luther. "I Have a Dream." Washington, D.C., August 28, 1963. https://avalon.law.yale.edu/20th_century/mlk01.asp.

Miller, Adam David. *Ticket to Exile: A Memoir*. Berkeley: Heyday Books, 2007.

Motley, Constance Baker. *Equal Justice Under Law: An Autobiography*. New York: Farrar, Straus & Giroux, 1998.

Sifford, Charlie, and James Gullo. *Just Let Me Play: The Story of Charlie Sifford, the First Black PGA Golfer.* Latham, N.Y.: British American Pub., 1992.

The Social Register: Richmond, Charleston, Savannah, Atlanta, 1911. New York: The Social Register Society, 1911.

Taft, Robert, and Betty Taft. *On the Bag: Seventy Years Remembered by Pinehurst's Hall-of-Fame Caddie Willie McRae.* Cincinnati: Stevens Publishing, 2013.

Updike, John. *Golf Dreams.* London: Penguin, 1998.

Washington, Booker T. *Up From Slavery: An Autobiography.* New York: Doubleday, 1901.

Wickham, DeWayne. *Woodholme: A Black Man's Story of Growing up Alone.* 1st ed. New York: Farrar, Straus, and Giroux, 1995.

Wright, Richard. *Black Boy: A Record of Childhood and Youth.* Cleveland: World Publishing Co., 1947.

Secondary Sources

Adler, Jeffrey S. *Murder in New Orleans: The Creation of Jim Crow Policing.* Chicago: University of Chicago Press, 2019.

Anderson, Devery S. *Emmett Till: The Murder That Shocked the World and Propelled the Civil Rights Movement.* Jackson,: University Press of Mississippi, 2015.

Armour, Tommy. *Tommy Armour's ABC's of Golf.* New York: Simon and Schuster, 1967.

Aron, Cindy S. *Working at Play: A History of Vacations in the United States.* New York: Oxford University Press, 1999.

Austin, Paula C. *Coming of Age in Jim Crow DC: Navigating the Politics of Everyday Life.* New York: NYU Press, 2019.

Ayers, Edward L. *The Promise of the New South: Life after Reconstruction.* New York: Oxford University Press, 1992.

Baker, Ray Stannard. *Following the Color Line: American Negro Citizenship in the Progressive Era.* New York: Harper Torchbooks, 1964.

Baldwin, Davarian L. *Chicago's New Negroes: Modernity, the Great Migration, & Black Urban Life*. Chapel Hill: University of North Carolina Press, 2007.

Baradaran, Mehrsa. *The Color of Money: Black Banks and the Racial Wealth Gap*. Cambridge, Massachusetts: Belknap Press, 2017.

Barkow, Al. *Gettin' to the Dance Floor: An Oral History of American Golf*. 1st edition. New York: Atheneum, 1986.

Bates, Beth Tompkins. *Pullman Porters and the Rise of Protest Politics in Black America, 1925-1945*. Chapel Hill: University of North Carolina Press, 2001.

Bay, Mia. *Traveling Black: A Story of Race and Resistance*. Cambridge, MA: Belknap Press, 2021.

Bayor, Ronald H. *Race and the Shaping of Twentieth-Century Atlanta*. The Fred W. Morrison Series in Southern Studies. Chapel Hill: University of North Carolina Press, 1996.

Bernstein, David E. *Only One Place of Redress: African Americans, Labor Regulations, and the Courts: From Reconstruction to the New Deal*. Constitutional Conflicts. Durham, NC: Duke University Press, 2001.

Berrey, Stephen A. *The Jim Crow Routine: Everyday Performances of Race, Civil Rights, and Segregation in Mississippi*. Chapel Hill: The University of North Carolina Press, 2015.

Blackmon, Douglas A. *Slavery by Another Name: The Re-Enslavement of Black People in America From the Civil War to World War II*. New York: Doubleday, 2008.

Blight, David W. *Race and Reunion: The Civil War in American Memory*. Cambridge, MA: Harvard University Press, 2002.

Bond, Julian. "Foreword." In *Emmett Till: The Murder That Shocked the World and Propelled the Civil Rights Movement*, edited by Devery S. Anderson, xiii–xv. Jackson,: University Press of Mississippi, 2015.

Boskin, Joseph. *Sambo: The Rise & Demise of an American Jester*. New York: Oxford University Press, 1986.

Brock, Julia. "Land, Labor, and Leisure: Northern Tourism in the Red Hills Region, 1890-1950." Ph.D., University of California, Santa Barbara, 2012.

Brown, Ashley Nicole. "The Match of Her Life: Althea Gibson, Icon and Instrument of Integration." Ph.D., The George Washington University, n.d.

Brown, Dona. *Inventing New England: Regional Tourism in the Nineteenth Century*. Washington, DC: Smithsonian Institution Press, 1995.

Brown, Leslie. *Upbuilding Black Durham: Gender, Class, and Black Community Development in the Jim Crow South*. Chapel Hill: University of North Carolina Press, 2008.

Brundage, W. Fitzhugh. "Introduction." In *The Folly of Jim Crow: Rethinking the Segregated South*, edited by Stephanie Cole and Natalie J. Ring, 1st ed., 1–16. Walter Prescott Webb Memorial Lectures ; No. 43. College Station: Texas A&M University Press, 2012.

———. *Lynching in the New South: Georgia and Virginia, 1880-1930*. Blacks in the New World. Urbana: University of Illinois Press, 1993.

Bryan, William D. *The Price of Permanence: Nature and Business in the New South*. Athens: University of Georgia Press, 2018.

Burns, Rebecca. *Rage in the Gate City: The Story of the 1906 Atlanta Race Riot*. Cincinnati: Emmis Books, 2006.

"Burton Smith." In *The National Cyclopaedia of American Biography, Being the History of the United States as Illustrated in the Lives of the Founders, Builders, and Defenders of the Republic, and of the Men and Women Who Are Doing the Work and Moulding the Thought of the Present Time*, 14:51–52. New York: J. T. White Company, 1910.

Caddoo, Cara. *Envisioning Freedom: Cinema and the Building of Modern Black Life*. Cambridge, Mass: Harvard University Press, 2014.

Cassanello, Robert. *To Render Invisible: Jim Crow and Public Life in New South Jacksonville*. Gainesville: University Press of Florida, 2013.

Castillo, Thomas A. *Working in the Magic City: Moral Economy in Early Twentieth-Century Miami*. First edition. Urbana: University of Illinois Press, 2022.

Clark-Lewis, Elizabeth. *Living In, Living Out: African American Domestics in Washington, D.C., 1910-1940*. Washington, D.C.: Smithsonian Books, 2010.

Clayton, Ward. *Men on the Bag: The Caddies of Augusta National*. Ann Arbor, Mich: Sports Media Group, 2004.

Cohen, Lizabeth. *A Consumers' Republic: The Politics of Mass Consumption in Postwar America*. New York: Knopf, 2003.

Corbett, Theodore. *The Making of American Resorts: Saratoga Springs, Ballston Spa, Lake George*. New Brunswick, NJ: Rutgers University Press, 2001.

Cox, Karen L, ed. *Destination Dixie: Tourism and Southern History*. Gainesville, FL: University Press of Florida, 2013.

Crenshaw, Ben, Carl Jackson, and Melanie Hauser, *Two Roads to Augusta, The Inspiring Story of How Two Men From Different Backgrounds Grew to Become Best Friends and Capture the Biggest Prize in Golf* (Greenwich, CT: The American Golfer, 2013).

Daniel, Pete. *The Shadow of Slavery: Peonage in the South, 1901-1969.* Urbana: University of Illinois Press, 1972.

David S. Cecelski. *Along Freedom Road: Hyde County, North Carolina, and the Fate of Black Schools in the South.* Chapel Hill: University of North Carolina Press, 1994.

Dawkins, Marvin P., Jomills H. Braddock, and Shelby Gilbert. "African American Golf Clubs in the Early Development of Black Golf." Western *Journal of Black Studies 42*, no. 1/2 (2018): 72–83.

Dawson, Michael C., and Lawrence D. Bobo. "One Year Later and the Myth of a Post-Racial Society." *Du Bois Review: Social Science Research on Race 6*, no. 2 (2009): 247–49.

Deaton, Thomas Mashburn. "Atlanta During the Progressive Era." Ph.D., University of Georgia, 1969.

Delmont, Matthew F. *Half American: The Epic Story of African Americans Fighting World War II at Home and Abroad.* New York: Viking, 2022.

Demas, Lane. *Game of Privilege: An African American History of Golf.* Chapel Hill: University of North Carolina Press, 2017.

Doyle, Bertram Wilbur. *The Etiquette of Race Relations in the South: A Study in Social Control.* Chicago: University of Chicago Press, 1937.

Earley, Lawrence S. *Looking for Longleaf: The Fall and Rise of an American Forest.* Chapel Hill: University of North Carolina Press, 2004.

Edwards, Elizabeth. *Raw Histories: Photographs, Anthropology and Museums.* Oxford: Berg, 2001.

Fairclough, Adam. "The Costs of Brown: Black Teachers and School Integration." *The Journal of American History 91*, no. 1 (2004): 43–55.

Foley, Barbara. *Spectres of 1919: Class and Nation in the Making of the New Negro.* Urbana: University of Illinois Press, 2003.

Freedman, Estelle B. *Redefining Rape: Sexual Violence in the Era of Suffrage and Segregation.* Cambridge, Mass,: Harvard University Press, 2013.

Gaines, Kevin K. *Uplifting the Race: Black Leadership, Politics, and Culture in the 20th Century.* Chapel Hill: The University of North Carolina Press, 1996.

Gates, Henry Louis. "The Trope of a New Negro and the Reconstruction of the Image of the Black." *Representations*, 24 (1988): 129–55.

Gems, Gerald R. *Before Jackie Robinson: The Transcendent Role of Black Sporting Pioneers*. Lincoln, Nebraska: University of Nebraska Press, 2017.

Gibson, Helen A. "Access to Labor and Leisure in Cars: Early Black Motorists' Automotivity in Miami." *Mondes Du Tourisme, no. 21* (June 1, 2022).

Giltner, Scott E. *Hunting and Fishing in the New South: Black Labor and White Leisure after the Civil War*. Baltimore: Johns Hopkins University Press, 2008.

Glenn, Cerise L., and Landra J. Cunningham. "The Power of Black Magic: The Magical Negro and White Salvation in Film." *Journal of Black Studies 40*, no. 2 (November 1, 2009): 135–52.

Godshalk, David Fort. *Veiled Visions: The 1906 Atlanta Race Riot and the Reshaping of American Race Relations*. Chapel Hill: University of North Carolina Press, 2005.

Goldberg, David E. *The Retreats of Reconstruction: Race, Leisure, and the Politics of Segregation at the New Jersey Shore, 1865-1920*. 1st edition. New York: Fordham University Press, 2016.

Goodson, Steve. *Highbrows, Hillbillies & Hellfire: Public Entertainment in Atlanta, 1880-1930*. Athens: University of Georgia Press, 2002.

Greene, Lorenzo J, and Carter G Woodson. *The Negro Wage Earner*. Washington, D.C.: The Association for the Study of Negro Life and History, 1930.

Gross, James A. *Rights, Not Interests: Resolving Value Clashes under the National Labor Relations Act*. Ithaca: Cornell University Press, 2017.

Hahn, Steven. *A Nation Under Our Feet: Black Political Struggles in the Rural South, from Slavery to the Great Migration*. Cambridge, Mass: Belknap Press of Harvard University Press, 2003.

Hale, Grace Elizabeth. "'For Colored' and 'For White': Segregating Consumption in the South." In *Jumpin' Jim Crow. Southern Politics from Civil War to Civil Rights*, edited by Jane Dailey, Glenda Elizabeth Gilmore, and Bryant Simon, 162–82. Princeton: Princeton University Press, 2001.

———. *Making Whiteness: The Culture of Segregation in the South, 1890-1940*. 1st Vintage Books ed. New York: Vintage Books, 1999.

Hall, Jacquelyn Dowd. "The Long Civil Rights Movement and the Political Uses of the Past." *The Journal of American History 91*, no. 4 (2005): 1233–63.

Harold, Claudrena N. *New Negro Politics in the Jim Crow South*. Athens: University of Georgia Press, 2016.

Harriet, Ramona. *A Missing Link In History: The Journey of African Americans in Golf*. 2nd edition. CreateSpace, 2015.

Harris, J. William. *Deep Souths: Delta, Piedmont, and Sea Island Society in the Age of Segregation*. Baltimore: Johns Hopkins University Press, 2001.

———. "Etiquette, Lynching, and Racial Boundaries in Southern History: A Mississippi Example." *The American Historical Review* 100, no. 2 (1995): 387–410.

Harris, Thomas Edward. "An Analysis of the Clash Over Issues Between Booker T. Washington and W. E. B. Dubois." Ph.D., Temple University, 1981.

Hawkins, Robert. "Brotherhood Men and Singing Slackers: A. Philip Randolph's Rhetoric of Music and Manhood." In *Reframing Randolph: Labor, Black Freedom, and the Legacies of A. Philip Randolph*, edited by Andrew E. Kersten and Clarence Lang. New York: NYU Press, 2015.

Hickman, Nollie. *Mississippi Harvest: Lumbering in the Longleaf Pine Belt, 1840-1915*. Jackson: University Press of Mississippi, 1962.

Hillyer, Reiko. *Designing Dixie: Tourism, Memory, and Urban Space in the New South*. Charlottesville: University of Virginia Press, 2014.

Himel, Matthew Taylor. "Greening Golf: Grass, Agriculture, and Pinehurst in the Sandhills." Ph.D., Mississippi State University, 2020.

Hourigan, Richard R. "Welcome to South Carolina: Race, Sex and the Rise of Tourism in Myrtle Beach, 1900–1975." Ph.D., The University of Alabama, 2010.

Hueber, David B. "The Changing Face of the Game and Golf's Built Environment." Ph.D., Clemson University, 2012.

Hunter, Tera W. *To 'joy My Freedom: Southern Black Women's Lives and Labors after the Civil War*. Cambridge, Mass.: Harvard University Press, 1997.

Jackson, Kenneth T. *Crabgrass Frontier: The Suburbanization of the United States*. New York: Oxford University Press, Incorporated, 1987.

James Jr., Rawn. *The Double V: How Wars, Protest, and Harry Truman Desegregated America's Military*. 1st edition. New York: Bloomsbury Press, 2013.

Jefferson, Alison Rose. *Living the California Dream: African American Leisure Sites during the Jim Crow Era*. Lincoln: University of Nebraska Press, 2020.

Jett, Brandon T. *Race, Crime, and Policing in the Jim Crow South: African Americans and Law Enforcement in Birmingham, Memphis, and New Orleans, 1920–1945*. Baton Rouge: Louisiana State University Press, 2021.

Johnson, Joseph Herman. "West Southern Pines: An Experiment in Negro Self Government," 1932.

Johnson, M. Mikell. *The African American Woman Golfer: Her Legacy*. Westport, Conn.: Praeger, 2008.

Jones, Jacqueline. *Labor of Love, Labor of Sorrow: Black Women, Work and the Family, from Slavery to the Present*. New York: Basic Books, 2010.

———. "'Lifework' and Its Limits: The Problem of Labor in The Philadelphia Negro." In *W.E.B. DuBois, Race, and the City: The Philadelphia Negro and Its Legacy*, edited by Michael B. Katz and Thomas J. Sugrue, 103–26. Philadelphia: University of Pennsylvania Press, 1998.

Jones, William P. *The March on Washington: Jobs, Freedom, and the Forgotten History of Civil Rights*. New York: W. W. Norton & Company, 2014.

———. *The Tribe of Black Ulysses: African American Lumber Workers in the Jim Crow South*. Urbana: University of Illinois Press, 2005.

Jong, Greta de. *You Can't Eat Freedom: Southerners and Social Justice after the Civil Rights Movement*. Chapel Hill: University of North Carolina Press, 2016.

Kahrl, Andrew W. *Land Was Ours: How Black Beaches Became White Wealth in the Coastal South*. Chapel Hill: University of North Carolina Press, 2016.

Kelley, Robin D. G. *Hammer and Hoe: Alabama Communists During the Great Depression*. Chapel Hill: University of North Carolina Press, 1990.

———. "'We Are Not What We Seem': Rethinking Black Working-Class Opposition in the Jim Crow South." *The Journal of American History 80*, no. 1 (June 1993): 75–112.

———. "Without a Song: New York Musicians Strike Out against Technology." In *Three Strikes: Miners, Musicians, Salesgirls and the Fighting Spirit of Labor's Last Century*, 119–56. Boston: Beacon Press, 2002.

Kendi, Ibram X., and Keisha N. Blain, eds. *Four Hundred Souls: A Community History of African America, 1619-2019*. New York: One World, 2021.

Kennedy, John H. *A Course of Their Own: A History of African American Golfers*. Lincoln: University of Nebraska Press, 2005.

King, Shannon. *Whose Harlem Is This, Anyway? Community Politics and Grassroots Activism during the New Negro Era*. New York: NYU Press, 2017.

Kinloch, Graham C., and Marvin P. Dawkins. *African American Golfers During the Jim Crow Era*. Westport, Conn.: Praeger, 2000.

Kirsch, George B. "Municipal Golf and Civil Rights in the United States, 1910-1965." *The Journal of African American History* 92, no. 3 (July 2007): 371–91.

Klarman, Michael J. *From Jim Crow to Civil Rights: The Supreme Court and the Struggle for Racial Equality*. Oxford: Oxford University Press, 2006.

Kruse, Kevin M. *White Flight: Atlanta and the Making of Modern Conservatism*. Princeton: Princeton University Press, 2005.

LaShier, William Seth. "'To Secure Improvements in Their Material and Social Conditions': Atlanta's Civil Rights Movement, Middle-Class Reformers, and Workplace Protests, 1960-1977." Ph.D., The George Washington University, n.d.

LeFlouria, Talitha L. *Chained in Silence: Black Women and Convict Labor in the New South*. Chapel Hill: University of North Carolina Press, 2015.

Lewis, Catherine M. *A Host to History: The Story of The Atlanta Athletic Club*. Atlanta: Bookhouse, 2012.

———. *"Don't Ask What I Shot": How President Eisenhower's Love of Golf Helped Shape 1950's America*. New York: McGraw-Hill, 2007.

Lewis, David Levering. *W. E. B. Du Bois, 1919-1963: The Fight for Equality and the American Century*. New York: Henry Holt and Company, 2001.

Link, William A. Atlanta, *Cradle of the New South: Race and Remembering in the Civil War's Aftermath*. Chapel Hill: The University of North Carolina Press, 2013.

Litwack, Leon F. *Trouble in Mind: Black Southerners in the Age of Jim Crow*. 1st ed. New York: Knopf, 1998.

Loewen, James W. *Sundown Towns: A Hidden Dimension of American Racism*. New York: Touchstone, 2006.

Lozano, Henry Knight. "Race, Mobility, and Fantasy: Afromobiling in Tropical Florida." *Journal of American Studies* 51, no. 3 (August 2017): 805–31.

Martin, C. Brenden. *Tourism in the Mountain South: A Double-Edged Sword*. 1st ed. Knoxville: University of Tennessee Press, 2007.

Martin, Thomas H. *Atlanta and Its Builders: A Comprehensive History of the Gate City of the South*. Vol. 2. Atlanta: Century Memorial Pub. Co., 1902.

Martin, Waldo. "In Search of Booker T. Washington: Up From Slavery, History and Legend." In *Booker T. Washington and Black Progress: Up From Slavery 100 Years Later*, edited by W. Fitzhugh Brundage, 38–57. Gainesville: University Press of Florida, 2003.

McDaniel, Pete. *Uneven Lies: The Heroic Story of African Americans in Golf.* Greenwich, Conn: *The American Golfer*, Inc., 2000.

McDougald, Elise Johnson. "The Task of Negro Womanhood." In *The New Negro: An Interpretation*, edited by Alain Locke, 1:369–84. New York: Albert and Charles Boni, 1925.

McGuire, Danielle L. *At the Dark End of the Street: Black Women, Rape, and Resistance: A New History of the Civil Rights Movement from Rosa Parks to the Rise of Black Power.* New York: Alfred A. Knopf, 2010.

McIntyre, Rebecca Cawood. *Souvenirs of the Old South: Northern Tourism and Southern Mythology.* Gainesville: University Press of Florida, 2011.

McLeod, Yanela G. *The Miami Times and the Fight for Equality: Race, Sport, and the Black Press, 1948–1958.* Lanham: Lexington Books, 2018.

———. "The *Miami Times*: A Driving Force for Social Change, 1948-1958." Ph.D., The Florida State University, 2014.

McMillen, Neil R. *Dark Journey: Black Mississippians in the Age of Jim Crow.* Urbana: University of Illinois Press, 1989.

Meisenholder, Haley C. "Not in My Back Nine: An Examination of Land Use Disputes Over Golf Course Redevelopments in America." Thesis, Massachusetts Institute of Technology, 2019.

Midgley, Claire, Gabriela DeBues-Stafford, Penelope Lockwood, and Sabrina Thai. "She Needs to See It to Be It: The Importance of Same-Gender Athletic Role Models." *Sex Roles 85*, no. 3 (August 1, 2021): 142–60.

Mixon, Gregory. *The Atlanta Riot: Race, Class, and Violence in a New South City.* Gainesville: University Press of Florida, 2005.

Mooney, Katherine C. *Race Horse Men: How Slavery and Freedom Were Made at the Racetrack.* Cambridge: Harvard University Press, 2014.

Moore, Louis. *I Fight for a Living: Boxing and the Battle for Black Manhood, 1880-1915.* Urbana: University of Illinois Press, 2017.

Moss, Richard J. "Constructing Eden: The Early Days of Pinehurst, North Carolina." *The New England Quarterly 72*, no. 3 (1999): 388–414.

———. *Golf and the American Country Club.* Urbana, Ill: University of Illinois Press, 2001.

Muncy, Robyn. *Creating a Female Dominion in American Reform, 1890-1935.* New York: Oxford University Press, 1991.

Myers, Edward L. *Experiences of A Caddy.* Philadelphia: Dorrance and Co., 1927.

Napton, Darrell E., and Christopher R. Laingen. "Expansion of Golf Courses in the United States*." *Geographical Review 98*, no. 1 (January 1, 2008): 24–41.

Natanson, Nicholas. *The Black Image in the New Deal: The Politics of FSA Photography.* 1st ed. Knoxville: University of Tennessee Press, 1992.

Nelson, Bruce. *Divided We Stand: American Workers and the Struggle for Black Equality.* Princeton: Princeton University Press, 2001.

Niedermeier, Silvan. *The Color of the Third Degree: Racism, Police Torture, and Civil Rights in the American South, 1930-1955.* Chapel Hill: University of North Carolina Press, 2019.

Nightingale, Carl Husemoller. "The Global Inner City: Toward a Historical Analysis." In *W.E.B. DuBois, Race, and the City: The Philadelphia Negro and Its Legacy,* edited by Thomas J. Sugrue and Michael B. Katz, 226–58. Philadelphia: University of Pennsylvania Press, 1998.

Nolan, William H. *Caddie Routine: A Treatise on How to Caddie.* North Bennington, VT: W.H. Nolan, 1941.

Norrell, Robert J. "Caste in Steel: Jim Crow Careers in Birmingham, Alabama." *The Journal of American History 73*, no. 3 (1986): 669–94.

———. *Up from History: The Life of Booker T. Washington.* Cambridge, MA: Harvard University Press, 2009.

Ortiz, Paul. *Emancipation Betrayed: The Hidden History of Black Organizing and White Violence in Florida from Reconstruction to the Bloody Election 1920.* Berkeley: University of California Press, 2005.

Pace, Lee. *The Spirit of Pinehurst.* Pinehurst: Pinehurst Inc., 2004.

Patterson, James T. *Brown v. Board of Education: A Civil Rights Milestone and Its Troubled Legacy.* New York: Oxford University Press, 2001.

Perloff, Richard M. "The Press and Lynchings of African Americans." *Journal of Black Studies 30*, no. 3 (2000): 315–30.

Perry, Imani. *May We Forever Stand: A History of the Black National Anthem.* Chapel Hill: The University of North Carolina Press, 2018.

Pomerantz, Gary M. *Where Peachtree Meets Sweet Auburn: The Saga of Two Families and the Making of Atlanta.* New York: Penguin Books, 1996.

Porter, Michael Leroy. "Black Atlanta: An Interdisciplinary Study of Blacks on the East Side of Atlanta, 1890-1930." Ph.D., Emory University, 1974.

Quirke, Carol. *Eyes on Labor: News Photography and America's Working Class.* Oxford: Oxford University Press, 2012.

Raiford, Leigh. *Imprisoned in a Luminous Glare: Photography and the African American Freedom Struggle.* Chapel Hill: University of North Carolina Press, 2011.

Reed, Wornie. "The Black Golf Caddy: A Victim of Labor Market Discrimination." *Challenge Online 14*, no. 1 (May 1, 2008): 61–71.

Reich, Steven A. *A Working People: A History of African American Workers Since Emancipation.* Rowman & Littlefield, 2013.

Rio, Cecilia M. "From Feudal Serfs to Independent Contractors: Class and African American Women's Paid Domestic Labor, 1863–1980." Ph.D., University of Massachusetts Amherst, 2001.

Ritterhouse, Jennifer. *Growing up Jim Crow: How Black and White Southern Children Learned Race.* Chapel Hill: University of North Carolina, 2006.

———. "The Etiquette of Race Relations in the Jim Crow South." In *Manners and Southern History*, 20–44. Jackson: University Press of Mississippi, 2007.

Robertson, Robert J. *Fair Ways: How Six Black Golfers Won Civil Rights in Beaumont, Texas.* College Station: Texas A&M University Press, 2005.

Robertson, Thomas Heard. "The Conversation Club and the Early Years of Golf in Augusta." *The Georgia Historical Quarterly 89*, no. 1 (2005): 57–81.

Schmidt, Raymond. "Pars and Birdies in a Hidden World: African Americans and the United Golfers Association." In *Separate Games: African American Sport Behind the Walls of Segregation*, edited by David K. Wiggins and Ryan A. Swanson, 179–201. Fayetteville, AK: University of Arkansas Press, 2016.

Schultz, Mark. *The Rural Face of White Supremacy: Beyond Jim Crow.* Urbana: University of Illinois Press, 2005.

Sharpless, Rebecca. *Cooking in Other Women's Kitchens: Domestic Workers in the South, 1865-1960.* Chapel Hill: University of North Carolina Press, 2010.

Shircliffe, Barbara. "'We Got the Best of That World': A Case for the Study of Nostalgia in the Oral History of School Segregation." *The Oral History Review 28*, no. 2 (January 1, 2001): 59–84.

Silber, Nina. *The Romance of Reunion: Northerners and the South, 1865-1900.* Chapel Hill: University of North Carolina Press, 1993.

Simmons, LaKisha Michelle. *Crescent City Girls: The Lives of Young Black Women in Segregated New Orleans.* Chapel Hill: University of North Carolina Press, 2015.

Simon, Bryant. *Boardwalk of Dreams: Atlantic City and the Fate of Urban America.* New York,: Oxford University Press, 2006.

———. "Race Relations: African American Organizing, Liberalism, and White Working-Class Politics in Postwar South Carolina." In *Jumpin' Jim Crow: Southern Politics from Civil War to Civil Rights*, edited by Jane Dailey, Glenda Elizabeth Gilmore, and Bryant Simon, 239–59. Princeton: Princeton University Press, 2001.

Sinnette, Calvin H. *Forbidden Fairways: African Americans and the Game of Golf.* Sleeping Bear Press, 1998.

Sistrom, Michael. "The Freedom Labor Union: Economic Justice and the Civil Rights Movement in Mississippi." In *Reconsidering Southern Labor History*, edited by Matthew Hild and Keri Leigh Merritt. Gainesville: University Press of Florida, 2018.

Smith, Mark M. *How Race Is Made: Slavery, Segregation, and the Senses.* Chapel Hill: University of North Carolina Press, 2006.

Smith, Shawn Michelle. *Photographic Returns: Racial Justice and the Time of Photography.* Durham: Duke University Press, 2020.

Sontag, Susan. *On Photography.* New York: Farrar, Straus and Giroux, 1977.

Sorin, Gretchen. *Driving While Black: African American Travel and the Road to Civil Rights.* New York: Liveright, 2020.

Springer, Robert Dee. "The Social Characteristics and Behavioral Patterns of the Members of an All-Negro Golf Club in the City of Atlanta, Georgia." Atlanta University, 1958.

Starnes, Richard D. *Creating the Land of the Sky: Tourism and Society in Western North Carolina.* Tuscaloosa: University of Alabama Press, 2005.

Sterngass, Jon. *First Resorts: Pursuing Pleasure at Saratoga Springs, Newport, & Coney Island.* Baltimore: Johns Hopkins University Press, 2001.

Sturkey, William. *Hattiesburg: An American City in Black and White.* Cambridge, Mass.: Harvard University Press, 2019.

Sudheendran, Kesavan. "Community Power Structure in Atlanta: A Study in Decision Making, 1920-1939 (Georgia)." Ph.D., Georgia State University, 1983.

Thompson-Miller, Ruth, and Leslie H. Picca. "'There Were Rapes!': Sexual Assaults of African American Women and Children in Jim Crow." *Violence Against Women 23*, no. 8 (July 1, 2017): 934–50.

Trotter Jr, Joe William. *Workers on Arrival: Black Labor in the Making of America*. Berkeley: University of California Press, 2019.

Tufts, Richard S. *The Scottish Invasion, Being a Brief Review of American Golf in Relation to Pinehurst and the Sixty Second National Amateur*. Pinehurst, NC: Pinehurst Publishers, 1962.

Tye, Larry. *Rising from the Rails: Pullman Porters and the Making of the Black Middle Class*. 1st ed. New York: Henry Holt, 2004.

Usher, Jess. "'The Golfers': African American Golfers of the North Carolina Piedmont and the Struggle for Access." *North Carolina Historical Review 87*, no. 2 (April 2010): 158–93.

Vivian, Daniel J. *A New Plantation World: Sporting Estates in the South Carolina Lowcountry, 1900-1940*. Cambridge: Cambridge University Press, 2018.

Wardlaw, James Tapley. "Leisure Time Activities of Negro Boys in the First Ward of Atlanta, Georgia." Atlanta University, 1934. Robert W. Woodruff Library, Atlanta University Center (ETD Collection for AUC).

Weatherford, Willis D. *A Survey of the Negro Boy in Nashville, Tennessee*. New York, N.Y: Association Press, 1932.

Wellman, Manly Wade. *The County of Moore, 1847-1947; a North Carolina Region's Second Hundred Years*. Southern Pines, N.C.: Moore County Historical Association, 1962.

Williams-Forson, Psyche A. *Building Houses out of Chicken Legs: Black Women, Food, and Power*. First Paperback Edition. Chapel Hill: The University of North Carolina Press, 2006.

———. *Eating While Black: Food Shaming and Race in America*. Chapel Hill: The University of North Carolina Press, 2022.

Wright, Gavin. *Sharing the Prize: The Economics of the Civil Rights Revolution in the American South*. Cambridge, Mass: Belknap Press of Harvard University Press, 2013.

Notes

1. "Cover Image", *Sports Illustrated*, April 17, 1972.
2. Ward Clayton, *Men on the Bag*: The Caddies of Augusta National (Ann Arbor, Mich: Sports Media Group, 2004), 93–95.
3. Thomas Heard Robertson, "The Conversation Club and the Early Years of Golf in Augusta," *The Georgia Historical Quarterly 89*, no. 1 (2005): 58.
4. "'Perfect Course' Opens; Here's Comment," *The Atlanta Constitution*, January 14, 1933, 9.
5. "Mr. Rockefeller Coming Very Soon," *Augusta Herald*, January 30, 1912; "The First American Golf," *New York Times*, January 2, 1917; Like many other golfing presidents, Taft was criticized for the amount that he played. Eugene Debs, president of the Socialist Party, chastised Taft for too much golf. "So Taft has sent the troops to the Mexican border and has gone to Augusta to play golf," he said in 1911. "To Augusta to Golf After Sending Troops," *Augusta Herald*, March 17, 1911.
6. "In the Lobbies," *Augusta Herald*, March 10, 1910.
7. 1910 US Census, Burke County, Georgia, Population Schedule, Militia District #60, Enumeration District 18, Sheet 25A, Dwelling No. 284, Peterson, digital image, Ancestry.com, Accessed 20 Feb 2023
8. 1920 US Census, Richmond County, Georgia, Population Schedule, Augusta, Militia District #1269, Enumeration District 106, Sheet 2A, Dwelling No. 8, Peterson, digital image, Ancestry.com, Accessed 20 Feb 2023
9. Robert K Nelson et al., "Mapping Inequality," accessed February 21, 2023, https://dsl.richmond.edu/panorama/redlining/.
10. 1930 US Census, Richmond County, Georgia, Population Schedule, Augusta, Ward 4, Enumeration District 123-20, Sheet 11A, Dwelling No. 228, Peterson, digital image, Ancestry.com, Accessed 20 Feb 2023
11. 1930 US Census, Richmond County, Georgia, Population Schedule, Augusta, Ward 4, Enumeration District 123-20, Sheet 11b, Dwelling No. 230, Peterson, digital image, Ancestry.com, Accessed 20 Feb 2023

12. 1950 US Census, Richmond County, Georgia, Population Schedule, Augusta, Enumeration District 161-76, Sheet 79, Dwelling No. 266, Peterson, digital image, Ancestry.com, Accessed 20 Feb 2023
13. 1940 US Census, Richmond County, Georgia, Population Schedule, Augusta, Enumeration District 121-33, Sheet 1A, Dwelling No. 7, Edwards, digital image, Ancestry.com, Accessed 20 Feb 2023
14. 1940 US Census, Richmond County, Georgia, Population Schedule, Augusta, Enumeration District 121-33, Sheet 2A, Dwelling No. 28, Bennett, digital image, Ancestry.com, Accessed 20 Feb 2023; 1940 US Census, Richmond County, Georgia, Population Schedule, Augusta, Enumeration District 121-33, Sheet 6A, Dwelling No. 106, Henderson, digital image, Ancestry.com, Accessed 20 Feb 2023; 1940 US Census, Richmond County, Georgia, Population Schedule, Augusta, Enumeration District 121-33, Sheet 6A, Dwelling No. 107, Aaron, digital image, Ancestry.com, Accessed 20 Feb 2023;
15. 1940 US Census, Richmond County, Georgia, Population Schedule, Augusta, Enumeration District 121-35, Sheet 8A, Dwelling No. 152, Home, digital image, Ancestry.com, Accessed 20 Feb 2023; 1940 US Census, Richmond County, Georgia, Population Schedule, Augusta, Enumeration District 121-35, Sheet 11A, Dwelling No. 216, Roland, digital image, Ancestry.com, Accessed 20 Feb 2023; 1940 US Census, Richmond County, Georgia, Population Schedule, Augusta, Enumeration District 121-35, Sheet 8B, Dwelling No. 157, Williams, digital image, Ancestry.com, Accessed 20 Feb 2023.
16. Clayton, *Men on the Bag*, 97.
17. Clayton, 102–3.
18. "Willie Hits Jackpot as Aide to Big Jack," *Fort Worth Star-Telegram*, April 13, 1966, 18.
19. "The Caddie Question," *The Golfer*, March 1899, 238.
20. Cliff Mosieh, "Negro Caddies to Be Brought North in 1930," *Davenport Democrat and Leader*, November 10, 1929, 25.
21. Clayton, *Men on the Bag*, 108–9.
22. Wynston Wilcox, "Jack Nicklaus Donates Money to Give Former Caddie a Headstone," *The Augusta Chronicle*, November 7, 2020, https://www.augustachronicle.com/story/sports/2020/11/07/jack-nicklaus-donates-money-to-give-former-caddie-headstone/114725126/.

23. "Ex-Slave, 113, Dies in Moore," *Charlotte Observer*, December 7, 1934, sec. B, 3.
24. Alleetah Hilton, "Uncle Demas Taylor of Taylortown," *Pinehurst Outlook*, April 21, 1930, 7.
25. Hilton, 7.
26. Litwack, *Trouble in Mind*, 120–22.
27. US Bureau of the Census, Reports of the Thirteenth Census Vol. 7 Agriculture Reports by States, with Statistics for Counties—Nebraska-Wyoming, (Washington, D.C.: US Bureau of the Census, 1914), 222
28. Neil R. McMillen, *Dark Journey: Black Mississippians in the Age of Jim Crow* (Urbana: University of Illinois Press, 1989), 124–30; Litwack, *Trouble in Mind*, 120–40; Pete Daniel, *The Shadow of Slavery: Peonage in the South, 1901-1969* (Urbana: University of Illinois Press, 1972).
29. Hilton, "Uncle Demas Taylor of Taylortown," 7.
30. Sturkey, *Hattiesburg: An American City in Black and White*, 46; Lawrence S. Earley, *Looking for Longleaf: The Fall and Rise of an American Forest* (Chapel Hill: University of North Carolina Press, 2004), 133.
31. Hilton, "Uncle Demas Taylor of Taylortown," 7.
32. Hickman, *Mississippi Harvest: Lumbering in the Longleaf Pine Belt, 1840-1915*, 141–43.
33. Himel, "Greening Golf," 132.
34. Hilton, "Uncle Demas Taylor of Taylortown," 7; Demus Taylor Chopping Wood, n.d., n.d., P045338, Tufts Archives.
35. US Bureau of the Census, Negro Population, 1790-1915, Part 6 Economic Statistics, (Washington, D.C.: Bureau of the Census, 1918) 505, 515
36. William P. Jones, *The Tribe of Black Ulysses: African American Lumber Workers in the Jim Crow South* (Urbana: University of Illinois Press, 2005), 18–28.
37. Manly Wade Wellman, *The County of Moore, 1847-1947; a North Carolina Region's Second Hundred Years.* (Southern Pines, N.C.: Moore County Historical Association, 1962), 92–95.
38. Wellman, 103; Matthew Taylor Himel, "Greening Golf: Grass, Agriculture, and Pinehurst in the Sandhills" (Ph.D., Starkville, Mississippi, Mississippi State University, 2020), 13.
39. Larry Robert Youngs, "Lifestyle Enclaves: Winter Resorts in the South Atlantic States, 1870–1930" (Ph.D., Atlanta, Georgia State University, 2001), 260.

40. Richard S Tufts, *The Scottish Invasion, Being a Brief Review of American Golf in Relation to Pinehurst and the Sixty Second National Amateur* (Pinehurst, NC: Pinehurst Publishers, 1962), 15–16.

41. Himel, "Greening Golf," 35–36.

42. "The Making of Pinehurst," *Pinehurst Outlook*, October 28, 1898, 1.

43. Himel, "Greening Golf," 57–58.

44. Richard J. Moss, "Constructing Eden: The Early Days of Pinehurst, North Carolina," *The New England Quarterly 72*, no. 3 (1999): 292.

45. Tufts, *The Scottish Invasion*, 17.

46. Tufts, 27–28; Youngs, "Lifestyle Enclaves," 197–99; Himel, "Greening Golf," 72–74.

47. McIntyre, *Souvenirs of the Old South*, 132–33.

48. "Gone Are the Days," *Pinehurst Outlook*, April 11, 1908, 6.

49. Yuhl, *A Golden Haze of Memory*, 14–18; McIntyre, *Souvenirs of the Old South*, 110–15; Silber, *The Romance of Reunion*, 79; Lozano, "Race, Mobility, and Fantasy," 808; by David W. Blight, *Race and Reunion: The Civil War in American Memory* (Cambridge, MA: Harvard University Press, 2002).

50. "The Gulf Coast: Louisville and Nashville Railroad" (Poole Brothers, 1929), 57–62, 3C2a/SE.L&N, USGA Archives; "Atlantic Coast Line: Tropical Trips, 1929-1930" (Poole Brothers, 1929), 24, 3C2a/SE.ACL, USGA Archives.

51. "Those Who Enjoy Outdoors Travel to Pinehurst, North Carolina" (Frank Presbrey Co, 1915), 3C2b/NC.Pine, USGA Archives.

52. Howard Freeman, "In The Rough," *Philadelphia Public Ledger*, December 15, 1930, DF_1.00 Folder 13, Tufts Archives.

53. "An Attractive Winter Resort," *Pinehurst Outlook*, March 4, 1898, 1; "Unequalled Advantages," *Pinehurst Outlook*, April 29, 1898, 1.

54. "Unequalled Advantages," 2.

55. "Fine Enertainment," *Pinehurst Outlook*, March 3, 1899, 1.; During the regular season, agricultural wages ranged from 30 to 75 cents per day, and rose to between 60 cents and $1.00 during harvest. Lorenzo J Greene and Carter G Woodson, *The Negro Wage Earner* (Washington, D.C.: The Association for the Study of Negro Life and History, 1930), 53–54.

56. Stanley B. Lacks, "Memories of Pinehurst: From a 92 Year Old Man," December 2008, 9, DF_217, Tufts Archives.

57. William H. Evans, "Six Courses for Pinehurst!," *Pinehurst Outlook*, March 29, 1913, 5.

58. Al DeMaree, "Colored Caddies Unconsciously Funny," *Brooklyn Times*, February 23, 1928.
59. "One of the Neutrals!," *Pinehurst Outlook*, February 27, 1915, 9.
60. Joseph Boskin, Sambo: The Rise & Demise of an American Jester (New York: Oxford University Press, 1986), 108.
61. "The Southern Golfer Subscription Advert," *The Southern Golfer*, January 15, 1924, Front Matter.
62. "Taft's Boy Charlie," *Washington Herald*, July 26, 1908, 8.
63. "Pinehurst, North Carolina," *USGA Golf Bulletin*, November 1904, Front Matter.
64. "Pinehurst, North Carolina," Front Matter; "Pinehurst, North Carolina," *USGA Golf Bulletin*, January 1904, 73; Himel, "Greening Golf," 83–86.
65. "Pinehurst, North Carolina," *Country Life in America*, November 1909, 17.
66. "We Are Waiting for You at Pinehurst, North Carolina," *Golf Illustrated & Outdoor America*, January 1915, Front Matter.; For other ads placed nationally that include Black caddies see: "Pinehurst, North Carolina," *Country Life in America*, December 1913, 107; "Pinehurst, North Carolina," *Country Life in America*, January 1916, 16.
67. "J.C. Bull to Leonard Tufts," September 14, 1923, DF_1 Folder 2, Tufts Archives.
68. "List of Property Owners and Valuations Colored and White," 1922, DF_146 Folder 13, Tufts Archives.
69. This phrase is borrowed from Gregory Mixon's study on the Atlanta Riot 1906. The "commercial-civic elite" were the leading men in real estate, finance, industry, and law. They often also filled positions in local governance however Atlanta's ward system removed the possibility of them holding ubiquitous control on all political positions. No single interest group held more power than the Atlanta Chamber of Commerce over the first half of the century, and no group better typified the "commercial-civic elite"; Mixon, *The Atlanta Riot*; Kesavan Sudheendran, "Community Power Structure in Atlanta: A Study in Decision Making, 1920-1939 (Georgia)" (Ph.D., Atlanta, Georgia, Georgia State University, 1983).
70. Isma Dooly, "Long Skirts Strongly Condemned by Women Physicians of Atlanta," *The Atlanta Constitution*, June 17, 1900, 14.
71. "Are Arranging For Golf Links," *The Atlanta Constitution*, October 25, 1905, 5.
72. "Golf Now King of Local Sports," *The Atlanta Constitution*, July 23, 1911, 2; "Scene at Golf Club During Southern Championship Meet," *The Atlanta Constitution*, November 7, 1912, 2.

73. Tilou Forbes, "The Social and Fraternal Clubs of Atlanta And Their Appeal to the Thousands Here Who Are to Lead the Hosts to Victory," *The Atlanta Constitution*, September 9, 1917, D2.

74. Burns, *Rage in the Gate City*, 87.; For more on Broyles' rule over the recorder's court see: Steve Goodson, *Highbrows, Hillbillies & Hellfire: Public Entertainment in Atlanta, 1880-1930* (Athens: University of Georgia Press, 2002), 138–40; William A. Link, Atlanta, *Cradle of the New South: Race and Remembering in the Civil War's Aftermath* (Chapel Hill: The University of North Carolina Press, 2013), 172; Thomas Mashburn Deaton, "Atlanta During the Progressive Era" (Ph.D., Athens, Georgia, University of Georgia, 1969), 273–74.

75. Thomas H. Martin, *Atlanta and Its Builders: A Comprehensive History of the Gate City of the South*, vol. 2 (Atlanta: Century Memorial Pub. Co., 1902), 205.

76. "'Jedge Briles' Caddy, 'Tater,' Comes To Grief," *The Atlanta Constitution*, July 21, 1911, 7.

77. Other documented examples of caddies convicted in Broyles' court include: Jim Thomas, the East Lake caddie master accused of theft; Ernest Evans accused of intent to sell liquor; and a group of caddies accused of theft; "Recorder Will Have Good Caddy Next Time," *The Atlanta Constitution*, November 5, 1912, 7; "Judge's Caddy Fined as Tiger," *The Atlanta Constitution*, December 19, 1911, 3; "Caddies in Daytime and Thieves at Night," *The Atlanta Constitution*, April 11, 1914, 7.

78. "Up and Down Peachtree," *Atlanta Georgian*, November 8, 1912, 4.

79. US Bureau of the Census, 1940 Census of the Population, vol. 3, The Labor Force, part 2. Alabama-Indiana, (Washington, D.C.: Bureau of the Census, 1940), 735-736

80. Trotter Jr, *Workers on Arrival*, 86–90; Bates, *Pullman Porters and the Rise of Protest Politics in Black America, 1925-1945*, 24; Tye, *Rising from the Rails*, 27–28.

81. Stewart F. Gelders, "If a Caddy Must Be an Ass, Why Not Employ an Ass As a Caddy," *The Atlanta Constitution*, December 5, 1923, 7.

82. 1900 U.S. census, Moore County, North Carolina, population schedule, East Carthage Precinct, enumeration district (ED) 68, sheet 17, dwelling 49, family 49

83. "Robert L. Taylor, Civic Leader, Dies at Taylortown," *Southern Pines Pilot*, December 26, 1952, 7.

84. "Uncle Demus Taylor, 106 Year Old Dies," *Southern Pines Pilot*, December 7, 1934, 1.

85. Charlie Sifford and James Gullo, *Just Let Me Play: The Story of Charlie Sifford, the First Black PGA Golfer* (Latham, N.Y.: British American Pub., 1992), 10–11.

86. Ben Crenshaw, Carl Jackson, and Melanie Hauser, *Two Roads to Augusta* (Greenwich CT: *The American Golfer*, 2013), 29-32.
87. "Pinehurst Caddies Happy Over New Rule," *Pittsburgh Courier*, January 15, 1938, 6.
88. Robert Taft and Betty Taft, *On the Bag: Seventy Years Remembered by Pinehurst's Hall-of-Fame Caddie Willie McRae* (Cincinnati: Stevens Publishing, 2013), 12.
89. Merrell W. Whittlesey, "Tee to Green," *Washington Post*, April 6, 1941, SP3.
90. Al Sharp, "Atlanta Clubs Face Shortage Of Caddy Boys," *The Atlanta Constitution*, June 1, 1941, D2
91. "Knew His Business," *Charlotte Observer*, April 2, 1905, 6.
92. "Rassie Wicker Notes," n.d., Box DF187.00, Folder 23, Tufts Archives.
93. Donald J. Ross, "Donald J. Ross to Leonard Tufts," February 27, 1924, Box DF137.01, Folder 6, Tufts Archives.
94. "Pinehurst Caddies Work Good System," *Covington Virginian*, March 16, 1926, 1.
95. *Pinehurst*, Pictoreel Sportscope 1938.
96. William H. Nolan, *Caddie Routine: A Treatise on How to Caddie* (North Bennington, VT: W.H. Nolan, 1941).
97. James W. Tufts, "Understanding Between A.A. Ruffner and James W. Tufts," October 28, 1901, Box DF137.01, Folder 24, Tufts Archives.
98. Pinehurst Country Club Board of Governors, "Special Meeting 1911," February 21, 1911, Box DF125, Folder 2, Tufts Archives.
99. Donald J. Ross, "Donald J. Ross to Richard Tufts," November 16, 1927, Box DF79.02, Folder 26, Tufts Archives.
100. "An Interview About Caddies," *Pinehurst Outlook*, January 7, 1933, 4.
101. Sharp, "Atlanta Clubs Face Shortage Of Caddy Boys," D2.
102. Donald Ross was in contact with golf clubs throughout the South regarding their caddie policies. On one occasion he sent letters to twelve different courses in North Carolina to ask their opinion on the regarding caddie employment on Sundays. Donald J. Ross, "Correspondence Concerning Caddies," n.d., Box DF79.02, Folder 26, Tufts Archives.
103. Pinehurst Country Club Board of Governors, "Special Meeting 1911."
104. Greene and Woodson, *The Negro Wage Earner*, 53
105. Ross, "Donald J. Ross to Leonard Tufts," February 27, 1924.
106. Sifford and Gullo, *Just Let Me Play*, 10–11.
107. "Busy Doings of Atlanta Golfers," *Atlanta Georgian*, October 30, 1906, 12.

108. "Negro Caddy Dies Trying to Rescue Drowning Youth," *The Atlanta Constitution*, April 15, 1922, 7; A similar incident occurred in 1963 when an aspiring artist who worked as a caddie died while diving for golf balls. "Drowning Ends Artist Dreams of 13 Year-Old Durham Boy," *Carolina Times*, July 6, 1963, 1.
109. "Busy Doings of Atlanta Golfers," 12.
110. "County Officers Declare War on Caddies," *The Atlanta Constitution*, June 15, 1923, 9.
111. "Officer Is Held in Caddy Slaying," *The Atlanta Constitution*, April 8, 1930, 8.
112. "Richard S. Tufts to Mr. H. P. Harding," March 30, 1933, DF_79.02 Folder 26, Tufts Archives.
113. "Special Laundry and Caddie Ticket," 1905, DC_22-L Folder 003, Tufts Archives.
114. "An Interview About Caddies," 4.
115. Ross, "Donald J. Ross to Richard Tufts," November 16, 1927.
116. "Trolley Extension Hearing Enlivened by Verbal Tilts," *The Atlanta Constitution*, June 16, 1922, 12.
117. "What the Judge Said," *Atlanta Daily World*, July 24, 1934, 6.
118. Michael Leroy Porter, "Black Atlanta: An Interdisciplinary Study of Blacks on the East Side of Atlanta, 1890-1930." (Ph.D., Atlanta, Georgia, Emory University, 1974), 104; Burns, *Rage in the Gate City*, 163–64.
119. Hunter, To 'joy My Freedom, 58–60.
120. Donald J. Ross, "Golf Course Perfection," *Pinehurst Outlook*, December 6, 1913, 1.
121. "Golf in the Rain," *Washington Evening Star*, April 3, 1901, 7; "Mo' Rain Mo' Rest," *The American Golfer*, February 1915, 295.
122. DeWayne Wickham, *Woodholme: A Black Man's Story of Growing up Alone*, 1st ed. (New York: Farrar, Straus, and Giroux, 1995), 67.
123. Wickham, 133.
124. "Thirteen Caddies In Lockup After Raid in Gainesville," *Atlanta Daily World*, August 11, 1935, 8.
125. The description of this scene was taken from DeWayne Wickham's experiences as in the caddie house. Wickham, *Woodholme*, 61, 66, 133.
126. Caddies Rolling Dice, 1913, 1913, Getty Images Image #146120166, Underwood Archives.
127. Wickham, *Woodholme*, 161–62.
128. Hazard, "Eastern Department," *The American Golfer*, January 1918, 407; Lochinvar, "Western Department," May 1915, 587; Ring W. Lardner, "Golf Amid the

Pyramids," *The American Golfer*, February 10, 1923, 5; Edward L. Myers, *Experiences of A Caddy* (Philadelphia: Dorrance and Co., 1927); "Develop New Term for 'African Golf,'" Los Angeles Herald, April 9, 1920, 17; "Southern Caddies Talk 'Golf Crops,'" *Buffalo Commercial*, March 15, 1920, 7.

129. "Caddie Book," 1911, Display Cabinet, Tufts Archives.

130. Wickham, *Woodholme*, 60.

131. A.W. Stanley, "African Golf in Vogue," *Greensboro Daily News*, August 22, 1926, sec. D, 3.

132. "Donald Ross to Richard S. Tufts," September 6, 1928, DF_137.01 Folder 16, Tufts Archives.

133. "Caddie Book," 1911, Display Cabinet, Tufts Archives.

134. Wickham, *Woodholme*, 152–57; W.N. Cox, "Breaks of the Game," *Greensboro Daily News*, July 27, 1929, 11.

135. "Number Ten Course," *Pinehurst Outlook*, February 2, 1935, 2; Stanley, "African Golf in Vogue," 3.

136. Louis Moore, *I Fight for a Living: Boxing and the Battle for Black Manhood, 1880-1915* (Urbana: University of Illinois Press, 2017), 161.

137. "Handbill to 'The Cahlina Revuei,'" April 10, 1934, DC_22-L Folder 004, Tufts Archives; "New Clubhouse At West End Opens Friday," *The Atlanta Constitution*, January 23, 1929, 9.

138. Taft and Taft, *On the Bag*, 20–21.

139. Taft and Taft, 20–22.

140. Richard Wright, *Black Boy: A Record of Childhood and Youth* (Cleveland: World Publishing Co., 1947), 143.

141. Sifford and Gullo, *Just Let Me Play*, 21.

142. Taft and Taft, *On the Bag*, 12–13.

143. Taft and Taft, 30.

144. Taft and Taft, 33–37.

145. H. C. S. Everand, "Golf in Theory and in Practice," *USGA Golf Bulletin*, September 1909, 161–67.

146. Lochinvar, "Western Department," *The American Golfer*, June 1915, 157–58.

147. J. Lewis Brown, "A Regrettable Incident," *Golf Illustrated*, August 1924, 13.

148. "Rules of Etiquette for Public Courses," *The American Golfer*, December 1916, 150, 152.

149. Joe Kelly, "Management of Public Courses," *The American Golfer*, June 17, 1922, 8, 26.
150. Robert A. Blodgett, "The Courtesy of the Game," *Golf Illustrated*, January 1931, 23.
151. Taft and Taft, *On the Bag*, 10–17.
152. Stephen A. Berrey, *The Jim Crow Routine: Everyday Performances of Race, Civil Rights, and Segregation in Mississippi* (Chapel Hill: The University of North Carolina Press, 2015), 20–22.
153. Berrey, 56; Grace Elizabeth Hale, "'For Colored' and 'For White': Segregating Consumption in the South," in *Jumpin' Jim Crow: Southern Politics from Civil War to Civil Rights*, ed. Jane Dailey, Glenda Elizabeth Gilmore, and Bryant Simon (Princeton: Princeton University Press, 2001), 175–76; J. William Harris, *Deep Souths: Delta, Piedmont, and Sea Island Society in the Age of Segregation* (Baltimore: Johns Hopkins University Press, 2001), 76; McMillen, *Dark Journey*, 24; Mark M. Smith, *How Race Is Made: Slavery, Segregation, and the Senses* (Chapel Hill: University of North Carolina Press, 2006), 84–86.
154. Ritterhouse, *Growing up Jim Crow*, 55–107; Berrey, *The Jim Crow Routine*, 4; Litwack, *Trouble in Mind*, 35; McMillen, *Dark Journey*, 26–27.
155. Robin D. G. Kelley's 1994 article "We Are Not What We Seem" is the work which demonstrated the existence of political actions in everyday scenarios throughout the Jim Crow South - as well as the ways that such actions informed longer term political change on a national scale. Robin D. G. Kelley, "'We Are Not What We Seem': Rethinking Black Working-Class Opposition in the Jim Crow South," *The Journal of American History 80*, no. 1 (June 1993): 75–112; Berrey, *The Jim Crow Routine*, 6; Ritterhouse, *Growing up Jim Crow*, 50; Litwack, *Trouble in Mind*, 41.
156. Grace Elizabeth Hale, *Making Whiteness: The Culture of Segregation in the South, 1890-1940*, 1st Vintage Books ed. (New York: Vintage Books, 1999), 128.
157. Innis Brown, "How Rockefeller Plays Golf," *The American Golfer*, April 10, 1920, 15.
158. "New Orleans and the Beautiful Mississippi Gulf Coast," *Chicago Daily Tribune*, February 5, 1926, 20.
159. "Negro Caddies Down South," *The Nashville American*, May 29, 1910, 5.
160. Edward L. Ayers, *The Promise of the New South: Life After Reconstruction* (New York: Oxford University Press, 1992), 427; Litwack, *Trouble in Mind*, 38.
161. Ross, "Golf Course Perfection," 1.

162. Stanley B. Lacks, "Pinehurst's Rags to Riches Decade," May 1999, 2, DF_217, Tufts Archives.
163. For more on Sundown towns, see: James W. Loewen, *Sundown Towns: A Hidden Dimension of American Racism* (New York: Touchstone, 2006).
164. "To Make Changes at East Lake," *The Atlanta Constitution*, February 26, 1912, 8.
165. Evans, "Six Courses for Pinehurst!," 5.
166. "In Club, Course and Play," *Golf Illustrated*, July 1929, 39.
167. Tufts, "Understanding Between A.A. Ruffner and James W. Tufts."
168. Taft and Taft, *On the Bag*, 33.
169. Taft and Taft, 18–19.
170. Howard Freeman, "In the Rough," *Philadelphia Public Ledger*, December 18, 1930, DF_1.00 Folder 13, Tufts Archives.
171. "Out of Bounds," *Pinehurst Outlook*, January 3, 1931, 7.
172. Harris, *Deep Souths*, 76; Ritterhouse, *Growing up Jim Crow*, 37; Litwack, *Trouble in Mind*, 35; Mark Schultz, *The Rural Face of White Supremacy: Beyond Jim Crow* (Urbana: University of Illinois Press, 2005), 84–85; Sturkey, *Hattiesburg: An American City in Black and White*, 84; Jones, *Labor of Love, Labor of Sorrow*, 113; McMillen, *Dark Journey*, 23–24.
173. "Richard S. Tufts to Raymond Barrett," October 28, 1926, DF_79.02 Folder 26, Tufts Archives.
174. Ross, "Donald J. Ross to Richard Tufts," November 16, 1927.
175. "An Interview About Caddies," 4.
176. "Pinehurst, North Carolina" (Frank Presbrey Co, n.d.), 2C2c/NC.Pine, USGA Archives.
177. A.W. Tillinghast, "The Humor of the Game," *Golf Illustrated & Outdoor America*, September 1915, 40.
178. The Colonel, "From the South," *The American Golfer*, April 1913, 528–29.
179. Hunter, *To 'joy My Freedom*, 59–61; Litwack, *Trouble in Mind*, 171; Jones, Labor of Love, Labor of Sorrow, 113–15; Sharpless, *Cooking in Other Women's Kitchens*, 147–51.
180. "Caddy Breaks Golfer's Jaw During Attack," *The Atlanta Constitution*, October 25, 1929, 14.
181. The Colonel, "From the South," 528–29.
182. "Golf in the Rain," 7; "Mo' Rain Mo' Rest," 295; "Golf Gossip," *Sandhill Citizen*, March 14, 1924, 1.
183. Litwack, *Trouble in Mind*, 118–19.

184. "The Caddy and His Little Peculiarities," *New York Tribune*, October 13, 1907, E8.
185. "Mo' Rain Mo' Rest," 295.
186. Hagen, "Golf Customs Differ Over United States," 12.
187. "Richard S. Tufts to Raymond Barrett," October 28, 1926.
188. Tommy Armour, *Tommy Armour's ABC's of Golf* (New York: Simon and Schuster, 1967), 93.
189. Bill Bennett, "Colored Caddies," *High Point Enterprise*, April 6, 1952, 2.
190. "An Interview About Caddies," 4.
191. W. Fitzhugh Brundage notes that "Jim Crow advocates repeatedly react their arguments to address contemporary conditions and anxieties." W. Fitzhugh Brundage, "Introduction," in *The Folly of Jim Crow: Rethinking the Segregated South*, ed. Stephanie Cole and Natalie J. Ring, 1st ed., Walter Prescott Webb Memorial Lectures ; No. 43 (College Station: Texas A&M University Press, 2012), 4.; Likewise, Leon Litwack highlighted White hypocrisy in discussions of Black agricultural labor where Black workers were stereotyped as simultaneously lazy and industrious. Litwack, *Trouble in Mind*, 173.
192. Chapple, "Sojourning 'Neath the Long Leaf Pines," 315.
193. "Out of Bounds," 7.
194. Bertram William Doyle, who first coined the term "racial etiquette" believed that Black accommodation to White expectations was part of a long term trajectory which in the end led to assimilation and equality. See: Ritterhouse, *Growing up Jim Crow*, 49; Boyle, Ritterhouse, *Growing up Jim Crow*, 49; Bertram Wilbur Doyle, *The Etiquette of Race Relations in the South: A Study in Social Control* (Chicago: University of Chicago Press, 1937).
195. John LaCerda, "Paradise for Golfers," *Nation's Business*, November 1950, 85.
196. Jack Tucker, "'Paradise, Suh!,'" *Rochester Democrat and Chronicle*, March 5, 1938, 16.
197. Evans, "Six Courses for Pinehurst!," 5.
198. Edward Ayers notes that the "openendedness" of negotiations between Black and White Southerners "kept Whites in a constant state of unease." Ayers, *The Promise of the New South*, 427.; Likewise J. William Harris explains that Black challenges "showed what whites knew… that the color line, like any human construction, could be eroded and swept away." Harris, *Deep Souths*, 82.
199. Hagen, "Golf Customs Differ Over United States," 12.
200. Taft and Taft, *On the Bag*, 14.

201. Taft and Taft, 14–15.

202. Bryant Simon notes that White southerners used racial etiquette as a tool to "convince themselves that African Americans accepted, even liked segregation." Bryant Simon, "Race Relations: African American Organizing, Liberalism, and White Working-Class Politics in Postwar South Carolina," in *Jumpin' Jim Crow: Southern Politics from Civil War to Civil Rights*, ed. Jane Dailey, Glenda Elizabeth Gilmore, and Bryant Simon (Princeton: Princeton University Press, 2001), 240.; See also: Ritterhouse, *Growing up Jim Crow*, 48.

203. Ayers, *The Promise of the New South*, 429; Ronald H. Bayor, *Race and the Shaping of Twentieth-Century Atlanta*, The Fred W. Morrison Series in Southern Studies (Chapel Hill: University of North Carolina Press, 1996), 94–97.

204. Historians have often focused on reactive violence as the dominant means of enforcing racial etiquette See J. William Harris' statement that "etiquette maintained boundaries; when crossed, violence restored them."; J. William Harris, "Etiquette, Lynching, and Racial Boundaries in Southern History: A Mississippi Example," *The American Historical Review 100*, no. 2 (1995): 393.

205. Rebecca Sharpless notes that, for Black cooks and domestics, economic threats were a major tool to encourage obedience. Sharpless, *Cooking in Other Women's Kitchens*, 136.

206. "Pinehurst, North Carolina," 1913, 3cb/NC.Pine, USGA Archives.

207. This line of argument owes much to Jennifer Ritterhouse who noted that "racial etiquette was not merely regulatory, but formative. That is it did not simply reflect the culture, but helped to make it." Ritterhouse's work was among the first to take racial etiquette's formative nature seriously. Most other discussions of the subject framed it as a symptom of Jim Crow society rather than a constructive feature. Jennifer Ritterhouse, "The Etiquette of Race Relations in the Jim Crow South," in *Manners and Southern History* (Jackson: University Press of Mississippi, 2007), 23.

208. Country Club of Jackson v. Turner, Series 2, Vol. 4 Southern Reporter: Cases Argued and Determined in the Courts of Alabama, Florida, Louisiana, Mississippi 718 (Supreme Court of Mississippi 1941).

209. Ritterhouse, "The Etiquette of Race Relations in the Jim Crow South," 28; Hale, "Chapter 7 'For Colored' and 'For White,'" 177; Simon, "Race Relations: African American Organizing, Liberalism, and White Working-Class Politics in Postwar South Carolina," 244; Smith, *How Race Is Made*, 54–56.

210. The 1906 Atlanta gubernatorial race was fought largely over the disenfranchisement issue. Hoke Smith's winning campaign relied heavily on the argument that political equality led directly to equality in social situations. Mixon, *The Atlanta Riot*, 1.
211. "Modern Instances," *The Nashville American*, June 17, 1901, 4; "State and Capital," Norfolk Landmark, June 13, 1901, 1; "Fifty Caddies on Strike," *Washington Evening Star*, June 12, 1901, 1.
212. "Modern Instances," 4; "Said of Richmond," Richmond Times, June 16, 1901, 4; "Seek Cool Places," *Richmond Dispatch*, May 26, 1901, 10; "Hermitage Golf Club Organized," Richmond Times, October 28, 1900, 2..
213. "Golf Caddies Strike," *Eagle River Review*, July 18, 1895, 3.
214. The author collected evidence of newspaper reports for 240 caddie strikes between 1895 and 1957. The evidence was compiled using digital newspaper archives. Given the limitations of keyword searches and Optical Character Recognition (OCR) it is likely that some recorded strikes were missed. However, the author searched extensively in multiple online archives to compile as representative a database of strikes as possible.
215. "Golf Caddies on Strike," *Butte Inter Mountain*, September 19, 1902, 8; "Caddies Strike for More Pay, Shorter Hours," The Robesonian, June 30, 1947, 8; "South Hills Club Caddies on Strike," Pittsburgh Post-Gazette, June 29, 1935, 2.
216. "Negro Caddies Strike, Yes, For Higher Wages," Miami News, February 12, 1918, 4.
217. "Said of Richmond," 4.
218. Moss, *Golf and the American Country Club*, 104–37.
219. According to Robin D. G. Kelley, between 1942 and 1944, "virtually every segment of organized labor committed to a no-strike pledge in support of the war effort." Robin D. G. Kelley, "Without a Song: New York Musicians Strike Out against Technology," in *Three Strikes: Miners, Musicians, Salesgirls and the Fighting Spirit of Labor's Last Century* (Boston: Beacon Press, 2002), 153–54.
220. "Playing Golf In the South," Jonesboro Weekly Sun, July 28, 1904, 7.
221. Robin D. G. Kelley, *Hammer and Hoe: Alabama Communists During the Great Depression* (Chapel Hill: University of North Carolina Press, 1990), 57–78; Kelley, "We Are Not What We Seem," 99.
222. William Seth LaShier, "'To Secure Improvements in Their Material and Social Conditions': Atlanta's Civil Rights Movement, Middle-Class Reformers, and Workplace

Protests, 1960-1977" (Ph.D., Washington, D.C., The George Washington University, n.d.), 117; Michael Sistrom, "The Freedom Labor Union: Economic Justice and the Civil Rights Movement in Mississippi," in *Reconsidering Southern Labor History*, ed. Matthew Hild and Keri Leigh Merritt (Gainesville: University Press of Florida, 2018), 194–96,

223. On occasion, Pinehurst had caddie shortages unrelated to the ones that occurred across the region. In 1924 Donald Ross informed Leonard Tufts that "We are feeling a shortage of caddies this year and I believe it is due, first to the shortage of rooming accommodations and second, to the low fees paid to them." Donald J. Ross, "Letter from Donald Ross to Leonard Tufts," February 27, 1924, DF_137.01 Folder 6, Tufts Archives.

224. "Fifty Caddies on Strike," 1.

225. For more on caddie tournaments, see Chapter 5.

226. "Junior Tourney Will Draw Many Players," *Asheville Citizen*, May 5, 1921, 9.

227. "Caddies Tourney Is Stopped by 'Strike,'" *Asheville Citizen*, May 24, 1921, 7.

228. "Caddies Tourney Is Stopped by 'Strike,'" 7.

229. "Caddies Must Return Monday, Board Says," *Asheville Citizen*, May 29, 1921, 17.

230. "Society and Personal," *Asheville Citizen*, May 26, 1921, 6; "Caddies on Strike at Asheville Country Club," *Charlotte Observer*, May 26, 1921, 1.

231. See Chapter 5.

232. "Junior Tourney Will Draw Many Players," 9.

233. Robert E. Harlow, "Caddies at Pinehurst, N.C., Tops," *New York Amsterdam News*, May 6, 1939, 19.

234. Mooney, *Race Horse Men: How Slavery and Freedom Were Made at the Racetrack*, 15, 231; Gerald R. Gems, *Before Jackie Robinson: The Transcendent Role of Black Sporting Pioneers* (Lincoln, Nebraska: University of Nebraska Press, 2017), 3.

235. Katherine Mooney notes a similar phenomenon in the horse racing world at the turn of the century, when White Americans consumed minstrel shows and images of Black jockeys as "ape-like black men jouncing ludicrously down the track toward disaster." In turn, "the men who administered racing wanted to see obsequious subordination and comical self-abnegation in the men who worked for them." Mooney, *Race Horse Men*, 229–30.

236. "City News in Brief," *Asheville Times*, September 21, 1898, 8.

237. Demas, *Game of Privilege*, 94.

238. Walter (Chick) Evans, "Evans Tells of Negro Caddies," *Rock Island Argus*, January 3, 1914, 6.

239. Evans' article makes reference to caddie master Jim. The caddie master at the time was Jim Thomas. Evans also discusses a caddie called "potatoes," who was supposedly "a famous fighter, whose life is a continual scrap." It is possible that Evans was referencing a caddie called Will Cook, known as "Tater," who came before the Atlanta Recorders Court a number of times. While Evans' article was likely somewhat sensationalized, these verifiable facts give it a degree of reliability. "Recorder Will Have Good Caddy Next Time," 7. For more on Cook, see Chapter 1.

240. "G.E. Horne to Richard Tufts," April 17, 1942, DF79.02 Folder 8, Tufts Archives.

241. Happy Walters, "The 19th Hole," *Washington Tribune*, September 8, 1934, 15.

242. Happy Walters, "The 19th Hole," *Washington Tribune*, November 3, 1934, 13.

243. "Negro Caddies Are on Strike," *Roanoke Times*, June 14, 1901, 4.

244. "Strikes and Strikes - It's Golfing Time," *Charlotte Observer*, March 23, 1937, B4.

245. Richard Moss notes that the country club in American life "commonly promoted itself as medicinal, as the malady brought on by the industrial city and modern life." One country club marketed itself as an "attempt to provide natural beauty, recreation, exclusivity, and 'perfect order' to people who could afford a very high price for such things." Moss, *Golf and the American Country Club*, 34–35.

246. For more on the social benefits that golfers received from employing caddies, see Chapter 1.

247. When Black workers organized for their working rights, Whites often responded with common tactics including blaming outsiders, employing strikebreakers, violence and arrests. Hunter, To 'joy My Freedom, 91–92; Steven Hahn, *A Nation Under Our Feet: Black Political Struggles in the Rural South, from Slavery to the Great Migration* (Cambridge, Mass: Belknap Press of Harvard University Press, 2003), 414–25; Leslie Brown, *Upbuilding Black Durham: Gender, Class, and Black Community Development in the Jim Crow South* (Chapel Hill: University of North Carolina Press, 2008), 43. 3

248. "Golf Notes," *Sandhill Citizen*, January 27, 1922, 2.

249. Hagen, "Golf Customs Differ Over United States," 12.

250. Bion Butler, "A National Asset," *Pinehurst Outlook*, March 4, 1916, 5.

251. Lee Pace, *The Spirit of Pinehurst* (Pinehurst: Pinehurst Inc., 2004), 104.

252. "Caddies Go On Strike Here at Golf Club But Fail To Get A Raise," *Cleveland Star*, July 31, 1935, 6.

253. Most labor laws passed between the 1870s and the 1930s that were, on the surface, racially neutral actually served to harm African American workers. The National Labor Relations 1935, or the Wagner Act, had little impact on the lives of workers like caddies in the South. Although the act guaranteed workers the right to organize without fear of retribution, it had key exclusions including domestic workers, agricultural workers and independent contractors. Southern democrats insisted on such exclusions to keep the majority of Black workers in the South from organizing. David E. Bernstein, *Only One Place of Redress: African Americans, Labor Regulations, and the Courts: From Reconstruction to the New Deal*, Constitutional Conflicts (Durham, NC: Duke University Press, 2001); James A. Gross, *Rights, Not Interests: Resolving Value Clashes under the National Labor Relations Act* (Ithaca: Cornell University Press, 2017), 20–21.
254. Wickham, *Woodholme*, 162.
255. "Caddie Strike Fails," *Washington Evening Star*, July 28, 1913, 14; "Strike of the Golf Caddies at Country Club Is Settled," *Washington Herald*, July 27, 1913, 8; "Interesting Golf Notes From the Local Clubs," *Washington Evening Star*, August 3, 1913, E4.
256. "Gainesville Perks up for Home Game," *Tampa Tribune*, November 14, 1937, C8.
257. "Fifty Caddies on Strike," 1.
258. "Caddy Strike a Floozie at the Very First Tee," *Washington Times*, July 12, 1910, 9.
259. "Columbus Golfers Quell Caddy Strike," *Birmingham News*, March 9, 1932, 9.
260. "Negro Sitdown Strike Caddies Sit Down Until the Blue Coats Come," *Miami News*, March 7, 1937, D7.
261. "Caddy Strike Halts as Leader Arrested," *Tampa Tribune*, February 24, 1929, 5; "Caddies Have Real Strike, Court Case 'n' Everything," *Richmond News Leader*, May 11, 1936, B1.
262. "Caddy Strike Halts as Leader Arrested," 5. Police played an active role in quelling Black labor organizing around the south. See also: Paul Ortiz, *Emancipation Betrayed: The Hidden History of Black Organizing and White Violence in Florida from Reconstruction to the Bloody Election 1920* (Berkeley: University of California Press, 2005).
263. For more on convict leasing and the exploitation of Black labor through the criminal justice system see Douglas A. Blackmon, *Slavery by Another Name: The Re-Enslavement of Black People in America From the Civil War to World War II* (New York: Doubleday, 2008); Talitha L. LeFlouria, *Chained in Silence: Black Women and Convict Labor in the New South* (Chapel Hill: University of North Carolina Press, 2015).

264. Historian Silvan Niedermeier notes that "torture demonstrated the white law enforcement officers' belief that they were entitled to wield absolute power over the black suspects in their custody."; Silvan Niedermeier, *The Color of the Third Degree: Racism, Police Torture, and Civil Rights in the American South, 1930-1955* (Chapel Hill: University of North Carolina Press, 2019), 38. For more on police violence see Jeffrey S. Adler, *Murder in New Orleans: The Creation of Jim Crow Policing* (Chicago: University of Chicago Press, 2019).

265. "Pinehurst, North Carolina" (R. and Avery Supply Co., n.d.), 3C2c/NC.Pine, USGA Archives.

266. Hagen, "Golf Customs Differ Over United States," 12.

267. Brandon T. Jett, *Race, Crime, and Policing in the Jim Crow South: African Americans and Law Enforcement in Birmingham, Memphis, and New Orleans, 1920–1945* (Baton Rouge: Lousiana State University Press, 2021), 3; Niedermeier, *The Color of the Third Degree*, 21–22.

268. "N.C. Caddies Win Sit-Down Strike," Arizona Gleam, May 7, 1937, 1; "Caddies Strike for More Pay," *Greenville News*, April 12, 1937, 6.

269. The classification of each strike by race was only done when the newspaper articles outrightly stated the race of the caddies. Although it might be assumed that some of the other strikes that occurred in the South were by Black caddies, the assumption could not be confirmed.

270. Taft and Taft, *On the Bag*, 14–15.

271. See Chapter 6.

272. In the 1960s, one golf course in Maryland began the practice of giving "Caddie Welfare" to those who sat in the caddy house all day without receiving a bag. DeWayne Wickham, who caddied at the club noted that "the two dollars we collected on days we sat around for nearly twelve hours without success wasn't welfare. It was an unemployment benefit." Wickham, *Woodholme*, 68.

273. Story taken from Charlie Sifford's account of the time he first met Howard Wheeler. Sifford's account suggests that the meeting took place the first spring that he arrived in Philadelphia, 1940. It seems unlikely that Wheeler would have been present in Philadelphia that year because he was living in Los Angeles until at least October 1940; Sifford and Gullo, *Just Let Me Play*, 28–31.; "Pennsylvania, U.S., Veteran Compensation Application Files, WWII, 1950-1966", digital image, s.v. "Howard Wheeler," Ancestry.com, accessed November 2021; "U.S., World War II Draft Cards Young Men,

1940-1947", digital image, s.v. "Howard Wheeler," Ancestry.com, accessed November 2021

274. Lucius "Melancholy" Jones, "Slant on Sports," *Atlanta Daily World*, September 4, 1938, 5.

275. Many accounts of Black golf history credit Sifford with six UGA National Opens. However, Sifford only won five. The 1952 Open which he is widely credited with winning was actually won by Teddy Rhodes. This correction was first noted by Raymond Schmidt; Raymond Schmidt, "Pars and Birdies in a Hidden World: African Americans and the United Golfers Association," in *Separate Games: African American Sport Behind the Walls of Segregation*, ed. David K. Wiggins and Ryan A. Swanson (Fayetteville, AK: University of Arkansas Press, 2016), 191n40; Kinloch and Dawkins, *African American Golfers During the Jim Crow Era*, 41.

276. Sifford and Gullo, *Just Let Me Play*, 108.

277. See Chapter 1 for more regarding the growth of Golf and racial hierarchy in the South.

278. Willis D. Weatherford, *A Survey of the Negro Boy in Nashville, Tennessee* (New York, N.Y: Association Press, 1932), 6–7.

279. Sifford and Gullo, *Just Let Me Play*, 12.

280. Al Barkow, *Gettin' to the Dance Floor: An Oral History of American Golf*, 1st edition (New York: Atheneum, 1986), 195.

281. Sifford and Gullo, *Just Let Me Play*, 15.

282. Taft and Taft, *On the Bag*, 188.

283. Kinloch and Dawkins, *African American Golfers*, 108, Kinloch and Dawkins, *African American Golfers During the Jim Crow Era*, 188.

284. Kennedy, *A Course of Their Own*, 5.

285. Joseph Herman Johnson, "West Southern Pines: An Experiment in Negro Self Government" (1932), 29.

286. "Number Ten Course," 2.

287. Kinloch and Dawkins, *African American Golfers During the Jim Crow Era*, 108.

288. Wickham, *Woodholme*, 151.

289. Wickham, 157.

290. Sifford and Gullo, *Just Let Me Play*, 16.

291. Sifford and Gullo, 16.

292. Barkow, *Gettin' to the Dance Floor*, 197.

293. This type of tournament is known as a shotgun start.

NOTES

294. Wickham, *Woodholme*, 152–56.
295. Taft and Taft, *On the Bag*, 187.
296. "The Last Word in Golf Club Making," *The American Golfer*, April 1910, 400.; For caddie wages, see Chapter 4.
297. "Rise in Price of Golf Clubs Is Threatened," *New York Times*, September 3, 1916, A2.
298. Taft and Taft, *On the Bag*, 186.
299. Barkow, *Gettin' to the Dance Floor*, 195.
300. Johnson, "West Southern Pines," 29.
301. Sifford and Gullo, *Just Let Me Play*, 16.
302. Ramona Harriet, *A Missing Link In History: The Journey of African Americans in Golf*, 2nd edition (CreateSpace, 2015), 17.
303. Caddies Playing Golf, n.d., n.d., Caddies, P010470, Tufts Archives.
304. Wickham, *Woodholme*, 151–52.
305. Sifford and Gullo, *Just Let Me Play*, 16.
306. Sinnette, *Forbidden Fairways*, 91.
307. Kinloch and Dawkins, *African American Golfers During the Jim Crow Era*, 116.
308. Barkow, *Gettin' to the Dance Floor*, 198.
309. Sifford and Gullo, *Just Let Me Play*, 16.
310. William Allen White, "As I See It," *New York Tribune*, July 23, 1922, 8.
311. Demas, *Game of Privilege*, 45–46.
312. "Caddies Meet at Lincoln Tourney," *Atlanta Daily World*, October 4, 1936, 5.
313. Sinnette, *Forbidden Fairways*, 39; Kinloch and Dawkins, *African American Golfers During the Jim Crow Era*, 102, 108–9, 122; Kennedy, *A Course of Their Own*, 4.
314. "One Armed Caddie Plays Hole in One At West End," *The Atlanta Constitution*, August 3, 1926, 18.
315. "Colored Golf Caddies Have The Answers, Says Writer," *Norfolk Journal and Guide*, February 19, 1938, 18.
316. Sifford and Gullo, *Just Let Me Play*, 19.
317. Mike Thomas, "Caddie Meet Won by 'Ike,'" *The Atlanta Constitution*, July 12, 1922, 10.
318. Ralph Dawkins Jr. remembered over 100 caddies from all over the state of Florida playing in the caddie tournament at Florida Country Club in Jacksonville, Florida; Kinloch and Dawkins, *African American Golfers During the Jim Crow Era*, 109.
319. "Negro Caddies Compete Today," *Charlotte Observer*, April 2, 1946, sec. B, 9.

320. "Negro Caddies Beaten in Match in Gate City," *Durham Sun*, August 21, 1939, sec. B, 4.
321. "Caddy Tournament Slated April 14," *The Atlanta Constitution*, April 3, 1930, 21.
322. At a caddie tournament in Savannah in 1929 a caddie named Elijah Green distinguished himself as an excellent talent among his peers. Green scored a one under par 73, including two birdies and an eagle in the first nine holes. His nearest competitor scored an 86. "Caddy Breaks Par To Lead Tourney," *The Atlanta Constitution*, July 31, 1929, 22.
323. Gary M. Pomerantz, *Where Peachtree Meets Sweet Auburn: The Saga of Two Families and the Making of Atlanta* (New York: Penguin Books, 1996), 172–73.
324. Harlow, "Caddies at Pinehurst, N.C., Tops," 19.
325. Kinloch and Dawkins, *African American Golfers During the Jim Crow Era*, 109.
326. Demas, *Game of Privilege*, 34–38; McDaniel, *Uneven Lies*, 24–25.
327. Demas, *Game of Privilege*, 102–4.
328. "The New Definition of an Amateur," *The American Golfer*, April 1915, 471.
329. "Defines Amateur Golf," *New York Times*, December 23, 1914, 11.
330. "Protests Ban on Negroes in Hale America Golf," *Chicago Daily Tribune*, May 26, 1942, 22.
331. Demas, *Game of Privilege*, 116; Kinloch and Dawkins, *African American Golfers During the Jim Crow Era*, 153.
332. "Southerner Wins National Golf Championship," *Chicago Defender*, September 6, 1930, 1.
333. Kinloch and Dawkins, *African American Golfers During the Jim Crow Era*, 41, 45; McDaniel, *Uneven Lies*, 51.
334. Jimmie Williams, "Golf's Popularity Big Sport Feature," *Chicago Defender*, January 2, 1932, 9.
335. Demas, *Game of Privilege*, 93–96.
336. "Southerner Wins National Golf Championship," 1; Demas, *Game of Privilege*, 92.
337. Ric Roberts, "Atlanta Golfers in California for National Meet," *Atlanta Daily World*, August 15, 1939, 5.
338. Kinloch and Dawkins, *African American Golfers During the Jim Crow Era*, 41,49.
339. "Southerner Wins National Golf Championship," 1; J. W. Smith, "Lincoln Golf Team Members End Matches for Free Trip," *Atlanta Daily World*, August 21, 1934, 5.
340. Kinloch and Dawkins, *African American Golfers During the Jim Crow Era*, 49–50.
341. Harlow, "Caddies at Pinehurst, N.C., Tops," 19.

342. The Pinehurst Golfers received brief mentions in some news articles about Pinehurst players. In 1954 they purchased the site of the Oakland Park Recreation Center for Negroes near Lakeview which they intended to turn into a golf course. After the purchase the group made a call for donations in the local newspaper, The Pilot. However no further mention of the project could be found, and other references to Oakland Park in the years that followed did not mention a golf course on the site. See: "N.C. Caddy Shoots 64 at Langston," *Baltimore Afro-American*, August 10, 1940, 19; "Negro Golf Course Outlook Bright," *Southern Pines Pilot*, April 30, 1954, 18; "Leading Negro of Vass Community Passed Saturday," *Southern Pines Pilot*, November 29, 1956, 18; "Golf Event Raises $50 for Hospital Fund," *Southern Pines Pilot*, June 9, 1950, 10.

343. "Boston Ready for National Golf Championships," *Chicago Defender*, August 9, 1941, 23.

344. James Tapley Wardlaw, "Leisure Time Activities of Negro Boys in the First Ward of Atlanta, Georgia" (Atlanta, Atlanta University, 1934), 64–65, Robert W. Woodruff Library, Atlanta University Center (ETD Collection for AUC).

345. Jimmie Williams, "Mashie-Niblick Shots," *Chicago Defender*, July 15, 1933, 8.

346. Joel W. Smith, "Down The Fairway," *Atlanta Daily World*, July 4, 1941, 7.

347. "Sports Fans Await 12th Annual Southern Open Golf Tournament," *Atlanta Daily World*, June 18, 1950, 7.

348. Roberts, "Atlanta Golfers in California for National Meet," 5.

349. Sifford and Gullo, *Just Let Me Play*, 32.

350. Demas, *Game of Privilege*, 209–13; McDaniel, *Uneven Lies*, 90.

351. Sifford and Gullo, *Just Let Me Play*, 123–25; Demas, *Game of Privilege*, 214.

352. Demas, *Game of Privilege*, 221–22.

353. "Yes Sir, J.C. Can Hit That Golf Ball: Rockville Gets Long Hitting Citizen," *United Golfer and Other Sports*, 1938, 11; Quoted in Sinnette, *Forbidden Fairways*, 40–43.

354. Hamilton actually went on to play three seasons in baseball's segregated Negro Leagues for the Homestead Grays in Washington, D.C. between 1940 and 1942. 1940 Census, Manatee County, Florida, Population Schedule, Bradenton City, Ward 3, Sheet 23A, Household 552, Digital image, Ancestry.com, accessed, 10 November 2021; "J. C. Hamilton," Seamheads Negro Leagues Database, accessed December 20, 2022, https://www.seamheads.com/NegroLgs/player.php?playerID=hamilo1jam.

355. "Statement on the Death of Charles L. Sifford," February 4, 2015, DCPD201500079, Administration of Barack Obama, https://www.govinfo.gov/content/pkg/DCPD-201500079/pdf/DCPD-201500079.pdf.
356. Tiger Woods, "History Was Made Last Night by My Grandpa," Instagram photo, November 25, 2014, https://www.instagram.com/p/vo_I4zy8dE/.
357. David Zucchino, "Putting the Cart Before the Caddies," *Raleigh News and Observer*, March 30, 1975, sec. V, 1.
358. J. W. Smith, "Roy Jones Shoots Sensational Putt," *Atlanta Daily World*, November 4, 1937, 5; "Golfers Try Dope On Victory in July," *Atlanta Daily World*, June 23, 1936, 5.
359. Russ DeVault, "Caddy Dies; Era Ends," *The Atlanta Constitution*, May 7, 1978, sec. D, 11.
360. One of the only attempts to answer the question focused largely on the disappearance of Black caddies from professional golf, rather than from the daily golf played by amateurs around the country. Wornie Reed, "The Black Golf Caddy: A Victim of Labor Market Discrimination," *Challenge Online 14*, no. 1 (May 1, 2008): 61–71.
361. Sharp, "Atlanta Clubs Face Shortage Of Caddy Boys," D2; Herb Graffis, "Making the Swing," *Golfdom*, January 1944, 4.
362. Whittlesey, "Tee to Green," SP3.
363. "Pinehurst Golf Play Continues," Greensboro Daily News, December 10, 1943, sec. B, 2; J Bryan III, "Privacy Unlimited," *Saturday Evening Post*, March 8, 1941, 96.
364. Stuart L. Klingelsmith, "Bag Cart Big New Factor in Golf Business," *Golfdom*, April 1947, 72.
365. For more on the changing attitudes toward service labor among Black workers and Black media, see Chapter 7.
366. John Budd, "Bag Cart Possibilities Call for Pro Studies," *Golfdom*, September 1947, 34.
367. "I.C. Sledge to Richard S. Tufts," March 10, 1943, DF79.02 Folder 8, Tufts Archives.
368. Budd, "Bag Cart Possibilities Call for Pro Studies," 34.
369. "First Caddy Cart," *The Golf Course Reporter*, July 1955, 27.
370. "Here's Faith," *Richmond News Leader*, March 11, 1933, 14.
371. Joseph Chamberlain, "Carts for Caddie Shortage," *Golfdom*, October 1941, 32.
372. Budd, "Bag Cart Possibilities Call for Pro Studies," 34.
373. Klingelsmith, "Bag Cart Big New Factor in Golf Business," 72.

NOTES

374. Herb Graffis, "Swinging Around Golf," *Golfdom*, July 1946, 11.
375. Klingelsmith, "Bag Cart Big New Factor in Golf Business," 72.
376. Budd, "Bag Cart Possibilities Call for Pro Studies," 34.
377. "Bag Carriers Offset Caddie Cut," *Golfdom*, October 1942, 31.
378. Klingelsmith, "Bag Cart Big New Factor in Golf Business," 72.
379. Guy Paulsen, "'Traffic Study' Shows Pros Big Job and Costs," *Golfdom*, February 1950, 58.
380. "Caddie-Masters Compare Their Work at WGA Meeting," *Golfdom*, May 1953, 48.
381. Harold Cliffer, "Pros Tell Space Needs in Pro Shop Architecture," *Golfdom*, May 1955, 56.
382. "Caddie-Masters Compare Their Work at WGA Meeting," 48.
383. Verne Wickham, "Bag Cart Traffic Is Course Wear Problem," *Golfdom*, April 1946, 33.
384. Walter Fuchs, "Meeting Demands of the Public Course Player," *The Golf Course Reporter*, August 1956, 8.
385. Chamberlain, "Carts for Caddie Shortage," 32.
386. Klingelsmith, "Bag Cart Big New Factor in Golf Business," 72.
387. Herb Graffis, "Golf Looks to New Frontier," *Golfdom*, February 1961, 20.
388. A 1962 article in *Golfdom*, claimed that the "golf car" was still the common usage, but by the end of the century they became known as golf carts. Herb Graffis, "Swinging Around Golf," *Golfdom*, January 1962, 3.
389. Vern Putney, "Golf Has Inspired Inventors Who Think Small," *Golf Course News*, March 1991, 42.
390. Tom Mascaro, "Meeting the Golf Cart Problem," in Summary of Proceedings (Annual Conference of the Mid-Atlantic Association of Golf Course Superintendents, Baltimore: Extension Service - University of Maryland, 1966), 10.
391. Dan Cordtz, "Golf Cars: Tiny Runabouts Grab a Growing Share of Divot Digging Dollars," *Wall Street Journal*, June 16, 1955, 1, 14.
392. Anthony Leviero, "Eisenhower and Nixon Are Partners on Links, Too," *New York Times*, September 12, 1953, 1; Cordtz, "Golf Cars: Tiny Runabouts Grab a Growing Share of Divot Digging Dollars," 1.
393. George Nivel, "How About Golf Cars?," *Golfdom*, March 1958, Pull Out.
394. Mascaro, "Meeting the Golf Cart Problem," 10.
395. Desmond Tolhurst, "Sales Continue Rising Trend," *Golfdom*, October 1966, 64.
396. "1970: The Year of the Golf Car," *Golfdom*, February 1970, 80.

397. William J. Freund, "Golf Cars, What's New - Part 1: Cars," *The Golf Course Reporter*, February 1961, 40.
398. TheGolfCourseReporter_196102_46 Ward Cornwell, "Golf Cars, What's New - Part 3: Superintendent Reports," *The Golf Course Reporter*, February 1961, 47.
399. Cordtz, "Golf Cars: Tiny Runabouts Grab a Growing Share of Divot Digging Dollars," 1.
400. The phrase "here to stay" was consistently used in golf industry periodicals and conferences. It appeared at least 20 times between 1951 and 1970.
401. T. M. Baumgardner, "Golf Car 'Traffic,'" in Proceedings (Seventeenth Annual Southeastern Turfgrass Conference, Tifton, GA: Georgia Coastal Plain Experiment, and Abraham Baldwin Agricultural College, 1963), 27.
402. Graffis, "Golf Looks to New Frontier," 19.
403. "Victor Electri-Car," *Golfdom*, April 1956, 32.
404. "Trouble Free! Rental Cart Service," *Golfdom*, June 1960, 88.
405. Mascaro, "Meeting the Golf Cart Problem," 12.
406. Peter V. Tufts, "Memo to the Management Committee," March 21, 1969, DF79.02 Folder 21, Tufts Archives.
407. Tolhurst, "Sales Continue Rising Trend," 68.
408. "Don't Put Members in Middle on Golf Car Policy," *Golfdom*, January 1959, 29.
409. "Don't Put Members in Middle on Golf Car Policy," 29.
410. Lizabeth Cohen, *A Consumers' Republic: The Politics of Mass Consumption in Postwar America* (New York: Knopf, 2003), 122–23; Kenneth T. Jackson, *Crabgrass Frontier: The Suburbanization of the United States* (New York: Oxford University Press, Incorporated, 1987), 246–71.
411. Graffis, "Golf Looks to New Frontier," 19.
412. "Trouble Free! Rental Cart Service," 88.
413. Tolhurst, "Sales Continue Rising Trend," 65.
414. "Buyers Guide to Golf Carts," *Golfdom*, February 1966, 68–76.
415. Jimmy Dudley, "Care and Handling of Golf Carts," in Proceedings (Seventeenth Annual Southeastern Turfgrass Conference, Tifton, GA: Georgia Coastal Plain Experiment, and Abraham Baldwin Agricultural College, 1963), 25.
416. Dudley, 24.
417. Tufts, "Memo to the Management Committee."

418. George L. Lanphear, "Golf Car Storage and Golf Car Paths," in Summary of Papers (34th International Turf-Grass Conference, San Diego, CA: Golf Course Superintendents Association of America, 1963), 8.
419. Tufts, "Memo to the Management Committee."
420. Mascaro, "Meeting the Golf Cart Problem," 12.
421. John D. Patterson, "Solving the Car Storage Problem," *Golfdom*, January 1969, 96.
422. "Richard S. Tufts to Peter V. Tufts," June 18, 1969, DF79.02 Folder 21, Tufts Archives.
423. Mascaro, "Meeting the Golf Cart Problem," 11.
424. John F. Gleason, "Is Your Golf Car Insurance Adequate?," *Golfdom*, August 1967, 38.
425. "The Logical Way to Ship Golf Cars!," *Golfdom*, January 1952, 14.
426. "Richard Tufts to Albert Tufts," January 31, 1966, DF79.02 Folder 26, Tufts Archives.
427. "Golf Notes," *Raleigh News and Observer*, May 18, 1975, sec. II, 6.
428. William J. Freund, "Golf Cars - Friend or Enemy?," *The Golf Course Reporter*, Conference Issue 1957, 60–61.
429. "Car Manufacturers Complete Basic Phase of Getting Organized," *Golfdom*, March 1964, 82.
430. Freund, "Golf Cars - Friend or Enemy?," 60–61.
431. Eugene Kinkead, "Caddy to A President," *Life*, May 11, 1953, 111.
432. Kinkead, 111.
433. President Dwight D Eisenhower And Willie "Cemetary" Perteet. In 1953, Getty Images Image #83123019, Augusta National; Catherine M Lewis, "Don't Ask What I Shot": How President Eisenhower's Love of Golf Helped Shape 1950's America (New York: McGraw-Hill, 2007), 173.
434. Clayton, *Men on the Bag*, 46–55.
435. William P. Jones, *The March on Washington: Jobs, Freedom, and the Forgotten History of Civil Rights* (New York: W. W. Norton & Company, 2014), x.
436. "Not A Man's Job," *Baltimore Afro-American*, April 13, 1957, 4; Other articles focused on Perteet include: Robert E. Clark, "Ike Wasted No Time Getting on Golf Course," *Atlanta Daily World*, April 19, 1957, 2; Louis Lautier, "Ike's Appointment of Cole Stirs Fear About Future of Public Housing," *Baltimore Afro-American*, March 14, 1953, 5; "What Afro Readers Say," *Baltimore Afro-American*, March 21, 1953, 4; "They Said It," *Baltimore Afro-American*, April 13, 1957, 5; Cliff W. Mackay, "News in

Tabloid," *Baltimore Afro-American*, March 14, 1953, 4; Robert E. Clark, "'Cemetery' Out As Ike's Caddy," *Chicago Defender*, May 4, 1957, 22; Fern Gayden, "'Cemetery' As Viewed By White Press, Shocking," *Pittsburgh Courier*, March 28, 1953, 29; William G. Nunn Jr., "An Open Letter to Our Commander-in-Chief!," *Pittsburgh Courier*, September 14, 1957, 18.

437. For more on the Double V campaign see: Rawn James Jr., *The Double V: How Wars, Protest, and Harry Truman Desegregated America's Military*, 1st edition (New York: Bloomsbury Press, 2013); Matthew F. Delmont, *Half American: The Epic Story of African Americans Fighting World War II at Home and Abroad* (New York: Viking, 2022).

438. Sharp, "Atlanta Clubs Face Shortage Of Caddy Boys," D2.

439. James L. Hicks, "Warns South Against Only Menial Jobs To 90 Per Cent of Veterans," *Atlanta Daily World*, April 11, 1946, 1.

440. "Plight of Negro Veterans Deplored," *Atlanta Daily World*, May 14, 1947, 2.

441. W. E. B. Du Bois, "The Winds of Time," *Chicago Defender*, April 14, 1945, 13.

442. Carl Husemoller Nightingale, "The Global Inner City: Toward a Historical Analysis," in *W.E.B. DuBois, Race, and the City: The Philadelphia Negro and Its Legacy*, ed. Thomas J. Sugrue and Michael B. Katz (Philadelphia: University of Pennsylvania Press, 1998), 226.

443. "Hydrogen Bomb Unit Accused of Race Bias," *New York Times*, September 19, 1951, 20.

444. "Still Little Hiring in Defense Set-Up," *New York Amsterdam News*, May 10, 1952, 25.

445. William O'Shields, "Pro Golf's Bars Higher than Baseball's: O'Shields," *Atlanta Daily World*, February 12, 1948, 5.

446. Roberts, "Atlanta Golfers in California for National Meet," 5.

447. Marion E. Jackson, "Sports of the World," *Atlanta Daily World*, July 3, 1954, 7.

448. Jackie Reems, "Reams of Sports," *New York Amsterdam News*, June 23, 1951, 16.

449. Andy Mitchell, "For Sale: $10,000 Bathroom," Mississippi Free Press, January 18, 1964, 5.

450. "Supreme Court Carried the Seed for Its Own Destruction, and the NAACP Encouraged It," Los Angeles Tribune, September 5, 1958, 8.

451. "The Powell Committee Hearings on Theatre," *New York Amsterdam News*, December 22, 1962, 55.

452. Walter White, "White Makes Retread Of Ike And His Anti-Bias Problem, 'Cemetery' Sans Comment," *New York Age*, June 6, 1953, 10.

453. Papers of the NAACP, Part 18. Special Subjects, 1940-1955, Series B: General Office Files: Abolition of Government Agencies-Jews, SERIES: Group II, Series A, General Office File, FOLDER TITLE: Eisenhower, Dwight D., 1953-1955., Library of Congress 157
454. Gayden, "'Cemetery' As Viewed By White Press, Shocking," 29.
455. Clark, "Ike Wasted No Time Getting on Golf Course," 2.
456. "Not A Man's Job," 4.
457. Langston Hughes, "Week By Week: Democrats and Republicans," *Chicago Defender*, January 5, 1960, 10.
458. Bryant Simon showed how, in coastal New Jersey, the use of Black service workers who pushed rolling carts on the Atlantic City Boardwalk was part of a "public performance of racial dominance." Bryant Simon, *Boardwalk of Dreams: Atlantic City and the Fate of Urban America* (New York,: Oxford University Press, 2006), 7; Likewise, Scott Giltner argues that "Having black subordinates in the field returned whites to a mythical era of racial control and projected to the world a solution for the South's "Negro problem." Giltner, *Hunting and Fishing in the New South*, 80.
459. This phenomenon can be found as a key catalyst in the disenfranchisement of African Americans in Georgia when, in 1906, Governor Hoke Smith argued that allowing political equality would encourage sexual intimacy between Black men and White women. Likewise, managers in industrial settings argued that "We hired them for this hot and dirty work and we want them [to stay] there. If we let a few rise, all the rest will become dissatisfied."; *Atlanta Journal*, Aug 1, 1906; quoted in Godshalk, *Veiled Visions*, 50–51; Industry manager quoted in Trotter Jr, *Workers on Arrival*, 86.
460. Kevin M. Kruse, *White Flight: Atlanta and the Making of Modern Conservatism* (Princeton: Princeton University Press, 2005), 106.
461. Giltner, *Hunting and Fishing in the New South*, 80 Also see Chapter 1 of this book .
462. Lozano, "Race, Mobility, and Fantasy," 829.
463. Kruse, *White Flight*, 125.
464. "Unemployment Used by Georgia Bigots to Stir up Race Hatred," *Baltimore Afro-American*, September 6, 1930, 3.
465. Kevin Kruse notes that White working classes in Atlanta had come to think of municipal services "as 'their' buses, 'their' parks, and 'their' pools." Kruse, *White Flight*, 107.
466. Mehrsa Baradaran, *The Color of Money: Black Banks and the Racial Wealth Gap* (Cambridge, Massachusetts: Belknap Press, 2017), 103–9.

467. Haley C. Meisenholder, "Not in My Back Nine: An Examination of Land Use Disputes Over Golf Course Redevelopments in America" (Thesis, Massachusetts Institute of Technology, 2019), 25–26; David B. Hueber, "The Changing Face of the Game and Golf's Built Environment" (Ph.D., Clemson, SC, Clemson University, 2012), 21; Darrell E. Napton and Christopher R. Laingen, "Expansion of Golf Courses in the United States*," *Geographical Review 98*, no. 1 (January 1, 2008): 28.
468. One of the courses was turned into a housing development while the other was bought by some of the members and saved from demolition. Over the subsequent years the golf course fell into disrepair before being restored in the 1990s as part of a community restoration project Catherine M. Lewis, *A Host to History: The Story of The Atlanta Athletic Club* (Atlanta: Bookhouse, 2012), 57; "Athletic Club To Vote on East Lake Sale," *The Atlanta Constitution*, March 9, 1968, 10.
469. "Golf Cars to Replace Caddies at May's Tam O'Shanter Club," *Golfdom*, February 1960, 25.
470. "All Work Together At East Lake Course," *The Golf Course Reporter*, Conference Issue 1960, 15.
471. Zucchino, "Putting the Cart Before the Caddies," 1.
472. Tye, *Rising from the Rails*, 235.
473. Greta de Jong, *You Can't Eat Freedom: Southerners and Social Justice after the Civil Rights Movement* (Chapel Hill: University of North Carolina Press, 2016), 2.
474. Cliff Wheatley, "Rapid Growth in Municipal Golf," *The Atlanta Constitution*, July 11, 1922, 10.
475. Jess Usher, "'The Golfers': African American Golfers of the North Carolina Piedmont and the Struggle for Access," *North Carolina Historical Review 87*, no. 2 (April 2010): 167; Kinloch and Dawkins, *African American Golfers During the Jim Crow Era*, 140–41.
476. James Bennett, "City to Open Golf Courses By June 29," *Birmingham Post-Herald*, June 20, 1963, 1; Usher, "The Golfers," 171–72.
477. George B. Kirsch, "Municipal Golf and Civil Rights in the United States, 1910-1965," *The Journal of African American History 92*, no. 3 (July 2007): 382.
478. The creation of separate spaces that were never actually equal marked White spaces as superior, and Black spaces as inferior, reinforcing the racial hierarchy that underpinned segregation. After *Plessy*, Whites segregated publicly funded spaces wherever possible. Any new municipal buildings or services came with segregation designed into them. Hale, *Making Whiteness*, 128–29; Ayers, *The Promise of the New South*, 432.

479. See Chapter 5.
480. Sharp, "Atlanta Clubs Face Shortage Of Caddy Boys," D2.
481. Whittlesey, "Tee to Green," Sp3.
482. In the 1930s, White supremacists in Atlanta criticized White golfers who hired Black caddies. "You men, who freely tip your caddies, your bootblacks, and your waiters, do you realize that there are several thousand unemployed White men in Atlanta?" "Unemployment Used by Georgia Bigots to Stir up Race Hatred," 3.
483. Demas, *Game of Privilege*, 47.
484. There is no evidence of any Black private courses in North Carolina, South Carolina, Mississippi, Louisiana, Alabama, or Texas, prior to 1950. Demas, 47; Kinloch and Dawkins, *African American Golfers During the Jim Crow Era*, 22.
485. Demas, *Game of Privilege*, 140–42.
486. "Negro Golf Course Proposed to Council," *Greensboro Daily News*, March 3, 1949, sec. B, 1.
487. "Mayor Says Negroes May Use Muny Course," *Knoxville News-Sentinel*, March 21, 1952, 14; "Council to Rule on Negro Golfing," *Knoxville News-Sentinel*, March 27, 1952, 2.
488. "Unreasonable Request," *Knoxville News-Sentinel*, April 10, 1952, 22.
489. "Private Meeting Set on Golf Course Issue," *Knoxville News-Sentinel*, April 19, 1952, 7.
490. "Let Negroes Play Golf, Say Readers," *Knoxville News-Sentinel*, April 14, 1952, 12.
491. "City's Four-Year Golf Loss $26,746," *Knoxville News-Sentinel*, April 8, 1952, 1.
492. "Council Rejects Low, OKs High Garbage Equipment Bid," *Knoxville News-Sentinel*, April 23, 1952, 6.
493. "Municipal Golf Course to Be Leased by City," *Knoxville News-Sentinel*, May 7, 1952, 1.
494. "Municipal Golf Course to Be Leased by City," 1; "Four Negroes, Barred From City Links, Sue," *Knoxville News-Sentinel*, May 21, 1952, 1.
495. "Four Negroes, Barred From City Links, Sue," 16.
496. Kinloch and Dawkins, *African American Golfers During the Jim Crow Era*, 147; Kirsch, "Municipal Golf and Civil Rights in the United States, 1910-1965," 387–89.
497. Discontent among Black Southerners was not a new thing. Throughout the late 19th century and the first half of the 20th, Black Southerners did not willingly accept segregation. In recent decades historians have emphasized the decades of struggle for Black Freedom that preceded the conventional mid-century definition of the Civil

Rights Movement, and encouraged a broader timeline of the "long civil rights movement." However, the 1950s and 1960s saw an explosion of political opposition to Jim Crow that was unprecedented in scale. For the purposes of clarity, and without detracting from Black struggles in the pre-WWII period, the Civil Rights Movement in this book refers to the vast social uprising for racial equality that occurred in the 1950s and 1960s. Jacquelyn Dowd Hall, "The Long Civil Rights Movement and the Political Uses of the Past," *The Journal of American History 91*, no. 4 (2005): 1233–63.

498. Kinloch and Dawkins, *African American Golfers During the Jim Crow Era*, 140, 144–48; Kirsch, "Municipal Golf and Civil Rights in the United States, 1910-1965," 382; Demas, *Game of Privilege*, 165–66; Yanela Gordon McLeod, "The *Miami Times*: A Driving Force for Social Change, 1948-1958" (Ph.D., Tallahassee, The Florida State University, 2014), 136–85.

499. McLeod, "The *Miami Times*," 137; Yanela G. McLeod, *The Miami Times and the Fight for Equality: Race, Sport, and the Black Press, 1948–1958* (Lanham: Lexington Books, 2018), 119.

500. Kinloch and Dawkins, *African American Golfers During the Jim Crow Era*, 145–48.

501. Some scholarly works refer to him as a "former caddie," while an article in the *Miami New Times* in 2000 called him a "caddie by profession. Kirk Nielson, "In the Rough," *Miami New Times*, February 24, 2000, 31; Kinloch and Dawkins, *African American Golfers During the Jim Crow Era*, 140.

502. 1940 US Census, Palm Beach County, Florida, Population Schedule, Delray Beach Precinct 28, Sheet 4A, Household 56, Rice, digital image, Ancestry.com, Accessed 26 Oct 2022

503. Joseph Rice, "U.S. World War II Draft Cards Young Men, 1940-1947" Database. Ancestry.com: 2011. Citing NAI: 7644725, Record Group Title: Records of the Selective Service System, Record Group 147; Box Number: 373

504. 1950 US Census, Palm Beach County, Florida, Census of Population and Housing, Delray Beach, Sheet 30, Dwelling 355, Rice, digital image, Ancestry.com, Accessed 26 Oct 2022

505. Demas, *Game of Privilege*, 164–65; Kinloch and Dawkins, *African American Golfers During the Jim Crow Era*, 140.

506. Robert J. Robertson, *Fair Ways: How Six Black Golfers Won Civil Rights in Beaumont, Texas* (College Station: Texas A&M University Press, 2005), xi-xii, 158.

507. James T. Patterson, *Brown v. Board of Education: A Civil Rights Milestone and Its Troubled Legacy* (New York: Oxford University Press, 2001), 66–67.

508. Jackson, "Sports of the World," 7.

509. Kirsch, "Municipal Golf and Civil Rights in the United States, 1910-1965," 151–52.

510. Kirsch, 384.

511. Demas, *Game of Privilege*, 152.

512. Constance Baker Motley, Equal Justice Under Law: An Autobiography (New York: Farrar, Straus & Giroux, 1998), 69; Quoted in Demas, *Game of Privilege*, 153.

513. Demas, *Game of Privilege*, 153.

514. Demas, 154; Kirsch, "Municipal Golf and Civil Rights in the United States, 1910-1965," 378.

515. "Atlantans Play Golf," *Baltimore Afro-American*, December 31, 1954, 1; "Dixie Fumes Over New Supreme Court Ruling," *Chicago Defender*, November 19, 1955, 1 Quoted in Demas, *Game of Privilege*, 157–58.

516. Kinloch and Dawkins, 143, 147

517. Demas, *Game of Privilege*, 149–51.

518. Bobby Clay, "Breaking Par against Racism: Holmes vs. Atlanta.," *Black Enterprise*, September 1, 1996, 110–12.

519. Usher, "The Golfers," 167, 171; Kirsch, "Municipal Golf and Civil Rights in the United States, 1910-1965," 371.

520. Usher, "The Golfers," 385.

521. "Confusing the Real Issue," *Louisiana Weekly*, March 30, 1957, 12.

522. "Says State Needs McKellar, Particularly If Republicans Win the Presidency," *Knoxville News-Sentinel*, April 17, 1952, 22.

523. "Municipal Courses Must Admit Negro Golfers," *Florida Star and News*, May 25, 1957, 1; "Negroes Win Right to Use Golf Course; Order Awaited," Palm Beach Post, May 23, 1957, 1, 23.

524. "Negroes Quick to Open Play On Houston Courses," *Fort Worth Star-Telegram*, June 3, 1954, 32.

525. "Other Dixie Cities Have Met Issue On Golf Courses," *The Atlanta Constitution*, July 11, 1954, 16.

526. "Negro Golfer Fires Hot 37," *Charlotte Observer*, January 10, 1957, 8.

527. Dick Young, "Heavy Play at Bonnie Brae," *Charlotte News*, January 16, 1957, 17.

528. "Negro Foursomes Use Golf Course," *Charlotte Observer*, May 27, 1961, sec. B, 1; "Whites and Negroes Play Golf in Charleston, S.C. 'Without Incident,'" Philadelphia Tribune, June 17, 1961, 4.

529. Walter Powers, "Four Negroes Play Golf on City Course at Sarasota," *Tampa Tribune*, February 12, 1959, 1; "Injunction," *Jackson Clarion-Ledger*, June 7, 1963, 10.
530. In 1941 the caddies at municipal courses were almost exclusively White. In the post-war years there is evidence that the municipal courses used a mix of White and Black caddies. Sharp, "Atlanta Clubs Face Shortage Of Caddy Boys," D2.
531. Reg Murphy, "Negroes Use Atlanta Golf Courses Without Incident; White, Colored Players Voluntarily Keep Segregated," Macon Telegraph, June 29, 1956, 5.
532. "Ala. City Officials Agree To Let Negroes Golf," *Chicago Defender*, June 24, 1963, 7; Bennett, "City to Open Golf Courses By June 29," 1.
533. Robert Dee Springer, "'The Social Characteristics and Behavioral Patterns of the Members of an All-Negro Golf Club in the City of Atlanta, Georgia" (Atlanta, Georgia, Atlanta University, 1958), 25.
534. Springer, 26.
535. Gladys Knight and The Pips, "Midnight Train to Georgia," track 1 on Imagination, Buddah, 1973.
536. Terrence Moore, "Long Wait for Hartsfield," *The Atlanta Constitution*, May 12, 1990, sec. F, 1.
537. Dick Forbes, "Augusta Steps Into Spotlight For Masters Week," *Cincinnati Enquirer*, April 3, 1983, sec. C, 4.
538. Bill Shirley, "The Course That's Really a Shrine," *Los Angeles Times*, April 7, 1983, sec. B, 1.
539. Dave Anderson, "Caddies Cross the Masters Color Line," *Rochester Democrat and Chronicle*, April 11, 1983, sec. D, 1.
540. Anderson, 1.
541. For more, see Chapter 5.
542. Lee Pace, "The Masters Blend of Different Facets Equals the Ultimate," *Durham Sun*, April 10, 1983, sec. B, 2.
543. Bob Sudyk, "So Much for Another Custom at the Masters," *Hartford Courant*, April 7, 1983, sec. D, 1, 16; Peter Oberjuerge, "Nobody's Slaves," *San Bernardino County Sun*, April 12, 1980, sec. C, 2; Wayne Hester, "Caddy Talk,", *Anniston Star*, April 15, 1979, sec. B, 1.
544. Demas, *Game of Privilege*, 77.
545. Lee Elder became the first black player to play in the Masters in 1975, two years before Roberts' death. Under Roberts' command the Masters was played 41 times, 39 of which involved no Black players.

546. Augusta National Archive, 1965, 1965, Getty Images Image #82746338, Augusta National.
547. Anderson, "Caddies Cross the Masters Color Line," 1; Shirley, "The Course That's Really a Shrine," 1.
548. "Blacks Fail to Qualify; Lunn Is Bonus Pick," *Bangor Daily News*, April 8, 1970, 24.
549. Ed Comerford, "Masters' Caddies Hoping to Carry for a Black," *Newsday*, April 12, 1974, 119.
550. "Art Wall Credits Negro Caddie For Helping Him Win Masters," *Alabama Tribune*, April 10, 1959, 3.
551. Tom McEwen, "Caddy's Boss in Tough Job," *Augusta Chronicle*, April 14, 1968, sec. B, 4.
552. Comerford, "Masters' Caddies Hoping to Carry for a Black," 119.
553. McEwen, "Caddy's Boss in Tough Job," 4.
554. "USGA's Caddy Rule Moved Up One Year," Kingston Daily Freeman, November 14, 1975, 20.
555. David Westin, "Issue Resolution Ended Tradition," *Augusta Chronicle*, April 11, 1992, sec. M, 3.
556. Bruce Berlet, "Holding the Bag Again, He's Not Unhappy," *Hartford Courant*, April 9, 1983, sec. C, 6.
557. Peter Oberjuerge, "All Black Caddy Corps Masters Augusta National Course," Fort Myers News Press, April 13, 1980, sec. c, 3.
558. Michael Carr, "National Sportscaster Says Masters Is Symbol of Racism," *Augusta News Review*, April 17, 1975, 5.
559. Howie Evans, "Sort of Sporty," *New York Amsterdam News*, April 18, 1970, 33; Other examples include "Black Caddy Chose Elder 10 Years Ago," *Chicago Defender*, April 9, 1975, 28; Maggie Hathaway, "Tee Time," *Los Angeles Sentinel*, April 17, 1975, sec. B, 3; Roosevelt Green Jr., "Speaking Out," *Augusta News Review*, May 9, 1974, 4.
560. "Shameful Policy Ends," *Augusta News Review*, November 21, 1982, 1.
561. Westin, "Issue Resolution Ended Tradition," 3.
562. Berlet, "Holding the Bag Again, He's Not Unhappy," 6.
563. Westin, "Issue Resolution Ended Tradition," 3.
564. Westin, 3.
565. Doug Stutsman, "Legendary Caddie Carl Jackson, Ben Crenshaw, Reunite in Par 3 Contest," *The Augusta Chronicle*, accessed December 21, 2022, https://www.augustachronicle.com/story/sports/pga/2022/04/07/

ahead-documentary-caddie-carl-jackson-returns-augusta-national-masters-champ-ben-crenshaw/9491114002/.

566. Clayton, *Men on the Bag*, 107.
567. Reed, "The Black Golf Caddy," 65–67.
568. *The Last Colored Caddy*, 2005.
569. According to the NCAA Demographics database, only 2% of D1 men's golf and 3% of D1 women's golf teams identify as Black. "NCAA Demographics Database," accessed February 8, 2023, https://www.ncaa.org/sports/2018/12/13/ncaa-demographics-database.aspx.
570. Martin Luther King Jr., "I Have a Dream" (Washington, D.C., August 28, 1963), https://avalon.law.yale.edu/20th_century/mlk01.asp.
571. Adam Fairclough, "The Costs of Brown: Black Teachers and School Integration," *The Journal of American History 91*, no. 1 (2004): 54–55; David S. Cecelski, *Along Freedom Road: Hyde County, North Carolina, and the Fate of Black Schools in the South* (Chapel Hill: University of North Carolina Press, 1994), 8–9.
572. Gavin Wright, *Sharing the Prize: The Economics of the Civil Rights Revolution in the American South* (Cambridge, Mass: Belknap Press of Harvard University Press, 2013), 223–28; Sturkey, *Hattiesburg: An American City in Black and White*, 308.
573. Jaime Diaz, "The Men the Masters Forgot," *Golf Digest*, April 1993, 132.
574. Maggie Hathaway, "Tee Time," *Los Angeles Sentinel*, August 24, 1967, sec. B, 2.
575. Clayton, *Men on the Bag*, 106.
576. Barbara Shircliffe, "'We Got the Best of That World': A Case for the Study of Nostalgia in the Oral History of School Segregation," *The Oral History Review 28*, no. 2 (January 1, 2001): 59–84.
577. John Updike, *Golf Dreams* (London: Penguin, 1998), 42.
578. *The Legend of Bagger Vance*, (Dreamworks, 2000)
579. Cerise L. Glenn and Landra J. Cunningham, "The Power of Black Magic: The Magical Negro and White Salvation in Film," *Journal of Black Studies 40*, no. 2 (November 1, 2009): 145.
580. Gary Crowdus and Dan Georakas, "Thinking about Power of Images: An Interview with Spike Lee," *Cinecaste*, 2001, 5.
581. Glenn and Cunningham, "The Power of Black Magic," 142.
582. Karen Crouse, "Treasure of Golf's Sad Past, Black Caddies Vanish in Era of Riches," *New York Times*, April 3, 2012, sec. Sports, https://www.nytimes.com/2012/04/03/sports/golf/from-a-symbol-of-segregation-to-a-victim-of-golfs-success.html.

583. Michael C. Dawson and Lawrence D. Bobo, "One Year Later and the Myth of a Post-Racial Society," *Du Bois Review: Social Science Research on Race 6,* no. 2 (2009): 247.

Index

A

Ansley Park GC 21, 222, 126
Athens CC 138
Atlanta Athletic Club...20-1, 32, 56, 61, 83, 155
Augusta CC 25-6, 145, 180
Augusta National Golf Club 26, 42, 144-6, 151-2, 156, 177-86, 188, 193
Armour, Tommy 65
Asheville CC 80-3
Avery, Nathaniel "Iron Man" 193

B

Ball, Robert "Pat" 114-7
Beal v. Holcombe 167-8, 172
Beecher, Lyman 133
Bendelow, Tom 20
Beard, Jariah 185, 188
Belle Meade CC 87
Bennett, Fred 182, 185
Bon Air GC .... xiii-xiv
Brookhaven GC 21-23, 32, 98, 109, 117
Brown v. Board of Ed. 168-70
Broyles, Nash R. 21-2
Bunn, Oscar 113-4

C

Capital City Club 21, 111, 126
Carolina CC (Charlotte) 43, 98-9, 102, 111
Carolina CC (Raleigh) 125-6, 155
Cobbs Creek GC 98
Columbia CC (MD) 90
Columbus (MS) CC 90
Cook, William "Tater" .... 21, 84[239]
Charleston Municipal GC 73
Crenshaw, Ben 185
Currie, Donald 31, 34, 60, 65-6

D

Dawkins Jr., Ralph 101
Dendy, John Brooks...83, 109, 117-20, 123, 159
Druid Hills GC 21, 23, 34-5, 117
Du Bois, W.E.B. 147

E

East Lake GC 20-1, 23, 32, 34, 61, 83-4, 98, 109, 117, 155
Eisenhower, Dwight D. .... xvi, 134-5, 144-6, 149-51
Elder, Lee .... 180[545], 181
Evans, Chick 83-4

F

Forsyth CC 93

G

Gainesville G&CC 89

H

Hagen, Walter 65, 68, 92
Hamilton, James C. 122-2
Hardin, Hord 184-5
Haywood, Gene 125, 155-6
Hartsfield, Zeke 119-20, 123, 159-60, 175
Hermitage GC 73-5, 85, 90
Holmes v. Atlanta 159-60, 167-72, 174
Holmes, Alfred "Tup" 159, 170-2
Hughes, Langston 151-2

J

Jackson, Carl 25-6, 185-6
Jackson CC 70
Jones, Bobby 23, 98, 106

K

King Jr., Rev. Dr. Martin Luther 187

L

The Legend of Bagger Vance 190-4
Louis, Joe 115, 178

M

Martin, Clyde 115
McRae, Thaddeus 27, 44, 69
McRae, Willie 42, 46-8, 53, 58, 68,
                                                94, 101, 104
McClady, Leon xvii
McDougal, Horace 115

N

NAACP 150, 165, 168-70
National Negro Open 83, 98,
                                                112, 116-7
New Lincoln G&CC 109, 118-20,
                                                126, 153, 159, 174
Nicklaus, Jack .... xi-xiii, xvii-xix,
                                                2, 186, 193

O

Olmsted, Frederick Law 11

P

Palmer, Arnold 180, 193
Peete, Calvin 181
Perteet, Willie "Cemetery" 143-7,
                                                149-52
Peterson Jr., Willie .... xi-xix, 2, 186-8, 193
PGA Tour 32, 121, 123, 179,
                                                181, 186, 193
Piedmont GC 20, 160
Pinehurst CC/Resort 2-3, 9-20, 24,
          26-36, 39-42, 45-8, 55-61, 64-70, 79,
          87-8, 92, 94, 100-1, 104-5, 112, 119-20,
                     124, 127-8, 136, 139-41, 156, 162, 193
Pioneer GC 174
Plessy v. Ferguson 161, 167
Presbrey, Frank 12, 17-9

R

Rhodes, Teddy 121, 147
Rice, Joseph 166-7, 169

Rice v. Arnold 166
Roberts, Clifford 179, 181
Robinson, Robert "Hardrock" 42-3
Ross, Donald 2, 12, 32, 36, 40,
                                                55-6, 60, 87-8
Ruffner, A.A. 30, 57

S

Sedgefield CC 40, 121
Shippen, John 113-4, 116
Sifford, Charlie 25, 32, 43, 97-100,
                     102, 105-7, 111, 120-3, 147, 171, 178, 181
Southern Open (UGA) 118, 120,
                                                159
Spiller, Bill 121, 147, 178
Stafford, Robert 42-3
Stewart, Walter 99, 107
Stirling, Alexa 23
"Swamp" 41, 107

T

Tam O'Shanter Club 155
Taylor, Nicodemus (Demus) 2-9,
                                                23-4, 29
Thomas, Jack 110
Tufts, James Walker 1-3, 9-12, 46
Tufts, Leonard 12, 14, 17-20, 46
Tufts, Peter V. 139
Tufts, Richard 46-7, 58, 101, 140

U

United Golfers Assn (UGA) 115-20,
                                                159, 171
USGA 16, 113-6, 122

W

Washington (D.C.) G&CC 89
Wheeler, Howard 97-8, 106-9,
                                                115, 117, 119-23
Whittle Springs GC 163-5
Wickham, DeWayne 37-8, 88, 102-3, 105
Woodholme CC 37, 102-3
Woods, Tiger 123, 178, 189, 192

About the Author

CRAIG J. GILL is a Scottish writer, researcher, and historian. Having grown up playing golf and caddying for the occasional American tourist in Edinburgh and the East Neuk of Fife, he completed an undergraduate degree in History and a Master's in American Studies at the University of Glasgow. He spent the subsequent five years in the U.S. South, studying the region's complex past. He earned a PhD in History from the University of North Carolina at Chapel Hill. Craig now lives in Vancouver, British Columbia—four thousand miles from his (and golf's) home country, but still deeply committed to illuminating a more holistic understanding of golf's rich past.

Printed in Great Britain
by Amazon

7a170cf1-a34c-4cd6-b453-dc24ee49c5e4R01